TREATING THE
ADULT SURVIVOR OF
CHILDHOOD SEXUAL ABUSE

Treating the Adult Survivor of Childhood Sexual Abuse

A PSYCHOANALYTIC PERSPECTIVE

Jody Messler Davies, Ph.D.
Mary Gail Frawley, Ph.D.

BasicBooks
A Division of HarperCollins*Publishers*

Designed by Ellen Levine

Library of Congress Cataloging-in-Publication Data
Davies, Jody Messler, 1952–
    Treating the adult survivor of childhood sexual abuse : a psychoanalytic
perspective / Jody Messler Davies, Mary Gail Frawley.
       p. cm.
    Includes bibliographical references and index.
    ISBN 0-465-06633-X
    1. Adult child sexual abuse victims—Rehabilitation. 2. Psychotherapy.
3. Psychoanalysis. I. Frawley, Mary Gail, 1950–
    II. Title.
RC569.5.A28D37 1994
616.85'83690651—dc20   93–34377
                                                        CIP

95 96 97 ❖/HC 9 8 7 6 5 4 3

THIS BOOK IS DEDICATED TO

My grandmother, Ida Wallach,
and in loving memory of Celia Messler,
Samuel J. Wallach, and Ned Messler
—J. M. D.

The memory of Martha Kivlan Quinn
—M. G. F.

Contents

Acknowledgments

WE HAVE BEEN fortunate to have the professional and relational support of many people during the writing of this book. Although there is some overlap between us in people we wish to thank, we, for the most part, sought out different colleagues and friends as we worked on this project, and thus we wrote separate acknowledgments.

First, however, we begin with some commonality. Wendy Greenspun catalyzed this collaboration, for which she has been both cursed and blessed by us, depending on how the writing was going at any given time. Mostly, we thank her for bringing us together. We also thank Jo Ann Miller and Stephen Francoeur of Basic Books. Jo Ann welcomed us as new authors, believing from the beginning in the value of our work. Stephen contributed humor, constancy, and balance as we struggled to bring this book to a publishable form.

Jody Messler Davies:

The opportunity to thank all of those whose knowledge, generosity, and support have contributed to the final version of this book is, indeed, a formidable task, as well as a long-awaited pleasure and privilege.

I wish to begin with the patients, whose courage and persistence in the face of overwhelming life circumstances has been a continuous source of inspiration and hope. Their stories, their faith, and their trust have changed my life and profoundly influenced my understanding of the psychoanalytic process.

To the many others who have supported this project at different points along the way, giving of their limited time with great generosity and enthusiasm: George Stricker, Elena Skolnick, Lewis Aron, Robert Mendelsohn, Lawrence Epstein, and Jerry Rittigstein. They have read long sections of the book, in some cases the entire manuscript, and have offered their criticisms and comments with directness, candor, and tact.

To those colleagues with whom I have struggled to understand the difficult and personally challenging work with adult survivors. They have shared their thoughts, their writing, and their most personal moments of triumph and self-doubt: Sue Shapiro, Madelyn Miller, Sue Grand, Richard Gartner, Wendy Greenspun, Judith Alpert, Michelle Price.

To the members of my study group for continuing to provide a place that is "safe enough," a place in which to learn, question, disagree, and ultimately create new ideas. My appreciation and affection to Susan Katz Flinn, Patricia Kennedy, Susan Shimmerlik, Linda Pasternack, and Carolyn Clement.

To Neil Skolnick, with whom I first contemplated the idea of commiting thoughts to paper. This book could not have been written without our earlier collaboration.

To Jonathan Slavin, who carried this manuscript half-way around the world and gave of himself, his ideas, and his spirit, time and time again, whenever asked, and without fail. My heartfelt thanks for his enthusiasm, his support, and ultimately for his frienship.

To Stephen Mitchell, the rarest of teachers, who has conveyed with such eloquence and respect the ideas of the past and the present, remaining all the while intrigued with new ways of thinking about and conceptualizing the analytic process. His work has served as a model of quality, dignity, and creative open-mindedness. My sincerest thanks for the generosity with which he has given of himself.

To my coauthor, Mary Gail Frawley, for the experience of a collaboration that has been generative in the truest sense of the word, as well as creative, respectful, and fun throughout. Over the past 3 years, we have worked, we have struggled, and we have played. In the end, it would be impossible to imagine doing this work without the truly safe context provided by her presence.

Finally, I turn to my family, without whose love, enthusiasm, and emotional sustenance this book would never have been written.

To my parents, Mark and Sandra Messler, who have given their love, confidence, and support, as well as so many weekends of "extra" babysitting.

To my daughters, Jocelyn and Shelby, with great love, for remaining proud of their mother and interested in her work, despite the many times it has infringed on our days together. "Okay girls, I am finally done."

At the heart of it all, I return as I always do, to Lee, empowered by his faith, sustained by his energy, and grateful, beyond words, for his love.

Mary Gail Frawley:

Jody and I were only acquaintances when this book was conceived. Over the past 3 years, we have become good friends as well as coauthors who have worked together with remarkable ease. I have come to cherish deeply her intellectual prowess, humor, generosity of spirit, and collegial support. To Jody, I say, "We did it! Let's do it again!"

The Derner Institute at Adelphi University has been my intellectual, clinical, and emotional home for almost a decade. I have been influenced, challenged, and held by many members of the Adelphi family, some of whom deserve special mention. George Stricker has been mentor, transferential father, colleague, and friend and has guided my professional footsteps for years. From the inception of this project, George gave generously of his time and knowledge. As the project drew to a close, he read the entire manuscript, offering valuable suggestions that enhanced the final draft. I want to convey to George my respect, gratitude, and affection.

At a demanding time during which he assumed the position of Acting Dean of the Derner Institute, Bob Mendelsohn read and commented on several key chapters of this book. In addition to his contribution to this project, Bob has been an important influence on my clinical work; his genius and capacity for play have impressed and moved me.

Larry Epstein and Jerry Ritigstein read the entire manuscript, for which I am very grateful.

As a doctoral student, I was excited by Irwin Hirsch's insistence that the therapist become a full partner in psychoanalytic journeys, enacting and observing with the patient key relational configurations. I am grateful to Irwin for reading the chapters on transference and countertransference and for arguing with me about my ideas about dissociation.

Moving to the wider psychoanalytic community, I want to thank Jonathan Slavin. Jonathan has graciously and generously extended himself to Jody and me as critic and professional supporter. As important as his interest in our work, however, is his friendship. Jonathan has become a friend whose company I enjoy and whose kindness was important to me at a time of significant change in my life.

I was most fortunate to enjoy the collegial support of a number of fine therapists in Rockland County. Steve Ratnow, Erica Wanderman, Gloria Stone, Ann Kuehner, Laura Woolis, and David Friedman are gifted professionals who are also friends. Over the years, they have contributed to my growth as a clinician and also have provided warm support and encouragement during the writing of this book.

Family and friends have been enormously loving and patient, as this book evolved from idea to finished product, generously tolerating unreturned phone calls, canceled engagements, and periods of absorption that excluded what should have been expectable responsiveness from me. To Martha Ann, Debbie, Kevin, Judy, Elizabeth and Gerritt, Michelle, Arlene, Tom (the master pipe bender) and Joanne, Bob and Laurie, Jenny, and Mary O'Hanlon go my gratitude and love.

Important journeys often are marked by unexpected twists and turns; they are more interesting and safely ventured in partnership with a trusted other. Lynn has been a steady, yet playful traveling companion, who has earned my respect, trust, deep gratitude, and love.

As an old college friend of mine once said, "One never knows where love may be lurking." For over 25 years, Dennis O'Dea has been the poet in my heart. As the writing of this book drew to a close, we found each other yet again, and, now, his love warms and enriches me.

Finally, I thank my patients, from whom I have learned much as I traveled with them on their journeys of recovery and reclaimed hope. Their courage, their determination to grow beyond the once unspeakable violations of their bodies and minds, their generous willingness to help me to help them have moved and inspired me. I sincerely hope these pages do justice to their creativity and persistence.

Introduction

WRITING AN INTRODUCTION is, perhaps, an author's most personal statement. It is a frame through which we hope the reader will view and interpret what we offer, and it is a final attempt, placed paradoxically at the beginning, to influence how one's thoughts and, in the case of psychoanalysis, one's clinical work will be received. We write this introduction at the end of our journey, aware that it is only as we ourselves emerge from our embeddedness in this project that we can hope to gain some perspective from which to view it.

When we began to contemplate this project more than 3 years ago, there was little written or discussed from a psychoanalytic perspective on the treatment of adult survivors of childhood sexual abuse. Those psychoanalytically oriented articles we could find did not integrate psychoanalytic theory into the growing body of empirical, clinical, and theoretical observation available from the sexual abuse and psychological trauma literature. Also unintegrated were current developments in cognitive psychology that dealt with the variety of ways in which traumatic memories were symbolized and encoded by patients. Indeed, even in private conversations with our colleagues about the problems inherent in treating sexual abuse survivors, we encountered disbelief, or an atmosphere of hushed secrecy, and awkward discomfort as if the very discussion were as forbidden as its topic.

Both of us were working at this time with a large number of adult survivors of childhood sexual abuse in psychoanalysis or psychoanalytically oriented psychotherapy. We both felt a strong need to communicate about aspects of treatment that seemed relationally challenging and paradigmatic of the work. Other analytically oriented clinicians who treated incest and sexual abuse survivors told us they were often steeped in self-doubt, even shame, about what they considered to be somewhat unconventional and turbulent treatments. They yearned for reassurance, guidance, and validation.

At the same time, we were also meeting other colleagues who expressed doubt or misgiving about the whole issue of early sexual trauma, its sequelae, and the centrality it should be accorded in treatment.

Much to our surprise, in the 3 years during which we wrote this book, there was an explosion of media attention on childhood sexual abuse and its aftermath. At best, these public and sometimes sensationalized exposés encourage incest and sexual abuse survivors to seek treatment for their psychic scars. At worst, the media circus surrounding the subject threatens to trivialize the long-standing pain experienced by many survivors or alienate clinicians unfamiliar with the sequelae of childhood sexual trauma who may view patients' disclosures of sexual abuse as conformity with the latest national fad. As we witnessed the widening popular focus on childhood sexual abuse, we felt even more strongly that psychoanalytically oriented professionals needed to engage in a comprehensive, critical dialog about the sequelae of early sexual trauma and the treatment of adult survivors.

Two separate lines of inquiry have served as point and counterpoint in an often embittered debate among analysts and between psychoanalysts and other clinical specialists. One line argues that it is the reality of the traumatic event, accompanied by the actual overwhelming of ego functions and symbolic capacities, that is ultimately more disruptive to adaptive functioning and thus more seriously demanding of clinical attention. The other line argues that it is more important to understand the way in which traumatic events become incorporated within unconscious fantasy, particularly sadomasochistic fantasy. Some psychoanalytic writers speak eloquently of the long-term developmental failures and particular vicissitudes of unconscious fantasy found among adult survivors but fail to integrate into their thinking the growing literature on traumatic stress and the specific posttraumatic stress reactions common to adult survivors. Others write movingly of the effect of real traumatic events on their patients but appear to suggest that a thorough abreactive reliving of these events will, in itself, unlock developmental arrests, rework the pathological reality distorting/preserving defenses marshalled by the traumatized survivor, and reformulate the internalized system of abusive relational matrices that continue to influence current interpersonal relationships.

Our heartfelt conviction, indeed our raison d'être for writing this book, became to offer our shared belief that this controversy has in itself become destructively misleading. It has led analytically oriented clinicians into an overly polemicized debate, fostering the perception that, clinically, one must choose between dealing with the realities of childhood abuse or with their internalized fantasied elaborations. We believe this choice to be unnecessary and hold that making such a choice too often contributes to the well-documented treatment failures in this area of clinical work. Both the reality of childhood sexual abuse and the fantasied elaborations of these traumatic

ment-to-moment, inextricably bound concordant and complementary coun-
terparts to the transference (Racker, 1968). Included in this definition of
countertransference are aspects of the work that have been previously conceptualized as the clinician's side of the working alliance: the real feelings
the therapist experiences for the patient—thoughts, feelings, fantasies, projective identifications, etc. that evolve in response to the patient's conscious
and unconscious, verbal and nonverbal communications; and responses derived primarily from the therapist's dynamically based conflicts and fantasies.

All of the clinician's reactions to the patient and all of the patient's reactions to the therapist are threads in the tapestry that is woven by both partici-
pants/observers to form the relational matrix within which and through
which the therapy unfolds. The therapeutic relationship thus forms both the
background and foreground (Pine, 1981) in which treatment occurs. As background, the relationship is the consistent holding environment (Winnicott,
1960a) in which the patient gradually learns to trust, a good enough
(Winnicott, 1960b) space that becomes safe enough for a patient to go on
being (Winnicott, 1962) while she relives, tames, and slowly integrates the
long split-off self and other representations originally splintered by traumatic
experiences. As foreground, the therapeutic relationship is "where the action
is." It is the arena in which abuse, neglect, and idealized salvation are reexperienced and in which therapist and patient participate in the emergence, identification, and working through of powerful, often chaotic, transference and
countertransference paradigms. It is within the relational matrix that state-dependent traumatic memories are triggered off by aspects of transference-
countertransference reenactment.

In our writing, we have attempted to describe, in as evocative a manner
as possible, the specific dissociative patterns and characteristic transference
and countertransference paradigms that emerge with some consistency in
our work. We realize that our patients do not represent a homogeneous,
monolithic group. Rather, the clinical process that emerges between each
patient/therapist dyad will be distinctive and unshared by any other pair.
Where we may err in the direction of overschematizing certain patient-
therapist interactions, as in the transference and countertransference chapters, we do so in an attempt to help clarify regressive reenactments of these
paradigms, which are always intensely passionate, and often are disorganizing to both the patient's and the therapist's experience of a shared reality.
Here, we attempt to provide a language of broadly stroked categories
through which the therapist can attempt to regain some sense of psychic
equilibrium, organizing and locating herself with some clarity in the heat of
the transference-countertransference moment. However, these are only landmarks, and we provide them in full recognition that they will take different
form within different therapeutic dialogues. We hope that our readers will

use them as such, without resorting to a reification of these categories that might result in a somewhat reductionistic approach to the wonderfully creative pursuit of psychoanalytically derived experience.

Likewise, in our use of such terms as "the child self" and "the adult self," we are not suggesting a new structure of mind but, rather, the most evocative images we can summon up to depict the regressive reenactment of certain traumatically dissociated aspects of self and object representation that can shift with mind-boggling rapidity between patient as subject and object, and therapist as subject and object. It is our experience that particular characters (such as "the abused child," "the abusing adult," "the idealized savior," and "the indifferent and denying parental other") are the archetypes that most often organize the dissociated self and object world of the sexually traumatized child and intrude, unpredictably, on the adult patient's understanding of her current interpersonal relationships. We do not approach our clinical work as a search for such preconceived prototypes, but it is a fact that we have seen these characters literally possess our patients and ourselves, shifting back and forth, and doing so with some regularity despite the striking differences among the patients and therapists involved. Sometimes, these personas jump out of the transference-countertransference process, filling the therapeutic space with their unmistakable presence. At other times, they make their presences felt in more subtle and insidious ways: a choice of word or phrase, a look in the eyes, a particular mannerism or gesture at one time attributed to a significant other in the patient's life, now emanating from the core of self as she occupies the treatment setting or emanating from the surprised and unsuspecting person of the internally occupied analyst.

In writing this book, we have struggled endlessly with the complex gender issues involved in our conceptualizations. We have seen both male and female survivors in treatment. However, our experience with female survivors far outweighs our experience with male survivors, in large measure, we believe, because women still represent the significant majority of those presenting for treatment with histories of childhood sexual abuse. It is also a fact, although often stated only implicitly, that most of the sexual abuse literature from which we draw conclusions involved studies of female survivors only. Our clinical examples, therefore, involve mostly women and, in most cases, we refer to our patients as "she." We do not want to understate in any way the traumatic legacies of countless numbers of young boys who have been sexually traumatized and who do appear regularly for psychoanalytically informed treatment. Although we believe that many of our formulations and recommendations will prove useful in treating male survivors, we are also aware that the literature to date suggests some differences between men and women in the way they deal with childhood sexual trauma (Gartner, 1993). We therefore regard our conceptualizations as they apply to men with a different degree of confidence, aware that a more comprehensive understanding of the male survivor awaits additional empirical and clinical investigation.

We also know that childhood sexual abuse is not a monolithic phenomenon but, rather, encompasses a range of sexual activities, levels of violence, ages of onset and termination, durations, and relationships between victim and perpetrator. Adult survivors with whom we usually work were sexually abused in childhood for several years. The abuse often began when they were quite young, between 3 and 7 years old, and frequently extended into adolescence. Abusive activities tended to be serious, including rape, sodomy, fellatio, cunnilingus, digital penetration of the child's genitals, and mutual masturbation of victim and perpetrator. Abusers were usually close relatives—mothers, fathers, uncles, grandfathers, brothers. Many of our patients disclosed their abuse to at least one other person when they were children. In most cases, they were ignored, disbelieved, or, in some other way, rebuffed. It is thus clear that we have in treatment a biased sample of the universe of sexual abuse survivors; it is a sample that is consistent, however, with adult survivors found in other clinical populations (Briere, 1989; Jehu, 1988).

To preserve confidentiality of past and present patients, we have identified them by pseudonyms. The case vignettes that appear here are composites based on the experiences of many different patients. In all instances, we have thoroughly disguised identifying details.

The major psychoanalytic books on the treatment of adult survivors of childhood sexual abuse (Kramer & Akhtar, 1991; Levine, 1990; Shengold, 1989) have been written primarily from a classical perspective in which the sequelae of early trauma are encapsulated within a drive/structure model of psychopathology. Treatment is conceptualized within a one-person model in which the patient's intrapsychic contents and processes are focused on. Our book, on the other hand, is written from a relational perspective and embeds the consequences of childhood sexual abuse within a model of psychopathology in which the internalization of early relationships is key. This book thus offers a psychoanalytic perspective on the treatment of adult survivors of childhood sexual abuse that is embedded in contemporary relational theories and, as such, offers an approach quite different from those of other psychoanalytic books on this subject.

There are many nonpsychoanalytic works on the treatment of adult survivors of childhood sexual abuse (Briere, 1989; Courtois, 1988; Herman, 1981, 1992; Jehu, 1988; Russell, 1986). These have contributed epidemiological information regarding the frequency and nature of childhood sexual abuse. They also have provided valuable information regarding common symptoms and sequelae of early sexual trauma and have suggested treatment approaches that range from behavioral to cognitive to an eclectic mixture of psychodynamic, cognitive, and behavioral approaches. Clearly, our book differs from these in offering a specifically psychoanalytic perspective.

Structure of the Book

Chapter 1 addresses the history of psychoanalytic thought on psychological trauma and childhood sexual abuse. Beginning with Freud and Sandor Ferenczi, in this chapter we offer models of trauma from four psychoanalytic perspectives: classical, ego-psychological, object relational, and self-psychological. It is our belief that psychoanalytic thinking about trauma must be enhanced by an understanding of psychological trauma and the contributions of the empirical sexual abuse field. Therefore, Chapter 2 reviews the developmental, cognitive, affective, self-experiential, relational, and behavioral sequelae of trauma as delineated within the psychological trauma literature. This chapter also discusses key epidemiological findings from the empirical sexual abuse literature. Chapter 3 provides our own integrative model of childhood sexual abuse in which we discuss the sequelae and treatment of adult survivors from a relational-psychoanalytic perspective, informed by the trauma and sexual abuse literatures. Chapters 1 to 3 thus set the stage for a discussion of specific treatment issues with these patients.

Dissociation is the hallmark of trauma. In Chapter 4, we discuss dissociation from theoretical and phenomenological perspectives and address in detail the clinical implications of working with patients for whom dissociation is an important mode of communication, defense, and adaptation. In this chapter we also review the differences between dissociated traumatic memories and what the current media have come to refer to as "repressed memories of abuse." In so doing we hope to help clarify some of the misunderstanding underlying this controversy.

Secrecy is another hallmark of trauma; the sexual abuse of children is most often wrapped completely in secrecy. Disclosure of past abuse is a critical step in the recovery of these patients. Thus, it is crucial that clinicians learn how best to facilitate disclosure of past sexual trauma. Chapter 5 therefore discusses disclosure and also addresses the ways in which traumatic memories are likely to be recalled. Frequently, these memories do not return in the symbolized, pictorial form we are used to but, rather, besiege and overwhelm the patient as body memories, flashbacks, dreams, and other disruptive phenomena.

In some ways even more destructive than the actual sexual abuse is the typical attack on the victim's sense of reality that is encapsulated within early sexual trauma. Chapter 6 describes the long-lasting disruption of the adult survivor's capacities to test reality and discusses her intractable propensity to doubt her own sense of reality and to preserve internalized relational bonds by distorting contemporary internal and external realities. Here, too, we hope to distinguish our approach from one which regards a return and abreaction of memory as the sole curative factor in treatment.

Therapists working with survivors of early trauma often find most disruptive the impressive array of violent, shocking, self-destructive behaviors in which these patients often engage. Because the continuity of the therapist's containing and interpretive functions is crucial in the face of self-destructive acts, Chapter 7 is devoted to a thorough discussion of two especially difficult problems: the erotization of fear and compulsive self-abuse.

It is within the transference and countertransference of psychoanalytic treatment that the real work of therapy is accomplished. It is here, within the relational paradigms evoked by and enacted within the treatment, that the patient's internalized world of traumatogenic self and object representations will come alive where they can be observed, put into play in the transitional space of the therapy, and eventually made explicit. Because of the centrality of the transference and countertransference, we devote three chapters to this area of treatment. Chapter 8 discusses the impact of trauma on development and expression of the transference and countertransference. Here we examine the effect of the patient's unorganized, unsymbolized experiences; her use of dissociation as a coping skill, defense, and vehicle for communication; the effect of the patient's general defensive constellation, particularly acting out and projective identification; and, finally, the impact of the clinician's personal attitudes toward or experiences with trauma and of his or her transference to more traditional psychoanalytic concepts. In Chapter 9, we discuss eight specific relational positions that emerge in work with these patients: the uninvolved, rejecting, nonabusing parent; the unseen, neglected child; the abuser; the abused; the omnipotent rescuer; the needy, sometimes entitled child; the seducer; the seduced. We stipulate that therapist and patient will each enact, again and again, each of these relational positions at various points during the therapeutic journey. We close our discussion of transference and countertransference in Chapter 10 with an extended case vignette that illustrates the points made in the preceding two chapters.

Chapters 11 and 12 are devoted to a summary and further delineation of a treatment model for adult survivors of childhood sexual abuse. In Chapter 11, we review the constituent elements of our treatment model: containment; recovery and disclosure of traumatic memories and fantasied elaborations; symbolization and encoding of memory and experience; integration of disparate self and object systems and of other reality-distorting defenses; internalization of a new object relationship found within the therapy. Chapter 12 is devoted to a discussion of the theoretical and clinical implications of our model. Here, we include thoughts on the therapeutic interplay between illusion and reality; traditional concepts of abstinence and neutrality in working with patients who have been abused; and the pathogenicity of projective identification in abused children and its centrality in work with adult survivors. We close with a reconsideration of the place of oedipal dynamics in psychological development and offer our views on the therapeutic stance evolving from this reconsideration.

We encourage the reader to regard this work not as a finished product but as a temporary stopping point in the ongoing dialog about the treatment of this important patient group. This invitation is made in a spirit of openness and is intended to stimulate disagreement and discussion, both within psychoanalysis and between psychoanalytic professionals and those from other branches of social work, psychology, and psychiatry. We expect to raise here at least as many questions as we answer, leading, we hope, to a professional dialog that steers an intellectually and clinically sound course between the stultifying silence of the past and the somewhat deafening cacophony of the present.

We ask you, then, to journey with us, through what is undoubtedly difficult terrain. Although we can surely provide certain landmarks and reassurances along the way, we begin each trip in full awareness that the experience will never be the same twice; no two clinicians will come away with the sense that they have journeyed the same road. The one truth that does serve us well through the inevitably dark moments of our work is the heartfelt conviction that childhoods marked by traumatic abuse will impose the template of such early trauma on the transference-countertransference experiences of the patient and therapist alike. We thus cling to the hope that in our most disorganized, despairing, and enraged moments (as well as in our most glorious and omnipotent experiences of rescue and salvation), we have come upon not insurmountable obstacles to therapeutic success but a conduit that can provide full access to the dissociated and otherwise unknowable self and object world of the adult survivor of traumatic childhood sexual abuse.

CHAPTER 1

Trauma and Childhood Sexual Abuse in Psychoanalysis

THROUGHOUT ITS HISTORY, psychoanalysis has struggled to decide what importance should be given to the role of actual childhood trauma, especially sexual abuse, in the genesis and treatment of adult psychopathology. Like the larger society, psychoanalysis discovered, denied, rediscovered, redenied, and is currently discovering yet again the significance of childhood sexual trauma as an etiological factor in later psychopathology. However, even when analytic thinkers have agreed that actual early trauma is an important pathogenic phenomenon, they have disagreed on how traumatic events are internalized by the child and expressed by the adult patient. Thus, treatment models vary widely. In this chapter, we review historical and contemporary psychoanalytic views of psychological trauma, especially childhood sexual abuse. An exhaustive review of this literature can be found elsewhere (Wolf and Alpert, 1991). Here, we offer a representative cross section of the theories of major psychoanalytic thinkers.

Sigmund Freud and the Seduction Theory

Any psychoanalytic consideration of childhood sexual abuse must begin with Freud's development and later renunciation of the seduction theory, a paradigm stipulating that hysterical neurosis derives from early sexual seductions. Although he never wholly rejected the notion that childhood seductions were pathogenic, Freud shifted his emphasis from the seduction theory to the Oedipus complex, on which he based his assertion that the neuroses were etiologically embedded in the unconscious fantasies of the psychoanalytic patient. Fantasy upset reality as the causal link to the neuroses, and the stage was set for Freud and his successors to interpret reports of early sexual victimizations as fantasies driven by the adult patient's unconscious childhood wishes. Thus, from early on, Freud's renunciation of the seduction theory moved psychoanalytic emphasis away from a conceptualization of the neuroses that attended to the central role of *real* childhood events and relationships.

Over the years, Freud's biographers and other psychoanalytic writers have presented polarized views on the meaning of the abandonment of the seduction theory. Some (Gay, 1988; Jones, 1961; McGrath, 1986) cite the renunciation of the seduction theory as a landmark achievement emanating from Freud's rigorously demanding self-analysis. Others (Krull, 1986; Masson, 1984; Miller, 1984) argue that the abandonment of the seduction theory led to an unfortunate invalidation of a central childhood experience. Furthermore, they suggest that the renunciation was primarily driven by idiosyncratic factors in Freud's life and psyche. We elect not to join the intensely polemical battle regarding the basis of Freud's rejection of the seduction theory. Although the psychobiographical analyses of the issues are fascinating and provide intriguing insights into Freud's personal life and psyche, the bitter controversy evoked by speculation about the reasons *why* he rejected the seduction theory distracts from serious consideration of the consequences of the retraction. At this point, we believe that it is more pertinent to review Freud's own arguments for and against the seduction theory.

On April 21, 1896, Freud introduced the seduction theory in an address before the Society for Psychiatry and Neurology in Vienna. His paper, the *Aetiology of Hysteria* (Freud, 1896), was based on his work with 18 female hysterics and expounded his theory on the cause of the disorder. Freud's conclusion was that "at the bottom of every case of hysteria there are one or more occurrences of premature sexual experiences, occurrences which belong to the earliest years of childhood" (p. 203). Freud firmly believed in this clinically driven theory, as demonstrated in the paper's closing remarks:

> Prepared as I am to meet with contradiction and disbelief, I should like to say one thing more in support of my position. Whatever you may think about the conclusions I have come to, I must ask you not to regard them as the fruit of idle speculation. They are based on a laborious individual examination of patients which has in most cases taken up a hundred or more hours of work. (p. 220)

Within 18 months, Freud reversed himself and repudiated the seduction theory in a letter to Fliess written on September 21, 1897 (in Masson, 1985): "Let me tell you straight away the great secret which has been slowly dawning on me in recent months. I no longer believe in my neurotica" (p. 264). In this letter, Freud cited several reasons for rejecting the seduction theory. First, he stated that he must doubt its validity, because his analyses of hysterics were not completely successful and because partial successes could be explained without reference to the seduction theory. Second, Freud doubted the frequency of childhood sexual abuse implied by his theory. Third, as he told Fliess, as there is no representation of reality in the unconscious, it was possible for the patient to weave fantasies in which the parents are cast into assaultive roles. Finally, Freud asserted that even in the psychoses, unconscious memories do not break through to consciousness. He thus doubted that in treatment unconscious memories of real events could break through the censoring mechanism of the conscious mind.

Let us consider and critique Freud's own arguments regarding his change of mind. First, the analyses of many patients, sexually abused or not, end prematurely for a variety of reasons. Furthermore, it is not infrequent that a patient leaves or wants to leave treatment when confronted with the memories of abuse. When a patient begins to remember and share memories of the sexual victimizations, the reality of the abuse often hits very hard. Until this point in treatment, the patient has worked to deny the reality of the abuse and fights against the pain of truly knowing about the assaults by relegating the memories to a state of fuzziness. Many survivors wish to leave therapy when they can no longer hide from the truth of their traumas. At this juncture, leaving seems preferable to enduring the pain evoked by memories. In addition, the memories, associated affects, and fantasy elaborations are activated and repeated in the transference process, so that the patient actually feels abused within the treatment. In 1896 Freud himself addressed the great distress experienced by a survivor in recalling details of the abuse:

> While they are recalling these infantile experiences to consciousness, they suffer under the most violent sensations of which they are ashamed and which they try to conceal, and, even after they have gone through them once more in such a convincing manner, they still attempt to withhold belief from them. (p. 204)

One can also hypothesize that some of Freud's female patients left analysis because of intense transference phenomena evoked by remembering early sexual assaults. Continued analysis with a male therapist, close in age and social status to the perpetrator—perhaps even a social acquaintance of the abuser—might have evoked a transference in which the patient expected Freud to reabuse her or betray her by sharing her memories with the perpetrator. Moreover, at this stage of his career, Freud still engaged in physical manipulation of his patients, massaging them or touching their heads with his hands. It is easy to imagine a female survivor of childhood sexual abuse running from a male analyst who occasionally touched her during treatment and onto whom she transferred expectations derived from her abusive experiences. Freud, at this point, had not developed a full understanding of transference and may have missed negative (or positive, especially erotically mediated) transference manifestations, particularly if the patient did not verbalize them.

Although all this is conjecture, it can plausibly explain premature terminations or only partially successful treatments. What is clear is that early terminations and incomplete analyses are not incompatible with continued allegiance to the seduction theory.

Second, Freud wrote to Fliess that he came to reject his theory because it
implied an improbable frequency of childhood sexual abuse. Once again,
Freud had anticipated this criticism in his 1896 paper when he stated, "children are far more often exposed to sexual assaults than the few precautions
taken by parents in this connection would lead us to expect" (p. 207). In
1896, then, Freud could believe that children were commonly abused sexually. By 1897, he questioned this premise. Why?

Part of the answer to that question is that Freud had no way of empirically validating the extent of sexual abuse in Victorian Vienna. As a bour-
geois father, he apparently could not conceive that children were abused in
numbers large enough to produce the frequency of hysteria seen in that day,
especially when one assumed that hysterics represented only some fraction
of the universe of sexually abused children. Considering that it was only in
the 1980s that empirically excellent studies (Russell, 1986; Wyatt, 1985) generated incidence rates of childhood sexual abuse at 38% of all American
women, we can understand Freud's resistance to accepting the frequency of
childhood sexual abuse implied by the incidence of hysteria.

In his third argument against the seduction theory, Freud offered what
later became the cornerstone of his new theory of the neurosis. He suggested
that his hysterical patients had fantasized the childhood victimizations, casting their parents into the roles of abusers. That reports of childhood sexual
abuse were fantasies was a criticism Freud anticipated when he presented
the 1896 paper, and, there he offered a rebuttal: "In the first place, the behavior of patients while they are reproducing these infantile experiences is in
every respect incompatible with the assumption that these scenes are anything else than a reality which is being felt with distress and reproduced
with the greatest reluctance" (p. 204).

This perspective is clearly consistent with our own experiences with patients who are disclosing details of their sexual abuse. In fact, the predominant fantasy presented by our patients is that the sexual abuse was not really
as bad as it sounds or that the abuser, often a parent or other trusted relative,
was not as self-serving as the memories suggest. Because acknowledging the
reality of the abuse is often tantamount to knowing that she was abandoned
by a desperately loved and needed parent, the patient protects herself from
the pain of that reality by fantasizing a less horrific early environment. Freud
supported this view in the 1896 paper when he said:

> There are, however, a number of other things that vouch for the reality of the
> infantile sexual scenes. In the first place, there is the uniformity which they ex-
> hibit in certain details, experiences always of the same kind, but which would

otherwise lead us to believe that there were secret understandings between various patients. In the second place, patients sometimes describe as harmless events whose significance they obviously do not understand, since they would be bound otherwise to be horrified by them. Or, again, they mention details without laying any stress on them, which only someone of experience in life can understand and appreciate as subtle traits of reality. (p. 205)

In 1896, then, Freud went to great lengths to argue that his patients' reports of sexual abuse could not represent fantasy material, and he marshaled convincing evidence to support his views. By 1897, he had changed his mind on this point too, in part because his self-analysis revealed to him that fantasies are potent psychological organizers.

Finally, Freud doubted the validity of the seduction theory, because it is unlikely, he said, that accurate memories of real childhood events could ever break through into consciousness. If even psychotics preserve the censorship of real memories, certainly analytic treatment cannot reverse that censoring process to release accurate memories. Many clinicians today would not require that verifiable, exact memories be produced before they believed the essential truths contained in patients' reports of childhood events. A patient may, for example, report an abusive experience that is a composite memory of several victimizing episodes and that is imbued with fantasy elaborations of the original trauma. The memory is inaccurate; the fact of the abuse is not. We do not believe, therefore, that a patient's failure to exactly reproduce accurate childhood memories required abandoning of the seduction theory.

We see, then, that Freud traveled a long distance in the 18 months between his presentation of the seduction theory in 1896 and his renunciation of it in 1897. By the time the oedipal conflict was emplaced as the central forerunner of neurosis, Freud had come full circle. The seduction theory was based on validation of a patient's childhood experiences with real people; it incriminated adults who used children to fill their own narcissistic needs. The oedipal conflict, on the other hand, insisted that childhood sexual abuse was fantasy material driven by unconscious childhood sexual wishes; it protected parents at the expense of the patient's reality. The seduction theory was based on clinical data obtained from actual patients. Theory based on the centrality of the oedipal conflict grew not from case material but, rather, from interpretations Freud made during his self-analysis (Gay, 1988).

Had Freud not rejected the seduction theory, he might have explicated further the role of all kinds of child abuse in adult psychological problems. Child abuse occurs in many forms—physical, sexual, emotional, or some combination of these. Both mothers and fathers perpetrate the abuses, and the victimized child often becomes an adult with serious psychological problems, including the dissociative phenomena seen in Freud's hysterics. Instead of expanding the seduction theory to account for all types of childhood trauma, Freud replaced the seduction theory with psychosexual theory and, in so doing, turned almost solely to the realm of fantasy to explain adult psychopathology. What is more, he issued a mandate to his professional progeny that rendered criticism of this powerful transferential father problematic. We know that Freud brooked no serious dissent from his views, roundly rejecting and expelling from the "family" such followers as Adler and Jung who dared to question major aspects of Freudian theory. For the most part, psychoanalysis was silent on the subject of early sexual trauma for many years. There were, however, exceptions, and Sandor Ferenczi stands out as an early continued supporter of the centrality of childhood sexual abuse in adult psychopathology.

Sandor Ferenczi

Ferenczi, who is currently enjoying a worldwide rehabilitation, was notable among members of Freud's inner circle for maintaining allegiance to a view of pathology centered on the etiological significance of childhood sexual trauma. His tenacity cost him Freud's approval and his standing in the early psychoanalytic community.

Freud's pupil, analysand, and, after Fliess, his closest friend, Ferenczi eventually jeopardized his relationship with Freud and his esteem within the psychoanalytic community by promulgating his belief that early sexual trauma was a common occurrence, frequently associated with adult psychopathology. In his seminal paper, *Confusion of Tongues Between Adults and the Child* (1932), Ferenczi validated the reality of childhood sexual abuse, poignantly described its impact on the child victim and adult survivor, and in so doing challenged Freud's reliance on instinctually driven fantasies as the basis of psychopathology. Ferenczi said:

> trauma, especially the sexual trauma, as the pathogenic factor cannot be valued highly enough. Even children of very respectable, sincerely puritanical families, fall victim to real violence or rape much more often than one had dared to suppose. Either it is the parents who try to find a substitute gratification in this pathological way for their frustration, or it is people thought to be trustworthy such as relatives (uncles, aunts, grandparents), governesses or servants, who misuse the ignorance and the innocence of the child. . . . The real rape of girls who have hardly grown out of the age of infants, similar sexual acts of mature women with boys, and also enforced homosexual acts, are more frequent occurrences than has hitherto been assumed. (p. 201)

In addition to validating the reality of childhood sexual abuse, Ferenczi referred to some of the pathological consequences of early sexual trauma: identification with the aggressor, pervasive guilt and shame, sexual dysfunction and perversion, and the profound splitting of the ego associated with dissociation. In this paper, Ferenczi clearly stated his belief that psychoanalysis had strayed too far from crediting the etiological importance of actual trauma in later psychopathology when he said: "By that I mean the recent, more emphatic stress on the traumatic factors in the pathogenesis of the neuroses which had been unjustly neglected in recent years. Insufficient deep exploration of the exogenous factor leads to the danger of resorting prematurely to explanations—often too facile explanations—in terms of 'disposition' and 'constitution'" (p. 196).

Ferenczi read this paper at the International Psycho-Analytic Congress at Wiesbaden, Germany, in September 1932. In so doing, he alienated the analytic community and provoked an irreconcilable break with Freud. So vicious was the attack on Ferenczi that his views were publicly correlated with his supposed emotional breakdown. Instead, Judith Dupont's publication of *The Clinical Diary of Sandor Ferenczi* (1988) portrays a man in full possession of his faculties and exquisitely sensitive to the psychological adaptation and resultant psychopathology of childhood sexual trauma.

Throughout his diary, Ferenczi discussed the devastating sequelae of childhood sexual abuse, struggling informally with those points he summarized in the 1932 paper. In reading the diary, we are struck continually by the congruence between Ferenczi's descriptions of his patients and what we see in our own consulting rooms. In addition to his cogent insights into the psychological sequelae of the actual seductions, Ferenczi was also keenly aware of the centrality of the maternal deprivation inherent in much sexual abuse, especially incest. He said, "But the most frightful of frights is when the threat from the father is coupled with simultaneous desertion by the mother" (p. 18), and he went on to describe the further ego fragmentation engendered by the mother's lack of protection of the child.

Ferenczi's discussions of the recovery of memories and of maternal emotional abandonment are but two topics sensitively addressed in a diary replete with clinically rich and theoretically interesting entries about the sequelae and treatment of childhood sexual abuse. We who work daily with adult survivors of incest and of other forms of childhood sexual abuse find in Sandor Ferenczi an analyst who, over 50 years ago, grasped many of the essential psychodynamics and therapeutic approaches salient to work with this clinical population. Through their treatment of Ferenczi, however, the members of the early psychoanalytic establishment issued an injunction against serious consideration of childhood sexual abuse that was powerfully effective for many years. Written psychoanalytic discourse on this central clinical phenomenon has been sparse, even up to today. Psychoanalytic writing on psychological trauma can be divided among four schools of thought: classical, ego-psychological, object-relational, and self-psychological.

The Classical Psychoanalytic Perspective

The classical psychoanalytic view of trauma is a direct descendant of Freud's position that, even when actual prepubertal sexual traumas occur, their significance lies in the reactivation in fantasy of earlier, primarily sadomasochistically formulated exposure to primal scene experiences. For Freud and the classicists, the pathogenicity of trauma derives neither from an overwhelming of the ego by unmanageable real events nor from a profound betrayal of relational bonds but, rather, from a regression to intense sadomasochistic fantasies. The pathogenic action, in other words, is intrapsychic rather than relational.

Phyllis Greenacre's work (1949, 1950, 1967) is an intermediate point between Freud's thinking and contemporary proponents of the classical perspective on trauma (Abend, 1986; Brenner, 1986; Dowling, 1986; Kramer & Akhtar, 1991; Levine, 1990; Shengold, 1989, 1992). Greenacre, like Freud, understands exposure to the primal scene as the prototype for all traumatogenic experience. Pathology results from regression to sadomasochistic fantasies, mediated by exposure to the primal scene and potentiated by prepubertal sexual experiences. It is the regression to fantasies belonging to a preoedipal level of psychosexual organization that, for Greenacre, is the most significant aspect of prepubertal sexual trauma. The effects of the actual traumatic events are minimized. In her review of several clinical case examples, Greenacre (1949) unfortunately not only fails to incorporate the disorganizing effects of the immediate sexual abuse described but also appears to view the abuse as related to the fact that her patients were very "seductive" little girls and, therefore, by implication, the unwitting instigators of their own molestations.

More contemporary classical psychoanalytic writers cite Fenichel's (1945) claim that trauma is unrelated to the quantity of stimulation experienced by the individual. According to Fenichel and, later, Abend (1986), Brenner (1986), Dowling (1986), and Shengold (1989, 1992), it is the conscious and unconscious meanings ascribed by the patient to particular events that render those events traumatic. Brenner (1986), for instance, stipulates that "the trauma, what is traumatic, is the subjective experience of the traumatized individual. It is what the event meant to the individual which is the trauma. It is the impact of the external stimuli, how they heightened fears, intensified sexual and aggressive wishes, resonated with feelings of guilt and remorse. All of this is what a psychically traumatic event actually is" (p. 203).

Leonard Shengold (1963, 1967, 1971, 1979, 1989), a contemporary classical psychoanalyst, employs the term *soul murder* to describe the phenomenological experience of recurrent abuse and deprivation. He encapsulates his clinical constructions within a drive theory paradigm in which he discusses the patient's need to distance from emotions, because feelings might lead to fantasies and, ultimately, to traumatic memories linked to fantasies, particularly those of an oral aggressive and sadomasochistic nature. The soul murder victim's alienation from her feelings results, Shengold says, in an "as-if" presentation of pseudorelatedness that disguises a deeply seated mistrust of others based on an experienced reality. Shengold further suggests that acceptance of the analyst as a separate, predominantly benevolent person is a difficult step that may take years marked by relentless testing of the analyst's constancy. In addition to the difficulty in overcoming a profound lack of trust, Shengold points out that acceptance of the therapist as substantially different from the patient's soul-murdering caretakers requires the patient to challenge and eventually relinquish the fantasy that the caretakers were in fact loving and emotionally generous. He says: "Experientially, the patient feels the terrible danger of losing the parents psychologically. . . . The imminence of the loss revives something at the heart of the child's traumatic anxiety (and the terrified child is very much alive within the adult): to be alone and beside oneself with distress and overstimulation, helpless in a terrible and destructive, or indifferent world" (1989, p. 315).

The giving up and mourning of the fantasied good parent is, Shengold suggests, the central issue of therapy with former victims. As this proceeds, the patient begins to feel intense rage and hatred that are frightening and against which the patient has defended through emotional isolation, psychical fragmentation, autohypnosis, denial, and perpetuation of relationships based on "masochistic bondage" (1989, p. 315).

Proceeding from earlier works by Fliess (1953) and Dickes (1965), Shengold stresses the centrality of what he calls "autohypnotic states" in the mental lives of adult survivors of soul murder. He believes that autohypnotic states essentially relieve the patient from the burden of being responsible for what is said and felt during the treatment hour. Though he maintains a classical drive model and views autohypnosis as "the ego's need to defend against drive tensions" (1989, p. 141), Shengold adds two very significant perspectives to the concept of autohypnosis. He stresses the possibility that autohypnosis can also be used to facilitate drive discharge, a phenomenon that transcends the drive functions. Here, alteration in consciousness is used to facilitate a traumatic reenactment, either within or outside the transference, and to deny the experience of significant gratification of libidinal and aggressive impulses. In addition, Shengold describes how the hypnotic state can bring about a "concentrated hypercathexis of perceptory signals" that enhances awareness of peripheral stimuli and evokes a state of "hypnotic vigilance" (1989, p. 143). Although it stems from the simultaneous need to defend against and gratify the derivatives of instinctual drive or their discharge, the process appears inadvertently to heighten the patient's sensitivity to a range of other experiences within the therapeutic relationship.

We see, then, contemporary classical analytic thinkers turning to a consideration of incest and childhood sexual abuse as important pathogenic events.

With some variation, most classicists find the primary impact of trauma located in the intrapsychic, fantasy-mediated organization of the patient. Treatment is embodied within a traditional analytic frame, in which verbal interpretation predominates as a mode of communication between the patient and the neutral, abstinent analyst.

The Ego-Psychological Perspective

An alternative contemporary psychoanalytic perspective on trauma, still based on classical metapsychological formulations, incorporates not only the unconscious meaning of the traumatic event but also stresses the extent to which the ego is overwhelmed and rendered nonfunctional by the excessive stimulation inherent in early trauma. Proponents of this ego-psychological viewpoint include Cooper (1986), Anna Freud (1967), Furst (1967, 1986), Gediman (1991), Kramer and Akhtar (1991), Krystal (1978, 1988), and Levine (1990). Anna Freud (1967) sets out the position subscribed to by the ego psychologists:

> Like everyone else, I have tended to use the term "trauma" rather loosely up until now but I shall find it easier to avoid this in the future. Whenever I am tempted to call an event in a child's or adult's life "traumatic," I shall ask myself some further questions. Do I mean the event was upsetting; that it was significant for altering the course of further development; that it was pathogenic? Or do I really mean traumatic in the strict sense of the word, i.e., shattering, devastating, causing internal disruption by putting ego functioning and ego mediation out of action? (p. 242)

As suggested by Anna Freud, in their determination of what is traumatic and what is not, ego-psychological writers emphasize the ego's complete incapacitation and the phenomenological experience of helplessness in the face of what is perceived by the individual to be life-threatening danger. Furthermore, some of these authors differentiate between events they consider to be "near-traumatic" and those that represent "catastrophic trauma." The first are situations in which the ego is threatened but ultimately mobilizes extreme defenses leading to neuroses or more severe character pathology. Catastrophic trauma, on the other hand, is defined by Krystal (1988) as "a surrender to what is experienced as unavoidable danger of external or internal origin" (p. 154). He goes on to distinguish between near-trauma and catastrophic trauma:

> Evaluation of the situation as one of inevitable danger and the surrender to it, initiates the traumatic process. The affective response to the signal of avoidable danger is fear, dread, or anxiety. The affective response to the perception of inevitable danger is the catatonoid reaction. (p. 154)

Within this model, childhood sexual abuse clearly represents catastrophic trauma that results in deficits in every area of ego functioning.

Another contemporary classical analyst writing about childhood sexual abuse and the adult survivor is Howard Levine (1990). He points to the primitive defensive constellation of the adult incest survivor and cites the centrality of dissociation in this population, saying, "From a diagnostic perspective, it may be useful to think of many of these analysands as having a split-ego organization, in which a healthier, neurotic part of the personality alternates with or lies buried beneath a more impulsive, primitive part of the personality" (p. 198). In addition, Levine is acutely aware that the severity of the original trauma engenders powerful transference/countertransference paradigms in which, because of the patient's uncertainty about the line between fantasy and reality, "the experience of the analytic situation becomes the trauma" (p. 199).

Levine thus credits the reality of the patient's childhood as the primary factor in the development of pathological fantasies regarding self and other that characterize the adult patient's interpersonal relationships, including the one with the therapist.

Selma Kramer (1990, 1991) also follows classical analytic treatment of adult survivors of childhood sexual abuse. Kramer describes the somatic decoding of traumatic events that is experienced by the patient as body memories in which the sexual abuse is relived as if it were happening in the present. In addition, she points to the problems in separation and individuation experienced by these patients and positions their sometimes entitled demands during treatment as the restarting of long-blocked developmental channels.

The ego psychologists thus assign more weight than the classicists to the impact of real, external events on the developing ego of the child. At the same time, they still emphasize the intrapsychic mediation of external events as central in resulting pathology. Like classical thinkers, ego-psychological clinicians pursue a primarily traditional, verbally interpretive mode of treatment with their patients. What to us remains insufficiently addressed in the ego-psychological model is the extent to which unsymbolized traumatic experiences, encrusted in a primitive core of unspeakable terror, intrusive ideation, and somatic sensations, exist cordoned off within the patient's psyche where they are unavailable to self-reflective verbal processes and traditional analytic examination.

The Object-Relational Perspective

The object-relational perspective on trauma, espoused by Fairbairn (1943), Khan (1963, 1964), Kluft (1990b), Miller (1981, 1983, 1984), Scharff (1982), Steele (1986) and implied by Balint (1979) and Winnicott (1960a, 1960b), although taking into account ego incapacitation and psychic helplessness in the pathogenicity of traumatic events, stresses most that early trauma signifies betrayal of the child by one or more important early objects. Here, object relations theorists intersect with psychodynamically oriented developmentalists (Bowlby, 1969, 1973; Stern, 1985) in emphasizing the primacy of early attachment bonds to significant objects. Thus, within this theoretical model, the central themes are not the magnitude of the overstimulation inherent in sexual abuse or the fantasy mediation of the traumatic event but the extent to which abusive behavior, especially by parents, represents a psychic abandonment and profound betrayal of the child. At issue are the primacy of the child's relationship to the abusive other and the parents' failure to protect the vulnerable child from intrusive abuse. According to object relations theory, it is the child's and, later, the adult's attempts to preserve actual and internalized relational bonds that result in symptoms, notably dissociation, and in character pathology.

W. R. D. (Ronald) Fairbairn (1943), a British Middle School object relations theorist, made important contributions to the psychoanalytic literature on the sequelae of childhood sexual abuse. He stressed the impact of actual relationships on a child's developing psyche and wrote poignantly, based on his work with sexually abused children, about the significance of exploitative contact with caretakers. He postulated that a relationship with a bad object is not only painful for the child but also shameful. Because early object relationships are based largely on identification, children whose parents are abusive or neglectful will feel that they themselves are bad. No matter how abusive or neglectful the parents are, the child needs them and therefore cannot reject them. The internalization of bad parental objects represents, according to Fairbairn, an effort to control them. He said, however: "But, in attempting to control them in this way, he is internalizing objects which have wielded power over him in the external world; and these objects retain their prestige for power over him in the inner world. In a word, he is 'possessed' by them, as if by evil spirits "(1943, p. 67). Certainly in our own work with sexual abuse survivors, we struggle with the "possession" of our patients by internalized abusive objects to whom the patient remains tenaciously affectively attached.

Fairbairn recognized that abused children dissociate. He pointed out that the child splits off, or dissociates, bad aspects of the object and of the self in relationship with the object in order to preserve a good image of much-needed caretakers and of the self. As the dissociation occurs, the child simultaneously represses awareness of these now split-off aspects of the self and other. In Fairbairn's model, repression takes place not to censor instinctual drives but, rather, to defend "the self against the awareness of its shameful deficiencies" (Grotstein, personal communication, 1992).

Alice Miller (1981, 1983, 1984), a former classicist who became more and more relationally oriented and eventually disavowed psychoanalysis entirely, expands on Fairbairn's work, highlighting the adult abuse survivor's tendency to protect parents by seeing them as more loving than they in fact were. Miller also emphasizes the extent to which analysts hear what they are prepared to hear and miss what does not fit into preconceived theoretical paradigms. It is also our contention that analysts and analytically oriented therapists fail to serve previously abused patients well when they focus too exclusively on intrapsychic fantasies and patterns.

The contemporary interpersonalist Darlene Ehrenberg's (1992) views on the impact of childhood sexual abuse are compatible with those of the object relationists. Ehrenberg particularly notes the stifling of all desire, sexual and otherwise, that often occurs as a result of sexual abuse. Like Fairbairn, Ehrenberg points out that children usually assume responsibility for their own abuse. They do this, first, because the sexual acts frequently correspond with age-appropriate fantasies and desires. Second, the child unconsciously identifies with the abuser's desires, making them her own in an attempt to relieve and cure the perpetrator. Ultimately, desire itself becomes so dangerous to the psychic equilibrium of the child, and then to that of the adult patient, that it is renounced in full. One vital aspect of psychoanalytic treatment with these patients, Ehrenberg says, is to work through their sense of responsibility for the abuse in order to unlock the capacity for desire.

Within object relations theory clinicians find treatment models that provide templates for the treatment of profoundly dissociated patients who must, in order to heal, regress during treatment. Although neither Balint (1979) nor Winnicott (1960a, 1960b), for example, directly address actual trauma, their treatment models emphasize the need of many patients to regress to the area of a "basic fault" (Balint, 1979), where verbal interpretation is at best meaningless and at worst assaultively intrusive. In work with regressed patients, Balint and Winnicott among others (Bollas, 1987; Khan, 1963; Ogden, 1986, 1991) deemphasize verbal interpretation and traditional analytic abstinence, stressing instead the containing functions of the therapist, in which nonverbal acceptance and management of regression are paramount. Certainly adult survivors of childhood sexual abuse require that the therapist be comfortable managing protracted regressive reenactments.

The Self-Psychological Perspective

Like object relationists, self psychologists underscore the relational aspects of trauma. They insist that developmental trauma occurs within an intersubjective field consisting of self and self-object; it is the profound disturbance between the child (self) and caregiver (self-object) that renders an occurrence traumatic. The concept of trauma was incorporated into Heinz Kohut's

(1971) general thinking about personality development and pathology and is addressed specifically by such contemporary self-psychologists as Ulman and Brothers (1988) and Stolorow and Atwood (1992).

Kohut (1971) stipulates that when early self-objects deprive or disappoint the child in traumatic ways, the basic psychic apparatus and the structure of the personality are adversely affected. He suggests that very early preoedipal trauma interferes with maintenance of the basic narcissistic homeostasis of the personality and results in "diffuse narcissistic vulnerability" (1971, p. 47). Later preoedipal trauma challenges successful drive control and leads to resexualization of drive derivatives and internal and external conflict. Finally, trauma during the oedipal period or latency results in incomplete idealization of the superego with a concomitant eternal search for approval from external figures.

Kohut took a broad view of trauma; object loss or disappointment in, deprivation from, neglect, or abuse by important figures in a child's life could constitute traumatic experience. Ulman and Brothers (1988), on the other hand, define trauma as a "real occurrence, the unconscious meaning of which so shatters central organizing fantasies (of self in relation to self-object) that self-restitution is impossible" (p. 3). The unconscious meaning of the shattering real event is expressed symbolically in the symptoms of post-traumatic stress disorder (PTSD), which Ulman and Brothers classify as a dissociative disorder emanating from a vertical split of the ego.

Ulman and Brothers assert that successful therapy with trauma patients rests on the therapist's ability to become for the patient a fantasized self-object that facilitates restoration and transformation of shattered fantasies of self (p. 4). They recommend a standard self-psychological analytic approach, using the intersubjective field created by therapist and patient to reconstruct and work through the unconscious meaning of trauma. They emphasize analysis of resistance to and ultimate development and working through of self-object transference fantasies.

Stolorow and Atwood (1992) agree with Ulman and Brothers that trauma occurs only within an intersubjective field. They stipulate that the essence of trauma involves a failure of affective attunement between caregiver and child (self and self-object) that results in a disrupted capacity for affect regulation in the trauma patient. It is, first, the pain of an initial rebuff from a caregiver and, second, the failure of the caregiver to attune to the child in a way that contains or relieves that pain that are traumatic. Stolorow and Atwood go on to cite the dissociation, chronic self-doubting, affective instability, pessimism, and self-blame characteristic of trauma survivors. They also indicate that, much as the abused child protects early objects by disavowing the reality of trauma, trauma patients may split off or blame themselves for disruptions in the intersubjective field of analysis. In treatment, therapeutic action occurs when the analyst is positioned within the transference as the longed-for parent who successfully affectively attunes to the patient's internal states, especially traumatogenic states. Finally, Stolorow and Atwood attend to the fierce dread of retraumatization as a central resistance in psychoanalysis with trauma patients.

Self- psychologists place trauma within a relational context, in which both the real event and the unconscious meaning of the real event as mediated by the trauma victim are emphasized. Like object relationists, they view the analytic relationship and the transference/countertransference constellations emerging within it as central aspects of therapy. What does not seem to be emphasized by these writers is the extensive regression that is often required in work with trauma patients.

Throughout the 100-year history of psychoanalysis, the study of early childhood trauma and of unconscious intraspsychic processes and development has shifted between point-counterpoint theories in an elaborately argued, often embittered, discourse on the etiological significance of specific precursors to adult emotional disorders. The relative importance of fact versus fantasy in the pathogenicity of traumatic events appears to have evolved as the emblematic substratum of such dialogs. Is it the reality of the traumatic event or the complex vicissitudes of its symbolic internalization that are disruptive to later functioning? Is it the impact of trauma on the structuralization of the ego or the nature of the unconscious fantasies evoked by the trauma that demand clinical attention? Or is it the effect of trauma on the internalized self and object world of the patient, signified by complex patterns of projective and introjective identification, that leads to pathology and therefore must be addressed during treatment? It is our contention that the pathogenicity of childhood sexual trauma derives from all these—and more. In addition to what we have learned from psychoanalytic thinking, we find additional important insights into early trauma and its sequelae in the trauma literature. It is only through combining psychoanalytic concepts emerging from each major school of thought with the wealth of data available in the trauma literature that we can arrive at an integrated conceptualization of childhood sexual abuse, its sequelae, and its treatment.

CHAPTER 2

Long-Term Sequelae and Diagnosis of Childhood Sexual Abuse

TWO BODIES of literature, one relating to psychological trauma and the other compiled by empiricists and clinicians in the sexual abuse field, combine with psychoanalytic theories to facilitate a comprehensive, multifaceted conceptualization of childhood sexual abuse, its sequelae, diagnosis, and treatment. It is only when contributions from each of these fields are interwoven that a rich, complex, and clinically useful model for the treatment of sexual abuse emerges.

The History of Trauma Research

Interest in the impact of trauma on an individual's psychology and physiology dates at least as far back as Pierre Janet's (1889, 1894, 1898, 1907, 1909, 1911) work on dissociation, which he viewed as the central organizing mechanism of trauma-related disorders. In a process parallel to what occurred within psychoanalysis after Freud's repudiation of the seduction theory, work in the field of trauma was suspended for the most part for many years after Janet's contributions. It was wartime that evoked renewed interest in the impact of trauma, as battlefield neurologists, psychiatrists, and eventually psychologists were faced with soldiers who were badly and pervasively disorganized by their wartime experiences. Attention to the acute and persistent aspects of war-related trauma particularly burgeoned after the Vietnam War (Card, 1983; Figley, 1978; Laufer, Frey-Wouters, & Gallops, 1985; Yager, Laufer, & Gallops, 1984), a war noted for the severity of the psychological impact felt by many of its soldiers.

In addition to work with war veterans, trauma researchers have investigated the recurrent sequelae of such other traumas as the Holocaust (Barocas, 1975; Bergman & Jucovy, 1982; Eitinger, 1980; Kestenberg, 1985;

Rakoff, 1966); Hiroshima (Lifton, 1967); natural and manmade disasters (Adams & Adams, 1984; Baum, Gatchel, & Schaeffer, 1983; Green, 1982; Green, Grace, Lindy, Titchener, & Lindy, 1983; Perry & Lindell, 1978); crime (Terr, 1979, 1983), including rape (Burgess & Homstrom, 1974a, 1974b, 1978; Frank, Turner, & Duffy, 1979; Kilpatrick, Veronen, & Resick, 1979; Sutherland & Scherl, 1970); and, more recently, child abuse, including sexual abuse (Herman, 1992; Kluft, 1990; Terr, 1990, 1991; van der Kolk, 1987). It is striking that survivors of very different traumas share many acute and long-term sequelae, suggesting that there are some response patterns to shock and trauma that are typical for our species.

The work of these trauma researchers has led to the nosological concept of post-traumatic stress disorder (PTSD) (American Psychiatric Association, 1987). As currently formulated in DSM-III-R, the diagnostic manual of the American Psychiatric Association, PTSD encompasses sequelae related to a wide variety of traumas, including both single and repeated events, associated with a spectrum of such events as war, disaster, crime, and accidents. The only unifying theme is that the traumatic experience be "outside the range of usual human experience" (American Psychiatric Association, 1987, p. 247). More recently, Herman (1992) has proposed a new nosological category, complex PTSD, reserved for survivors of prolonged, repeated trauma, such as hostages, prisoners of war, battered spouses, and victims of childhood physical and sexual abuse (p. 121). Complex PTSD reflects the profound psychological and physiological disruptions commonly found among survivors of prolonged trauma, including adult survivors of childhood sexual abuse. Repeated childhood sexual trauma affects every aspect of an individual's functioning: cognitive, affective, self-experiential, relational, and behavioral. Psychoanalysis enriches our clinical work with adult survivors of childhood sexual abuse with contributions from classical, ego-psychological, object-relational, and self-psychological perspectives, but the trauma literature extends our clinical conceptualizations by providing a psychobiological model of the consequences of trauma.

Developmental Aspects of Trauma

Developmentalists such as John Bowlby (1969) have long suggested a biological substrate to a child's attachment to important early objects. It is not surprising, therefore, that when early attachment bonds are disrupted through neglect and abuse, the child suffers physiological as well as psychological effects. Animal and human research suggests that disruptions of attachment affect operation of select neurotransmitters and the endogenous opioid and endocrine system (van der Kolk, 1987). Longlasting, even permanent, neurobiological abnormalities can be engendered by childhood abuse and deprivation that are reflected in the adult patient's tendency to swing between hyperarousal and hypoarousal to internal and external stimuli. This characteristic often is manifested clinically in sometimes rapid shifts between unformed, uncontainable panic, and equally unsymbolized, crushing depression. Recognizing that adult surivors of childhood sexual abuse labor under the impact of neurobiological impairments mediated by disrupted early attachment highlights the importance of the therapeutic relationship, specifically the containing and holding functions of the therapist.

Cognitive Sequelae of Trauma

Psychological trauma has a disorganizing effect on an individual's ability to encode, process—through assimilation and accommodation (Piaget, 1968)— and store memories of the traumatic events (Fine, 1990; Fish-Murray, Koby, & van der Kolk, 1987; Janoff-Bulman, 1985; van der Kolk, 1988; van der Kolk & Ducey, 1989). By definition, trauma overwhelms. Part of what is overwhelmed in a sexually traumatized child is the ability to cognitively contain and process the enormity of the relational betrayal and physical impingement with which she is faced. Even if the child has reached the level of operational metaphoric thinking, the trauma engenders a regression to more concrete, sensorimotor iconic cognitive organization (van der Kolk, 1988). Here, too, biology plays a part in the response to trauma.

The encoding of memory involves the taxon system, which encodes information according to quality, and the hippocampus, which matures later and locates memories in space and time (van der Kolk, 1988). Severe or prolonged stress suppresses hippocampal functioning and potentiates the taxon system, leading to unsymbolized, context-free encoding of the traumatic experiences that renders the memories unavailable to linguistic retrieval. It becomes one function of the therapist to allow the adult survivor to relive traumatic memories sensorimotorically, that is, through body memories, and to help the patient symbolize these memories for the first time. Sensorimotor abreaction and symbolic transformation and integration are crucial. Obviously, symbolization can only proceed from reliving; abreactive reliving without symbolization and integration, however, is retraumatizing. Among other things, it engenders physiological hyperarousal without compensatory structuralization of experience.

In addition to affecting the traumatized individual's encoding and storage of traumatic events, trauma has long-term implications for the survivor's ability to engage in sublimatory, productive fantasy. Comparing the Rorschach responses of Vietnam combat veterans suffering from PTSD with those of combat veterans without PTSD, van der Kolk and Ducey (1989) conclude that the PTSD veterans show a biphasic response to the trauma.

They are either dominated by chronic, intrusive, disorganizing, unsymbol-ized "memories" of the trauma, or they avoid to the extreme any involve-ment in affect-potentiating mental activity, such as fantasizing, that might evoke a reexperience of the trauma, or they have both reactions. These researchers conclude that the PTSD veterans are unable to "symbolize, fan-tasize, or sublimate" (p. 267). Fish-Murray, Koby, and van der Kolk's (1987) analysis of abused children reveals similar all-or-nothing patterns with regard to fantasy.

In our own work with adult patients who were sexually abused as chil-dren, we also note a bifurcated ability to fantasize; a similar finding has been noted by Bollas (1989). Not always, but often, the patient is able to engage in transforming, sublimatory fantasies about aspects of her life, such as work, that are associationally disengaged from the traumatic history. In these areas, the patient can use fantasy creatively to plan, problem-solve, and ex-periment. When mental activity turns to areas of life associationally linked with the earlier traumas, however (e.g., sexual relationships with men, the expression of aggression toward authority figures), we find the biphasic pat-terns described by van der Kolk and Ducey (1989). The patient is alterna-tively overwhelmed and dominated by unsymbolized versions of the trauma and then rigidly defends against, and detaches from, any mental ac-tivity whatsoever.

For instance, Adrianna was abused sexually and physically by her father. A successful investment banker, this patient has a full, rich fantasy life about relatively nonconflictual aspects of her life such as her career, advancing her education, entertaining friends in her home. When she becomes involved with a man or contemplates visits with her family, however, Adrianna por-trays the biphasic pattern described above. When having sex with a boyfriend, for example, she may at times be overwhelmed by body sensa-tions or "memories" reminiscent of her abuse—her thighs are experienced as huge, and her anus contracts with pain (her father penetrated her anally). At other times, she becomes utterly numb and rigid during sex, reporting that her brain is "dead" and devoid of mental activity. Adult sexual relations clearly evoke the emergence of traumatic memories that overwhelm her cog-nitive capacities, as once did the actual traumatic events.

In addition to the impact of trauma on memory and fantasy, trauma re-sults in a constellation of cognitive symptoms. These include inflexible cog-nitive schemata (Fish-Murray, Koby, & van der Kolk, 1987), intrusive thoughts, or flashbacks of the trauma (Herman, 1992; Terr, 1991; van der Kolk, 1988); dichotomous thinking (Fine, 1990), misattribution of blame and responsibility for past and present events (Young, 1988), and a sense of a foreshortened future (Terr, 1991). From the trauma literature, we thus obtain a picture of the pervasive and persistent cognitive disruptions engendered by psychological trauma.

Affective Sequelae of Trauma

Trauma research has identified an affective response pattern characteristic of survivors of psychological trauma of all kinds. The pattern is marked by the survivor's shift between states of affective numbing and intense hyperarousal (van der Kolk & Greenberg, 1987). The inability to modulate arousal often leads to inappropriate motoric discharge of unbearable anxiety when the individual is hyperaroused and to similarly inappropriate emotional and psychomotor constriction in the state of psychic numbing.

When an individual is subjected to stress, the autonomic nervous system is aroused to stimulate a stress response. In such a chronic trauma as child abuse, autonomic arousal occurs again and again in an ongoing situation of physical and relational impingement, in which the child cannot intervene effectively. Autonomic arousal becomes a generalized organismic reaction to stress, in which the connection between the severity of the perceived threat and the degree of arousal is broken. The survivor, unable to discern between degrees of actual danger, responds to many stressors with autonomic hyperarousal that can result in such seemingly inexplicable behavioral reactions as temper outbursts or terrified withdrawal.

Animal research suggests that neurotransmitters and endogenous opioids also are involved in the trauma survivor's inability to modulate arousal and, thus, affective response (van der Kolk & Greenberg, 1987). For instance, norepinephrine and dopamine depletion, resulting from inescapable stress, leaves the traumatized individual psychobiologically hypersensitive to later arousal. Research with animals also implies that organisms subjected to prolonged stress develop a physiological dependence on the analgesia resulting from the release of endogenous opioids that is stimulated by trauma. This can lead to an active search for stressful stimuli in order to achieve a state of soothing calm, even numbness. As the endogenous opioid effect recedes, the organism suffers symptoms consistent with opioid withdrawal, including anxiety or aggressive displays.

The trauma survivor's tendency toward hyperarousal stems in part, then, from ongoing alterations in neurochemical operations. It is vital that the psychodynamically oriented clinician appreciate these neurobiological sequelae of trauma when treating patients who were sexually abused as children. The trauma literature indicates, for instance, that psychopharmacological agents, particularly some antidepressants, noradrenergic activity inhibitors, benzodiazepines, lithium, and carbamazepine, may help modulate the hyper- and hypoarousal states of the adult trauma survivor (Silver, Sandberg, & Hales, 1990; van der Kolk & Greenberg, 1987). Such psychotropic intervention is sometimes a necessary adjunct to psychodynamic psychotherapy that allows the patient to modulate affective arousal enough to make more constructive use of therapy.

Dissociation: The Impact of Trauma on the Organization of Self

Dissociation, although affecting an individual's cognitive, affective, relational, and behavioral functioning, leads first and foremost to a disruption of the organization of self. Unlike repression, which is a horizontal division into conscious and unconscious mental contents, dissociation involves a vertical splitting of the ego that results in two or more self states that are more or less organized and independently functioning. These two or more ego states alternate in consciousness and, under different internal and external circumstances, emerge to think, behave, remember, and feel. Such dissociated states are unavailable to the rest of the personality and, as such, cannot be subject to psychic operations of elaboration. They are likely to make their presence felt via the emergence of recurrent intrusive images, violent or symbolic enactments, inexplicable somatic sensations, recurrent nightmares, anxiety reactions, and psychosomatic conditions.

Colin Ross (1989, p. 89) asserts that dissociation exists on a continuum that includes what is normal biological (forgetting that one got up in the middle of the night to go to the bathroom), normal psychosocial (daydreaming during a boring lecture), abnormal biological (amnesia after a concussion), and abnormal psychosocial (amnesia for incest). It is abnormal psychosocial dissociation as defined by Ross that commonly coexists with trauma, including childhood sexual abuse.

Pierre Janet (1898) first linked trauma and dissociation almost 100 years ago. Janet believed that memory was an act of creative integration by which human beings organized, encoded, and categorized experiences into already existing cognitive schemata (van der Kolk, Brown & Van der Hart, 1989). Here is the early precursor of Piaget's bipolar dialectic between assimilation and accommodation. When an event in a person's life was too bizarre, terrifying, or overstimulating to fit into such preexisting schemata, Janet believed that it was split off from consciousness into a separate system of "fixed ideas" (Janet, 1898). There they became incorporated into their own system of organization, untouched or unmodulated by the rest of the individual's experience.

With Freud's discovery of and emphasis on repression as the central defense mechanism in neuroses, discussion of dissociation for the most part faded after Janet. Although dissociation was mentioned occasionally over the years (Dickes, 1965; Fairbairn, 1954; Fliess, 1953; Sullivan, 1956), it is only recently that trauma researchers integrated the concept into a model of the psychological regulatory processes evoked by trauma. Now, most trauma writers (Braun, 1986; Figley, 1986; Green, Wilson, & Lindy, 1985; Herman, 1992; Hilgard, 1977; Kluft, 1990b; Putnam, 1989; Spiegel, 1986; Van der Hart & Horst, 1989; van der Kolk, 1987; Wilson, Smith, & Johnson, 1985) view abnormal psychosocial dissociation as defined by Ross (1989) as a hallmark of trauma. In fact, van der Kolk & Kadish (1987) state that "Except when related to brain injury, dissociation always seems to be a response to traumatic life events" (p. 185).

Richard Kluft (1984) and Braun and Sachs (1985) propose similar etiological models of dissociation. First, the individual is likely to have some biopsychological predisposition to dissociate. This is akin to innate hypnotizability. Next, these researchers suggest that there is a severely traumatic life event with which the individual attempts to cope through dissociation. Kluft (1984) stipulates that severe dissociation indicates that the traumatized person engaged in ongoing dissociative activities after the initial trauma and that the environment failed to provide sufficient restorative experiences to intervene in continued dissociation. Braun and Sachs (1985), in their discussion of severe dissociation, state that the initial trauma is followed by other traumatic events that chain the dissociated experiences affectively.

David Spiegel (1986) offers another compelling etiological factor in dissociation certainly at work in the incestuous family. Spiegel cites the double bind as a powerful generator of dissociative phenomena in the individual predisposed to this psychic mechanism. In a double bind, the family issues a primary injunction to the child that is utterly contradicted by a second, more subtle injunction; finally the child is prohibited from openly addressing the contradiction (Spiegel, 1986, p. 67). In essence, the child is directed to "become two contradictory people simultaneously" (p. 69) and, furthermore, is made to understand that there can be no comment on this demand. Dissociation, suggests Spiegel, allows the child to become, in fact, two separately functioning people without being conscious of the contradiction.

It is clear that a child faced with ongoing sexual abuse and who is developmentally predisposed to dissociate exists in a world consistent with the models proposed by Kluft (1984), Braun and Sachs (1985), and Spiegel (1986). There is a triggering traumatic event—the first episode of sexual abuse—that is repeated over time in a family environment that all too often fails to restoratively provision the victim. Rather, the family double binds the child by insisting that she simultaneously become a demure "good girl" and a sultry sexual partner to the perpetrator and further enjoins her not to know about or point out the contradictory demands. The child in this situation employs dissociation during the abusive assaults and often, over time, resorts to this now tried-and-true mechanism whenever she wishes or needs to escape an aversive reality. We see this most dramatically in patients who, generally submissive, depressed, and inhibited, in a dissociated state enact wildly aggressive or sexually provocative behavior and later have no or only hazy memories of their seemingly ego alien activities. Here, we find a patient quite literally divided, self-state against self-state. This patient is unable to achieve ordinary self-consciousness, for to do so would unleash long warded-off terror, rage, and desperate helplessness associated with the early sexual traumas. In fact, the trauma literature (Spiegel, 1986) suggests that it is often only when the adult survivor can stand to reenter the affective state of primitive confusion, sense of impending annihilation, and utter helplessness that the memories of traumatic events can be reclaimed, symbolically encoded for the first time, and integrated into the consciousness of the adult patient.

Relational Sequelae of Trauma

The trauma survivor's capacity to form and maintain relationships, particularly intimate ones, is limited by the long-term effects of trauma. Trauma writers suggest that these interpersonal deficits are linked to the survivor's identity diffusion and tendency to react to others based on expectations forged during the trauma.

Mitchell Young (1988) describes the "inert identity" of the trauma survivor, saying, "The inert identity is composed of separation, disintegration, and stasis and is not able to experience connection, integrity, and movement" (p. 39). Adult survivors of childhood sexual abuse indeed often conform to Young's depiction of inert identity. Although they may have painstakingly constructed a public persona that is superficially friendly, vibrant, and efficacious, this identity is experienced as inauthentic and extraordinarily fragile. Just below the surface of this often impressively functioning veneer, the trauma survivor is trapped in an inner world of fragmentation, dissociation, terror, and rage. Often frightened that others will discover the hidden truths about them, trauma survivors, including patients with histories of sexual abuse, remain essentially disconnected from others. As Young points out, these patients are frozen in time, unable to flexibly respond to present-day relational demands and opportunities.

In addition to interpersonal problems emanating from trauma survivors' diffuse identities is their tendency to form a "traumatic transference" (Spiegel, 1986, p. 72) to others, including the therapist. Within a traumatic transference, the trauma survivor may exhibit rapidly shifting relational postures, ranging from extreme dependency and vicious abuse to stark terror or cold aloofness that lead to chaotic interpersonal relationships or isolation. Real mutuality and intimacy born of shared authenticity are impaired.

The trauma survivor's capacity for relational intimacy is also disrupted by the symptoms of PTSD, including affective swings between hyperarousal and psychic numbing. Finally, the sexual abuse survivor's tendency to experience disorganizing flashbacks, especially during sexual engagement with a partner with whom the patient has grown emotionally close, renders intimacy painfully difficult to achieve.

The Effects of Trauma on Behavior

Perhaps the most dramatic manifestation of trauma is the survivor's reenactment of traumatic events through self-destructive actions. The patient with a history of psychological trauma frequently presents with a truly spectacular array of self-damaging behaviors, ranging from nonlethal forms of compulsive self-abuse to acute and persistent suicidality. Traumatized patients frequently cling tenaciously to these behaviors, which seem, for a long time, impervious to therapeutic intervention. Although psychoanalysis provides various important dynamic understandings of traumatic reenactments, the trauma literature offers a psychobiological explanation of the addiction to ongoing trauma.

As already noted, animal research indicates that the security of a child's early attachments affects the endogenous opioid system, with insecure attachment resulting in decreased brain opioid activity. In addition, high levels of stress have been found to activate the opioid systems of animals (Amir, Brown, & Amit, 1980; Miczek, Thompson, & Shuster, 1982). Van der Kolk (1989) concludes that, partially as a result of the attachment deficits and chronic hyperarousal that come with child abuse, adult survivors may require higher external stimulation of the endogenous opioid system to counteract hyperarousal and achieve a state of calm. They therefore develop a chemical and psychological addiction to exposure to the traumatic situations that in some ways mimics the drug addict's. According to van der Kolk (1989) such enactments as self-mutilation produce an altered state of consciousness that calms and soothes the trauma survivor. Furthermore, terminating situations reminiscent of the original trauma(s) may engender withdrawal symptoms not unlike those experienced by the addict. This addictive quality, combined with the temporary tranquilizing effectiveness of self-abuse or other traumatic reenactments, contribute to the intractability of the trauma survivor's enacting behavior.

In addition to compulsive repetition of trauma, the neurobiologically mediated shifts from hyperarousal to psychic numbing result in seemingly unpredictable changes in behavior. When hyperaroused, a normally placid, even withdrawn, patient may become openly aggressive, verbally assaulting the therapist and others or motorically discharging affect (e.g., by throwing things or stamping feet). The same patient, when psychically numb, may become rigid, withdrawn, and virtually unresponsive to attempts to make contact. Finally, a patient whose use of dissociation results in severe fragmentation of the ego may exhibit very different behaviors when another self-state emerges. For instance, a usually conservatively dressed, well coiffed patient who usually sits poised on the couch may suddenly muss her hair and curl into a ball when in a more primitively organized self state.

The trauma literature enhances our understanding of the adult survivor

TABLE 2.3
Adult Symptoms of Childhood Sexual Abuse

Amnesia for All or Specific Periods of Childhood

Physical Complaints

Migraine headaches
Gastrointestinal problems
TMJ (temporomandibular joint) disorder
Ulcers
Gynecological difficulties

Sleep Disturbances

Nightmares
Insomnia
Fear of the dark
Fear of someone breaking into the house at night

Sexual Dysfunction

Physiological dysfunction
    Arousal disorder
    Vaginismus
    Anorgasmia
    Dyspareunia
    Sexual anesthesia
Aversion to men
Promiscuity
Prostitution
Intense shame at self as sexual being

Other Symptoms

Anorexia or bulimia; compulsive overeating
Distorted body image
Shame during pregnancy; feeling that it is "wrong" to be pregnant
Parenting problems, especially with daughters
Self-mutilation
Suicidal ideation; suicide attempts
Low self-esteem
Chronic, free-floating guilt
Chronic shame
Depression
Subjective feeling of being wholly, inherently bad
Subjective feeling of not belonging, not fitting in, being different
Difficulty trusting others, particularly men
Social alienation or isolation, or compulsive socializing and a need to please
PTSD symptoms
History of adult rape, sexual and/or physical victimizations
Chronic dissociation

Research in the area of childhood sexual abuse is still young; the majority of the literature in the field has been published only within the last 15 years. For a long time, studies, mostly drawn from clinical samples, simply listed symptoms reported by adult survivors without verifying the discriminative power of these markers. More recently, an emergence of research has provided data successfully differentiating abused from nonabused women on the basis of certain symptom clusters (Bagley & Ramsay, 1986; Briere, 1988; Briere & Runtz, 1986, 1988; Gold, 1986; Surrey et al., 1990). These studies indicate that, as more sophisticated, methodologically impressive research is conducted on the long-term effects of childhood sexual abuse, it becomes clearer that women who were sexually abused as children give evidence of specific symptoms and behaviors that are correlated with their histories of abuse and that set them apart from women who have no abuse histories.

Diagnostic Considerations: Post-Traumatic Stress Disorder and Borderline Pathology

Psychological trauma survivors, including adult survivors of childhood sexual abuse, elicit a number of diagnoses on both Axis I and Axis II of the DSM-III-R (American Psychiatric Association, 1987). The affective disruptions stemming from the patient's tendency to shift from hyperarousal and psychic numbing often warrant an Axis I mood disorder or anxiety diagnosis. The cognitive symptoms, combined with the patient's use of dissociation, can lead to diagnoses of various dissociative disorders and to the misdiagnosis of psychotic conditions. Patients are also often assigned such Axis II diagnoses as histrionic personality disorder, schizotypal personality disorder, and, very often, borderline personality disorder.

Recently, trauma and sexual abuse researchers have begun to investigate a specific diagnostic issue that has profound implications for psychodynamically oriented clinicians: the relationship between early trauma and adult borderline pathology. It also addresses the possible overlap between PTSD and what traditionally has been conceptualized as borderline personality disorder, or borderline ego organization (Kernberg, 1984). These studies (Herman, Perry, & van der Kolk, 1989; Perry, Herman, van der Kolk, & Hoke, 1990; Saunders, 1991; Shearer, Peters, Quaytman, & Ogden, 1990; Stone, 1990; Stone, Unwin, Beacham, & Swenson, 1989) suggest that many patients assigned a borderline diagnosis report, when asked, histories of early trauma and, conversely, that many patients who report actual childhood trauma show borderline pathology. For instance, Herman (1989) found that 81% of patients who met criteria for borderline personality disorder gave histories of major childhood trauma, including childhood sexual abuse; this was significantly higher than for patients diagnosed with only borderline traits or with no borderline pathology. Ross (1989) goes as far as to say that "borderlines don't have either personality disorders or psychoses: They have chronic trauma disorder" (p. 149).

Research on this crucial diagnostic clarification is in its infancy, and conclusive results await us only in the future. These early studies certainly suggest, however, that we consider the possibility that patients presenting with borderline pathology are, in fact, suffering from the sequelae of early trauma. At this point, we can examine a well-accepted psychodynamic diagnostic model of borderline ego organization (Kernberg, 1984) to determine if these diagnostic criteria are compatible with a view of borderline pathology as etiologically linked to early trauma.

Otto Kernberg (1984) proposes a model for differentiating between neurotic, borderline, and psychotic ego structures. Patients in the borderline range of ego functioning, as stipulated by Kernberg, have symptoms and psychological regulatory mechanisms consistent with those described in much of the literature on borderline pathology (Gunderson, 1984; Masterson, 1976; Meissner, 1988; Searles, 1986; Volkan, 1987). What we find on closer examination, however, is that these patients also conform to the description of trauma survivors emerging from the trauma literature.

One of the primary diagnostic criteria in Kernberg's model is the extent to which the borderline patient presents with identity diffusion, defined as an inability to integrate contradictory representations of self and other. This kind of identity diffusion is completely consistent with the disturbances in identity and object relations described in the trauma literature, as emanating from the traumatized individuals' use of dissociation, their inert identities (Young, 1988), and their tendency to form traumatic transferences to others (Spiegel, 1990).

The next criterion for the diagnosis of borderline ego structure is the defensive constellation of the patient. Borderlines are said to use primarily "low-level defenses" (Kernberg, 1984), such as splitting, projection, projective identification, denial, primitive idealization and devaluation, omnipotence, and acting out. Dissociation could be added. All of these defenses incorporate some aspect of splitting, which is an adaptive and necessary defense for the trauma victim. The trauma literature is clear that repression is insufficient to cope with the overwhelming assault on the ego embodied by psychological trauma, especially child abuse. Other defenses, based on splitting, are required for the trauma victim to survive; they are the only methods by which the victim can preserve some semblance of good self and other representations.

Another diagnostic criterion of borderline pathology is the patient's usually intact reality testing that falters under increasing internal or external stress or decreasing environmental structure. Once again, we find compatibility here with the trauma survivor's tendency to shift between usually accurate reality testing and a loss of that capacity under stress, especially when internal or external stimuli trigger the emergence of warded-off memories of traumatic events. These lapses often correspond to the appearance of a wildly terrified, desperately confused, primitively organized dissociated ego state that is frozen in time in a traumatized condition.

Kernberg also describes "nonspecific" manifestations of ego weakness associated with borderline pathology: an intolerance for anxiety, poor impulse control, deficits in the ability to sublimate, and a lack of superego integration marked by primitively sadistic and highly idealized object representations. All of these markers of borderline pathology are also compatible with indicators of psychological trauma. The survivor's tendency to regress when hyperaroused is akin to the anxiety intolerance described here. Similarly, the borderline patient's poor impulse control can be conceptualized as the trauma victim's neurobiologically driven addiction to ongoing traumatic stimulation as well as their tendency to relate to others via a traumatic transference that elicits dramatic "flight or fight" behaviors. Sublimatory ineffectiveness, likewise, is consistent with the traumatized patient's bifurcated fantasy life, in which sublimatory mental activity is at times foreshortened by overwhelming, unsymbolized memories and fantasy elaborations of earlier abuse. Finally, the unintegrated superego of the borderline patient fits a model of trauma in which the survivor is dominated by internalized sadistic objects defensively offset by highly idealized compensatory objects.

Current research does not allow us to conclude that all borderlines are really trauma survivors or that all adult trauma survivors exhibit borderline ego structure. However, the available research, combined with the diagnostic symmetry between criteria for borderline pathology and chronic PTSD compel us to consider that the borderline patient before us may be a survivor of early psychological trauma. Herman et al.'s (1989) studies, in fact, suggest that the more severely borderline the patient, the more likely it is that early trauma took place. The possibility that a borderline patient has a history of actual trauma should therefore be seriously considered. Practitioners can question these patients about early traumatic events, including childhood sexual abuse, and can attend to derivatives, dreams, and, especially, transference and countertransference phenomena with an openness to their traumatic roots.

CHAPTER 3

An Integrative Model of Childhood Sexual Abuse

IN THIS CHAPTER we move from the theoretical and experimental to the clinical and attempt to organize what we have learned from reviewing both the psychoanalytic and the contemporary research literature into an integrated model for the psychoanalytic treatment of adult survivors of childhood sexual abuse. We focus on the pervasive developmental arrests and defensive accommodations that manifest themselves in the emergence of particular recurrent clinical phenomena woven as leitmotifs throughout the therapeutic process, as well as the particular sequelae of chronic childhood trauma whose dramatic effects often disorganize therapist and patient alike, foreclosing prematurely on the therapeutic process and its promise for change.

From the extensive literature on posttraumatic and delayed, posttraumatic stress reactions, it is clear that such a severe and chronic trauma as childhood sexual abuse exerts a defining influence on all aspects—cognitive, emotional, behavioral, and relational—of the adult survivor's internal organization and understanding of the world. Most powerfully affected is the adult patient's organization of self and object representations. The often mutually incompatible representations of parent as perpetrator and otherwise loving other, as well as the polar experiences of self which grow up around such disparate object representations come to be tolerated and ultimately internalized via the defensive process of dissociation. Though we are respectful of the enormous contribution made by trauma researchers, without whose understanding of the traumatic process effective treatment would be impossible, we remain sceptical that the kinds of "cathartic" and "abreactive" treatment suggestions which grow out of some of this literature can be sufficient in accomplishing the kinds of internal changes we deem necessary. If one of the goals of treatment is to help the patient to understand the way in which his or her particular internal organization of self and object images makes its presence felt in the difficult external world of interpersonal relationships, something way beyond the abreactive recovery of traumatic memory is required.

It is our belief that it is only within a relational-psychoanalytically oriented framework, that the full complexity of the human mind and its remarkable adaptation to abuse can come to be appreciated. It is within this model that symbols, fantasies, ego disruptions, and experiences of abandonment and betrayal are shaped and given meaning by dint of their function and significance within a system of complex self-object configurations. Here complex relational patterns—current, transferential, and past—provide the key to understanding the particular systems of self- and object-related imagery through which the patient organizes experience; the dissociation employed to prevent the traumatic memories and their associated fantasies from infiltrating and poisoning more benign representations; and the splitting, projection, and projective identifications that are the hallmarks of the adult survivors' internal object world and current interpersonal difficulties.

Four Points of Interface

There are four particular areas of interface where trauma theory can help to illuminate the psychoanalytic process with adult survivors of childhood sexual abuse and the kinds of clinical adjustments that may become necessary in the course of treatment.

The Symbolic Encoding of Traumatic Memory

A classical approach to traumatic memory deemphasizes the importance of the actual sexual abuse itself, stressing instead the primacy of meaning with which these events become imbued for the particular individual. Here it is the system of fantasies that grows up around experiences of abuse, the way in which such experiences reactivate and intensify earlier pregenital, primarily sadomasochistic organizations of fantasy and experience that are of primary importance.

In contrast, however, trauma research informs us that the more overwhelming the actual experiences of sexual abuse are, that is, the more sadistic the forms of abuse, the earlier the age of onset, the more central the relationship between victim and perpetrator, the more overwhelmed and disorganized the patient will become. Such a view, which stresses the traumatic overwhelming of the ego, implies dysfunctions in all areas of psychological organization—affective, cognitive, and self-regulatory. Here the organizing, synthesizing, symbolizing functions of the ego are overstimulated and flooded, both by the psychological regression precipitated by childhood abuse and by the physiologically mediated hyperreactivity secondary to experiences of childhood terror. These experiences thus become ones of unformulated experiential chaos. With no self-reflective observing ego to provide even the rudiments of containment, meaning, and structure to the traumatic events, the child exists in a timeless, objectless, and selfless nightmare of unending pain, isolation, and ultimately psychic dissolution. Memories of such abuse, when they do return, do so only in the form of intrusive idetic imagery, radical and inexplicable mood shifts, somatically experienced symptomatology, panic attacks, and so on. One patient's recovery of early abuse memories began with repeated episodes of midnight awakenings in which she felt that she was choking on some "horrid liquid substance" that she "could neither swallow nor bring up." Another patient had recurring images of a man standing menacingly at her door each night as she fell asleep. "It seemed like a hallucination, yet I knew that I wasn't crazy. I had an overwhelming sense of impending danger that I could not shake."

Embedded in the continuum between verbally encoded memory and such unformulated experience is a fundamental question that cuts to the core of a major therapeutic debate. Is the traumatic experience embedded in a fantasy-imbued meaning that can be verbalized, experienced, and made available to traditional psychoanalytic interpretation; or has the ego regression precipitated by trauma rendered symbolic functions inoperative? To the extent that the traumatic experiences remain unsymbolized, they lie encrusted in a primitive core of unspeakable terror and phenomenologically meaningless panic, intrusive ideation, and somatic sensation. As such, they exist outside the usual domain of recalled experience, unavailable to self-reflective processes and analytic examination. Only an approach that integrates what we have come to understand about the symbolization and encoding of traumatic memory within the framework of a relationally oriented psychoanalytic approach can provide an arena for working through such traumatic memories.

Dissociated Systems of Self and Object Representation

From a review of the trauma literature one comes away with an unshakeable belief in the inextricable connection between recurrent childhood abuse and the defensive process of dissociation. Although the concept of dissociation is reviewed in some detail in chapter 4, we wish to emphasize here the enhancement one achieves by incorporating this concept within a psychoanalytic perspective. The research literature speaks of the dissociation of traumatic events and the memories of those events, which remain unintegrated and unconnected with the remainder of the individual's experiences. Our integrative model stresses that it is not only the memory of specific traumatic events that comes to be dissociated from other experiences but also the organization of mutually exclusive systems of self and object representations that have been formed in relationship to such traumatic moments. It is only via the reactivation of such dissociated systems of self and object representations that the therapist working with an adult survivor can help the patient to integrate these otherwise inaccessible images that so influence his or her interpersonal experience of the world. In other words, it is not only the memories of specific abusive experiences that we should seek to integrate more effectively but also each patient's multiple experiences of self as they exist in relationship to defensively fragmented aspects of her internal object world. Here is the contemporary analog to Janet's work on dissociation and to our own current integrative approach to treating traumatogenic disorders.

Sudden Regressions and Experiences of Disorganization

The developmental literature, regardless of the particular psychoanalytic orientation, presupposes that the consolidation of ego development and self integrity begins around a secure attachment to a loving and protective other. This attachment provides the secure base, the backdrop of safety, order, predictability, and control that allows the young child to begin his relationship to our complex, dangerous, and oftentimes, overstimulating world. This secure relationship becomes the haven from which young children draw their confidence in their capacity to control external events; the omnipotence, if you will, that potentiates the child's active engagement in what might otherwise seem to be overwhelming developmental tasks. It is also the retreat to which the child withdraws for soothing and comfort when that omnipotence is challenged or thwarted by experiences of failure and frustration.

The intensity and primacy of this early parental bond and the developmental chaos that accompanies its disruption have been well documented in both human and primate research. Van der Kolk (1987) sees the loss of this secure base as the "earliest and possibly most damaging psychological trauma" (p. 32). From this point of view, it is both the parent who abuses and the parent who fails to protect who are guilty of primary betrayal; of abrogating essential and fundamental parental responsibility. Brandt Steele (1986) stresses this point:

> We are convinced, however, that the more significant element, at least from the standpoint of production of psychological damage, is not the strength of the stimuli themselves, but the failure of the protective shield which would enable the psychic apparatus to assimilate or counteract the stimuli. . . . It is easier in diagnosing traumatic maltreatment of children to count the bruises and fractures or sexual assaults than it is to establish how much love, care, and protection was not there. Likewise, it is easier in treatment to describe past events of physical and sexual trauma than it is to reconstruct the more significant but less easily accessible deficits in the protective shield. This is especially difficult if the abuser is at the same time a primary care giver (pp. 61–62).

Children deprived of this ongoing sense of well-being become anxiously attached and fearful. Even the most severe abuse, paradoxically, intensifies, rather than discourages, this desperate clinging behavior. Pynoos and Eth (1985), who have written extensively on the manifestations of posttraumatic stress disorders in abused children, make similar observations. They describe these children as unable to modulate aggression either toward others or toward themselves. They note extensive self-destructive and self-mutilating behavior, perseverative, rhythmical attempts at self-soothing, cognitive changes, time distortions, a tendency toward magical thinking, and a lifelong vulnerability to severe depressive episodes.

Certainly, adults who were sexually abused as children, particularly in cases where such abuse was perpetrated by one or both parents, find it impossible to evoke the presence of loving and protective internal objects at times when states of panic threaten acute regressive disorganization. As no parent or loving other appeared to put an end to the nights of terror-filled abuse, the adult survivor becomes unable to call upon internal representations of protective internal objects to help soothe, contain, and ultimately control flashback experiences of panic, disorganization, and physiologically mediated states of intense hyperarousal. Indeed, the trauma literature would warn us that survivors demonstrate a decreased ability to use symbolic mental operations at all, and under the sway of such arousal and disorganization, where mental processes fail, the trauma survivor becomes used to responding to threats or perceived threats via action rather than thought.

The same literature also informs us that even the most arbitrary events, because they were in the past associated with abusive situations, can trigger the kinds of acute regressions about which we speak. When such triggers emerge from the patient's experience of intense transference-countertransference involvements, the object-related nature of the regression can make it appear even more abrupt, intense, and disruptive. Thus, it is imperative that the clinician working with an adult survivor of childhood sexual abuse become familiar and comfortable with the kinds of abrupt shifts, dramatic mood changes, and disorganizing regressive episodes that become one of the defining hallmarks of this complex work. In the absence of any external or internal loving and supportive objects, it is ultimately between patient and therapist that this net of safety must be woven in order to allow for the unfolding and emergence of such toxic and dangerous internal representations.

Hyperreactivity and Trauma Response to Arbitrary Stimuli

In chapter 2, we reviewed the biochemical changes that occur after early and chronic childhood abuse. It is now well accepted within the trauma field that such intense, "all-or-nothing" responses include generalized overreactivity, startle responses, extreme irritability, nightmares, intrusive thoughts, flashbacks to traumatic events through the evocation of state-dependent memories, and ultimately the kind of regression and disorganization of thought processes just described. Of particular importance in the clinical understanding and management of these symptoms is the finding that, in traumatic stress reactions, habituation to the original traumatic stimulus can occur, and apparently neutral, yet associated stimuli come to elicit such traumatic response (van der Kolk, 1988). Certainly, this list of symptoms is familiar to those working with adult survivors of childhood sexual abuse and perhaps with the broader category of patients we have become used to thinking of as manifesting severe borderline pathology.

Clinical manifestations of these processes abound in work with adults who were sexually abused as children. One patient would begin to tremble and sweat at the mere taste of peanut butter. She reported feeling dizzy and "fuzzy-headed"; unable to organize her thoughts following such exposure. It was some time before the patient was able to fully understand this symptom. Although peanut butter does not appear to be directly related to the incestuous experiences between this patient and her father, peanut butter sandwiches were the lunch they always shared on the days when her mother left them alone together. It had thus become a simple, classically learned conditioned stimulus, associatively linked with incestuous memories, evoking a physiological response even before these memories were recovered in treatment.

Such connections are invaluable to an understanding of the physiological processes that connect psyche to soma. They help to explicate certain psychoanalytic explanations of this relationship, such as Joyce McDougall's conceptualization of somatic symptomatology as rooted in the foreclosure of symbolic representation (1989) or Henry Krystal's understanding of alexithymia as the severence between affect and its representational links (1988). Awareness of these symptoms is useful, too, in sensitizing us to the possible presence of early traumatic experience. Patients with histories of trauma often present with a multitude of startling and medically inexplicable somatic complaints. Such presentation or experiences of medical confusion and undiagnosable symptomatalogy should alert the clinician to the possibility of childhood abuse in the patient's history.

The Clinical Presentation of Traumatic Childhood Abuse

Moving from theory and research to clinical practice, one can cull from these four perspectives an integrated-relational point of view—a composite picture, if you will, of adult survivors of traumatogenic childhood abuse as they present for treatment.

Preeminent in the clinical presentation of adult survivors is the juxtaposition of what appears to be rather primitive, intrusive, and disruptive symptomatology in otherwise functional, often highly successful individuals. This is likely to be the first derivative of the underlying dissociative processes that the clinician is likely to observe—one that often gives rise to diagnostic mystification. It is not uncommon for adult survivors to present with a laundry list of prior diagnoses that are wide-ranging, contradictory, and confusing to those not familiar with this population. The first clinical vignette at the end of this section describes a patient who was diagnosed by her former therapist as "paranoid schizophrenic with borderline features"! In extended consultation, these patients may be dramatically different from day to day; even from minute to minute, with different levels of ego organization apparent at different points in time, always in different emotional and relational contexts.

Because they are usually highly functional individuals who perpetually totter on the brink of evoking their dissociated world of primitive, paranoid, or chaotic experience, these patients are frightened, rigid, and often hypervigilant. They must always remain cognizant of any interpersonal, transferential, or environmental triggers to their dissociative experience. They appear always ready to flee the session at a moment's notice in what one can regard to be the clinical manifestation of fright/flight/freeze reactions common to trauma survivors. They are cautious about what they say to the analyst. They choose their words carefully. It is difficult, if not impossible, for them to play. Often, they are distraught, bordering on the hysterical.

Adult survivors of childhood sexual abuse usually present as either highly emotional and reactive to internal and external stimuli; or as emotionally cold, detached, split off, even dead. Here both extremes speak to their inability to modulate affective responses; in one case, the reaction is markedly avoidant; at the other extreme, such a defense cannot be marshaled. The clinical picture is quite different, but both patients act in response to their own vulnerability to regressive, disorganizing, traumatic reenactment. In one case, the patient is perpetually in crisis, moving from one terrifying reenactment to another with only brief respites in between. In the other, the patient feels herself to be constantly avoiding the ultimate fall into chaos, disorganization, psychosis. There is a dim awareness that on the other side of emotional deadness lies a searing and uncontrollable pain. Such patients often present dreams of falling through bottomless holes, having the earth open beneath their feet, being swallowed up into some unknown and limitless place, and so on. Our patients are terrified of the couch, prolonged silences, vague therapeutic responses, or any other such technique that hurtles them, out of control, into an objectless state. As they have not yet learned to play with thoughts and ideas, they cannot allow their images of self and other to wander freely. Boundaries are either nonexistent or rigidly maintained. Terror is concrete, and transferentially the analyst is always on the brink of becoming the abusing or abused other, with the patient playing the complementary role. Of course, such depictions represent the extremes, and often this very dissociation allows one aspect of the patient's persona to interact in a lively, playful, and emotionally responsive way. However, one is always aware with adult survivors of the hypervigilance that controls access to the interior, guarding the dissociated, abused child from further painful entanglements.

Also common is a history replete with confusing somatic symptoms, undiagnosable illnesses, hospitalizations, and invasive but inconclusive medical procedures. Frequently, these patients show signs of noticeable physiological distress, even during the initial consultation. Trembling, hand shaking, sweating, blushing, excessive belching or flatulence, vulnerability to temperature changes in the therapist's office, and so on can all be presenting parts of the clinical picture. Such histories and such presentations reflect, in our opinion, the confluence of three different factors: the physiological changes secondary to histories of severe abuse; the fact that specific abuse memories are often encoded in specific somatic states that recur with regularity, particularly at times of acute stress; and, finally, the fact that invasive medical procedures (like addictive acts of self-abuse) represent reenactments of the painful, intrusive, sexual abuse.

Let us turn to three very different case descriptions that will illustrate some of the phenomena discussed. Each is the description of a patient presenting for an initial consultation. In each case, the patient turned out to be a survivor of childhood sexual abuse.

Case 1

Melissa was 22 at the time of her initial consultation, although she appeared to be no older than 15. She was casually, almost sloppily, dressed in jeans and a torn tee shirt. Speaking exclusively in a little girl whisper, she had a helpless, almost pathetic, waiflike quality that made the analyst imagine that the wind had blown her in and might soon sweep her up and blow her out. She cried continuously during the initial consultation, trembling excessively and sweating profusely. She would blush noticeably whenever direct eye contact was maintained. Melissa's mother was dying, and her current therapist was on the verge of moving out of state and discontinuing treatment. The patient described a history of dysfunctional family interactions, ongoing contact with youth groups and counselors that she herself had sought out, and minor skirmishes with drug and alcohol abuse, as well as dangerous sexual promiscuity and illegal acting-out. Melissa felt desperate and suicidal. She begged the analyst to accept her for treatment, saying that she "would do anything if you take me."

A startlingly different Melissa arrived for her next session. She came dressed in a tailored and sophisticated business suit, with her previously curly and unruly hair swept up away from her face. She was appropriately made up, projecting a stunning impression. She spoke in a deeper and more resonant voice, and the analyst was struck with the change in both her vocabulary and the depth of her thought processes. When asked about the same issues she had discussed two days before, her emotional reactions were strikingly different. For instance, where she had been dissolved in tears about her mother's imminent death on Monday, on Wednesday she replied, "I always hated my mother and she hated me. . . . She's a bitch. . . . I don't expect I'll miss her much. . . . I only cried the other day because that's what you're supposed to do when your mother is dying." Also of note on Wednesday was the fact that the patient had much less access to childhood memories than she had revealed on Monday. Her recollections were more anecdotal and her emotional availability far more restricted.

After recovering from her own shock, the analyst commented on how different the patient seemed that day. Melissa laughed, for the first time in that session, rather heartily and explained as if it was the most natural thing in the world, "Oh, that was on Monday. . . . I'm little on Monday, because I don't go to school or work. . . . You saw me in my play clothes. . . . Today you get the grown-up me." The patient then described what she had not mentioned previously, that she held a very responsible job and was currently working on her applications to medical school. She explained that she knew her mother would be dead by then and that, with the inheritance she would receive, she could easily afford to be a full-time student!

Melissa's former therapist described her in a phone conversation as "a paranoid schizophrenic woman with borderline features." The former therapist appeared to be trying to integrate divergent personal experiences of this patient by employing a diagnostic label that itself made no sense. This struggle can clearly be a formidable one—and may go far in explaining the frequent history of such wild diagnoses in the presentation of adult survivors.

Case 2

Emily was a married, 34-year-old mother of three children ages 2, 6, and 9. She had been hospitalized following a serious suicide attempt and was referred for treatment after her discharge. She had a long history of recurrent depression beginning in early adolescence. She described her family as alternately emotionally abusive or neglectful and absent and would or could say little else about them. There had been one other suicide attempt at age 16 and a brief hospitalization at this time. The suicide attempt had been attributed to the breakup of a high school love affair, but the patient remembers that, "there was something else at the time . . . something I can't quite remember. I'm not sure that I knew exactly what it was then either, but it was there, and I thought that I couldn't bear to deal with it. I remember I tried to tell my therapist in the hospital. It had something to do with my father. I remember that he laughed and said that I was being dramatic and looking for attention. I don't know, but it was the oddest thing . . . because no one in my family ever asked me why I tried to kill myself. If your kid did something like that, wouldn't you at least ask her why?"

Emily survived her college years in what could only be considered as a drug- and alcohol-induced stupor, moving from one promiscuous and dangerous sexual affair to another. These relationships were always tinged with aggression and involved overt sadomasochistic enactments. Although bright, she barely passed her course work and would have dropped out of college had she not met her present husband at the end of her junior year. She recalled in that initial consultation how good he was to her: "He was the only good person in my life . . . he took care of me, and I was really able to clean up my act for a few years. I knew that there was no way he could tolerate the person I had been . . . that dirty, evil thing."

In the context of this relationship, and with the help of antidepressants and tranquilizers, Emily was able to live a reasonably comfortable life over the next several years. She viewed her husband as "her rescuer" and believed that marriage and a family would put her nightmare of parental neglect and self-induced suffering to an end. Indeed, her husband seemed to identify with his role of savior; he was tender and attentive; determined to save the wounded little girl he sensed beneath the surface of his wife's chaotic life story. With the birth of their children, however, his attentions were drawn more and more away from his wife in their dyadic relationship into the ongoing stresses and demands of fatherhood and family life. Emily grew more and more enraged at what she experienced as his abandonment, becoming slowly and inexorably more symptomatic. She became more severely depressed, this time plagued with recurrent panic attacks that ultimately kept her confined to the house on most days. She suffered from persistent nightmares from which she would awake sweating, hyperventilating, and terrified. She remembered almost nothing of the contents of these dreams, except that they were violent and that she was in extreme danger.

Six months prior to her last suicide attempt, Emily had undergone an elaborate medical workup to determine whether or not she was suffering from multiple sclerosis. She was experiencing recurring tingling, numbing, and muscle weakness in different parts of her body. The symptoms, though severe at times, eluded diagnosis and corresponded to no known neurological pathways. She became very involved in the medical procedures and was noted to deal with this crisis better and more calmly than she had with anything in recent history. Her suicide attempt came 5 weeks after her doctors determined that they could find nothing wrong with her.

Emily spoke rapidly or not at all. She was highly emotional and extremely reactive to even her minutest perceptions of the therapist's behavior, attitudes, or reactions to her. Her thinking was often chaotic and disorganized, and she seemed to bolt from one crisis state to another with barely time to catch her breath. After 2 months of twice-a-week treatment, Emily was able to begin the recovery of incest memories that involved explicit sadistic torture.

Case 3

Delores, age 28, had been editor of the Law Review at her prestigious Ivy League law school. She was enormously successful academically and upon graduation had been pursued for the most highly coveted jobs. In addition to being brilliant, she was beautiful, articulate, and impeccably coordinated. She earned a great deal of money and lived in lonely high style. Although warmly related, Delores had few friends. Women, she felt, were intimidated by her; and she could only relate to men as platonic friends. Most of her close friends were married men with whom she had close working relationships but little social contact outside of the office. She was enormously disturbed by what she regarded as her sexual frigidity and her inability to maintain an ongoing sexual relationship. She had experimented in relationships with both men and women but felt equally nonresponsive to both. Recently, she had begun to wonder whether "anything sexual" had happened between her and her father (also a successful trial attorney) when she was younger, and although she was starting to believe that it had, she had no particular memories of such experiences. She began an analysis.

Only after several months, and within the context of a period of particularly intense positive transference and yearning for greater closeness with the analyst, was Delores able to reveal what she had consciously withheld before. First, that she still sucked her thumb at night as a way of calming her anxieties about letting go and drifting off into sleep. And, second, that she had a long and unremitting history of non lethal wrist cutting that was occasionally incorporated into her masturbatory and sexual fantasies. Intense anxiety interfered with her ability to engage these fantasies in the context of a real sexual encounter and was perhaps one reason behind her sexual unresponsiveness. Delores's own suspicions about childhood sexual abuse were now joined by those of her analyst.

Therapeutic Implications

Childhood sexual abuse is a form of chronic trauma, in which the abusive other overstimulates and overwhelms the young child's ego capacities to the extent that it renders them essentially inoperative. Where such abuse is perpetrated by a trusted family member, particularly a parent, the child loses not only his own capacities but also any ability to rely on the auxilliary ego capacities of the mother and father. The abusive parent cannot be relied on, and revelation of the abuse to the other parent threatens the dissolution of the entire family. To a young child, this represents a threat to his very existence. It is at this psychic crossroad that dissociation plays its crucial adaptational role. In an effort to preserve the remnants of a trusting capacity to depend upon the parents for emotional and physical sustenance, the young victim of traumatic abuse essentially sunders her ego, i.e., her experience of self and other, internal and external, in two. One represents business as usual, the daytime self, the part that responds to the parent's denial of the traumatic abuse by imposing its own denial. No one speaks of the other, nighttime self. It exists only as part of a dreamlike state whose very existence assumes an air of vague unreality in the light of day.

Because the reality of the abuse can never be spoken about, no verbal links exist between the experiences of the two dissociated aspects of self. The abused child enacts but is, in most cases, rendered speechless by her terror and by the ego regression psychically and physiologically mediated by such terror. The denying child is bound to maintain this wordlessness by the strictest familial collusion and by her awareness of the precariousness of her own continued survival. Without the ability to encode via verbal representation, her horrifying experiences, there can be no communication between these two experiences of self.

In cases of chronic abuse, what begins as a dissociated aspect of experience becomes organized into a cordoned-off system of internalized self and object representations that protects the remainder of the personality from the horrifying and psychically disorganizing effects of the trauma. The abused child becomes encased within her own world—a world that admits only abusers, victims, saviors, and those who choose to stay defensively uninvolved or unaware. She lives there perpetually without the language to announce what is happening to her. Although surely weakened by the enormous effort required to maintain such a psychic cleavage and by the vague, dreamlike awareness that "something is not right," the child is freed to develop and mature relatively spared from the poisonous effects of such toxic introjects and concomitant identifications.

The presence of such dissociation goes a long way toward explaining the breadth of clinical presentation described. The fact that the patient's psychic world is organized around at least two different loci of experience and incorporates, as it were, two entirely different and mutually exclusive systems of self and object representations, gives rise, in each case, to ego capacities reflective of essentially different life histories. One comes to expect, then, in working with adult survivors the presence of symptoms usually associated with more profound forms of psychopathology in the context of what appear to be higher functional capabilities. One also comes to expect, however, that these capacities will vary from day to day, within session, and certainly, as memories of abuse begin to emerge. Analysts working with adult survivors of childhood sexual abuse become acquainted with the reality that there are at least two different patients in treatment and that analytic technique will vary according to which system of self and object representations is being evoked and enacted within the transference-countertransference process at any given time.

However, the absence of words—the fact that, in so many cases, the patient has never semantically encoded what has happened to her—presents perhaps the most challenging dilemma for the analyst undertaking such work. Analysts are used to relying on words: Language is, and has always been, our medium. It is not difficult for the uninitiated, both therapist and patient, to be seriously set off course by the language of disembodied images, dreamlike states, somatic memories, and physiological states of hyperarousal and disorganization so common in work with adult survivors. How to reach such crucial aspects of experience, where no words exist; how to evoke an experience of self and other, defensively dissociated from more palpable self or object representations; how to encourage and support the patient's need to believe in a reality that expresses itself only in mood changes, bodily states, disorganized images, and illusively fleeting intrusive thoughts? Ultimately, it is the reestablishment and reenactment of specific transference-countertransference paradigms in the analysis and the capacity of such transferential reenactments to evoke state-dependent memories embedded within and organized around those unintegrated experiences of real or fantasied relationships to others that provide the initial bridge to traumatogenic memory and a therapeutic opening in the vague and turbulent states we have described.

A case illustration may highlight some of these issues. Jenny was a 28-year-old woman who had recently moved to this part of the country in order to complete a residency program in internal medicine. In an initial phone contact, the patient informed the therapist that she had had a long history of violent incest; and, although she knew of the therapist's interest in this area and was reassured that she would, therefore, be sensitive to many of the related issues, she did wish to make clear her belief that she had completely dealt with the issues of her sexual abuse in a previous therapy several years earlier.

She wished to return to treatment now, because she felt great anxiety at beginning her residency and was even aware of several disruptive physiological manifestations of this anxiety, for which she knew that there was no medical cause. The patient described recurring mild-to-moderate anxiety attacks, accompanied by nausea, light-headedness, and difficulty concentrating. She would sweat profusely and was aware of her heart racing. Because these episodes appeared to occur only at the hospital, Jenny had assumed them to be related to her initial insecurities about beginning a new aspect of her professional career. However, with time and her growing comfort on the job, these attacks had not ceased or even diminished.

Upon presenting herself at the therapist's office, the patient appeared attractive, appropriately dressed, and highly articulate. Alhough she claimed to be calm, "because as I told you I've been through all this before," there seemed to be an excessive amount of shifting, hand wringing, finger twisting, and hair twirling belying her reported nonchalance. Her body seemed to be in perpetual motion.

Jenny reported having been the victim of rather violent and sadistic sexual abuse at the hands of her father, beginning around the time of her fifth birthday and continuing until she began to menstruate at age 12. Though she detailed that the abuse had involved instances of fondling, digital penetration, and forced fellatio, her images were vague, the depiction highly clinical, and her affect detached and strikingly removed. The therapist began to wonder how much of the patient's experience and its accompanying affect remained dissociated. She therefore commented on the patient's ability to speak of such events in so calm a manner and was reassured by the patient that this apparent calm was only as a result of her prior treatment. "After all," she announced in a startling turnabout, "I'm not one of those people who dissociated a lot of my experience. I always remembered that I was abused, so it wasn't so shocking to talk about."

However, it remained of note, as treatment progressed, that Jenny never spoke of explicit aspects of her abuse. In addition, when asked by the therapist if she thought that, given her history, her anxiety attacks might be connected to the fact that she was examining so many naked bodies on a daily basis, she appeared mystified, as if she had never made the connection between her own somatic experiences, the specific memories she had worked on in her treatment, and the external triggers that might precipitate a regression to those states. It became increasingly clear, that although Jenny remembered the fact that she had been sexually abused, the specific memories, fantasies, and affects related to those experiences were still partially dissociated, unsymbolized, and, therefore, unintegrated. Gaining access to these warded-off childhood experiences became the clinical challenge.

One day, approximately 5 months into the treatment, the patient reported that she had always, since childhood, slept with the same large stuffed dog. With a mixture of amusement and embarrassment, she admitted to continuing this practice into the present and wondered, rather playfully, what this could mean psychologically. The therapist replied to her: "The meaning aside, I wish we could speak to that little puppy ... I'm sure he'd have a lot to tell us about what things were like for you." The patient's mood seemed to shift, she became more serious, almost tearful, and her voice had a somewhat trancelike, faraway quality. (We believe that, here, the analyst's shift to a child's worldview [one could talk to this stuffed puppy] allowed for the subtle shift in access to past experience that could then work its way into the analytic space.) The session proceeded in the following way:

> PATIENT: I used to hold him, you know, at night when my father did those things. I held on to him so tight, I used to worry that he couldn't breathe. That I would hurt him.
>
> THERAPIST: Do you remember what he felt like when you held him? [Again attempting to maximize the evocation of a particular experience by helping the patient focus on what might be a piece of non-threatening and available memory associatively linked to more traumatogenic and, as yet, unsymbolized aspects.]
>
> PATIENT: He was so soft. I remember I used to rub the fur against the side of my cheek ... and ... [crying now] he had a hard stuffed little nose that was glued on. I used to suck and bite on that and make everything else go away. ... [Patient closes her eyes.]
>
> THERAPIST: If you make everything go away now, we leave that little girl with no one but her puppy to talk to. I wish we could talk to her, so that we might try to help.

Here the physical transformation was striking. The patient curled up in her chair, wrapping her arms around her body. She began to tremble uncontrollably and to breathe rapidly with small gasping breaths. Her quiet crying became a wailing that was alarming to see. As she cried, she shook her head "no" in a violent manner; she could or would not speak to me of what she was experiencing. "No, no, no," was all she could say. She would not speak for the remainder of the session, and attempts to help her to do so began to feel intrusive and prodding. Alhough the patient was somewhat calmer by the end of the session, she clearly left the office in an agitated and psychically vulnerable state. Although the therapist called that evening to see how she was doing and to remind the patient of her availability, the answering machine picked up, and it appeared that Jenny was not answering the phone.

Jenny canceled her next two scheduled appointments. When the therapist was finally able to prevail upon her to return, she insisted that she could not speak of the images she had seen, and she was sure that doing so would overwhelm her, make it impossible for her to function at work, and essentially ruin her entire life. She was convinced that she would end up on the inpatient unit of a psychiatric hospital if she continued any further in treatment. Jenny was reassured that her fear of going crazy was experienced by many adults in the process of recovering memories of childhood abuse. The therapist explained that the fear of being destroyed by what she had to say was essentially a memory of the fear felt by the abused child, who was told over and over again that speaking of the abuse would lead to the destruction of the family or her extradition from it. Indeed, even maintaining conscious awareness of the abuse could be experienced as bringing the patient to the edge of an even more horrific psychic death. Jenny was assured that, although the process was painful, her words no longer contained the destructive potential that they had when she was a child. They would be unlikely, therefore, to precipitate a psychotic break. The therapist then added that she and Jenny would take things very slowly, as the patient was ready, using extra contacts, double sessions, temporary medications, and so on to make sure that Jenny would not be retraumatized in the process of working these issues through.

The patient was reassured by the support and the understanding that her terror could be contained and shared in the treatment setting. She therefore began over the next few weeks, in what was clearly the voice of a much younger child, to recount and at times relive aspects of the abuse she had endured as a young child—aspects that had not up to this time been spoken of to anyone. The story that emerged was one of horrifying sadism, helplessness, and coercive submission. It would appear that the return of these dissociated experiences was at least in part triggered by activation of the patient's identification with her father in the process of carrying out oftentimes painful medical procedures on her own passive patients.

The implications for analytic work are therefore multidimensional. The analyst must find a way to help the patient to contain the overstimulation, hyperarousal, and mental disorganization that are the psychological and physiological hallmarks of abuse and will accompany any attempt to enter the split-off world of the abused child. In so doing the analyst serves a holding function that makes possible the recovery of traumatogenic memories and ultimately their verbal symbolization. One cannot stress enough that the analytic work at this stage involves not only the recovery of memories but also the need to verbalize them again and again, thus establishing clear linguistic encoding of the heretofore unrepresentable pathogenic experiences. Such words will make it possible for the abused child and the adult who has grown up only partially aware of her to speak to each other for the first time. The patient can begin to integrate pieces of her experience that have, for too long, remained isolated from each other. She can also mend, in such a way, the internal splits in self and object representation that have defensively maintained traumatic memories in isolation, and given rise to complicated difficulties in present-day interpersonal relationships.

However, the experience of verbalizing recovered memories serves more than a symbolizing and integrating function. In the process itself, an essential shift will occur in the patient's internalized matrices of self and object representations; a shift that introduces and ultimately provides a pathway for the internalization of an entirely new object-related experience. Here the presence of the analyst provides an adult who will contain, listen, and believe in the child's inexpressible nightmare. The analyst will by dint of his or her presence and listening function inalterably change the traumatogenic situation of isolation and psychic foreclosure as it reemerges in the analytic setting, thereby facilitating symbolization and integration and minimizing the possibility that this emergence will be experienced as a retraumatization by the patient. Without such containment, the reemergence of traumatic material will represent only a dissociated reenactment within the transference and not the necessary type of integrative work.

Having internalized the childhood reality that certain words carried the potential of literally destroying her world, for better or for worse, the patient has grown up with those magical beliefs in the omnipotent destructiveness of her own words still intact. As the analyst perseveres and survives, in a Winnicottian sense, the patient works through her imprisoning ties to persecutory objects and internal representations of self that grow out of identifications with such objects. As these toxic introjects and self representations infuse the analytic relationship, giving rise to maddening cycles of ever-shifting transference-countertransference reenactments, the working-through process itself bears testimony to the fact that speaking the unspeakable words, which have by now become infused with an omnipotent destructiveness, will not destroy the patient, the analyst, or their growing bond to one another.

Here, for the first time, analyst and patient create a transitional space (Winnicott, 1951), where the patient is free to play with thoughts, ideas, words, and symbols that previously carried too much hate and destructive potential to be expressed. In elevating the patient's belief in her own destructive potential from the concrete to the symbolic, and by doing so in the context of a new object relationship that is accepting of both the patient's loving and hating internal identifications, the treatment progresses in a way that inalterably changes the nature of the patient's intrapsychic and interpersonal reality. Love and hate can comingle for the first time, thus providing a bridge for the integration of internally dissociated experiences and simultaneously enriching and enlivening the patient's ongoing relationships in her interpersonal world.

In optimal situations, the diffusion of the patient's magical beliefs in the power of her own rage also allows her to experience that others can be angry with her without seeking her destruction. The murderous wishes of the parents can be separated from the everyday annoyances and dissatisfactions of others. With the growing capacity to tolerate experiences of love and anger both within the self and within the object comes perhaps the first real opportunity for the kind of intersubjective experience in the analysis that lays the groundwork for the achievement of any real intimacy in the patient's world outside treatment. The ever-widening scope of tolerable self representations and the concomitant capacity to incorporate contradictory images of and fantasies about the analyst must, as they are internalized, lead to a facilitation of this process in other relationships as well. The capacity to touch and be touched to explore the interior of another as one allows that other into the self must in both its symbolically sexualized and desexualized forms begin in the treatment setting itself.

An integrated model for the psychoanalytically oriented treatment of adult survivors of childhood sexual abuse is thus based on the progressive unfolding of five specific and heretofore foreclosed intrapsychic capacities. They are (1) the therapeutic containment of the physiological and psychological hyperarousal and disorganization secondary to chronic trauma; (2) the recovery of pathogenic memories and fantasied elaborations; (3) the symbolization of memory and fantasied elaborations; (4) the integration of dissociated self and object representations; and finally (5) the internalization of a new object relationship, within which these capacities will be enfolded and by dint of which they will become internalized.

In laying forth this plan, we have attempted to stand with one foot firmly planted in an understanding of the trauma and sexual abuse research literature, and the other in our continued belief in the the centrality of the analytic relationship. Abreaction and symbolization of memories, as described in much of the trauma literature, seem insufficient in accomplishing the kind of change necessary. It is only when such abreaction and symbolization occur within the containing and holding context of a new therapeutic relationship; when that relationship becomes the vehicle for untangling and verbally encoding distorted, fragmented, and dissociated experiences of self in relation to other; when that relationship facilitates the diffusion of heretofore omnipotently imbued destructiveness and thus potentiates the unfolding of true transitionality and intersubjectivity in personal thought and relationship, that therapeutic work can be internalized in a meaningful and permanent way. The containing, symbolizing, and integrating function of the explanatory words and theories generated between patient and analyst will be effective only in so far as they become the symbolic representation of the all-important object relationship in which they were first uttered.

CHAPTER 4

Dissociation

What Is Dissociation?

DISSOCIATION IS THE PROCESS of severing connections between categories of mental events—between events that seem irreconcilably different, between the actual events and their affective and emotional significance, between actual events and the awareness of their cognitive significance, and finally, as in the case of severe trauma, between the actual occurence of real events and their permanent, symbolic, verbal mental representation.

When a child is subjected over time to a trauma, such as sexual abuse by a trusted parent, the enormity of the betrayal and of the physical and psychological violation is too great for the ego to tolerate. The continued survival of the child is felt to be at risk, because the actuality of the abuse jeopardizes this primary object bond and challenges the child's capacity to trust and, therefore, to securely depend. To protect the self from such overwhelming fear of annihilation and, further, to shield oneself from cognitively knowing about the event(s), the individual's experience of consciousness splits vertically. Coexistent with the ego state(s) that knows about the trauma and affectively reacts to it, is an ego state that, although somewhat depleted, is ignorant of the catastrophic events.

Traditionally, then, dissociation is defined as a process by which a piece of traumatic experience, because it is too overstimulating to be processed and recorded along the usual channels, is cordoned off and established as a separate psychic state within the personality, creating two (or more) ego states that alternate in consciousness and, under different internal and external circumstances, emerge to think, behave, remember, and feel. Such dissociated states are associatively unavailable to the rest of the personality and, as such, cannot be subject to psychic operations or elaboration. The adult survivor of childhood abuse will experience the dissociated traumatic states in the form of memories of the trauma that are unavailable at other times; recurrent intrusive images connected to the trauma but otherwise unrecognizable; violent or symbolic acting out; inexplicable somatic sensations; recurrent nightmares; anxiety reactions; and psychosomatic conditions.

Dissociative pathology of varying degrees plays a significant role in the intrapsychic organization of most patients who have suffered chronic sexual abuse in childhood. This would appear to be particularly true when such abuse involves a parent or close and trusted other. Although some have disagreed with this formulation (Shengold, 1992), researchers in the area of PTSD have continued to demonstrate the link between severe trauma and dissociation (Figley, 1986; Green, Wilson, et al., 1985; Herman, 1992; Hilgard, 1977; Kluft, 1990b; van der Hart & Horst, 1989; van der Kolk, 1987; van der Kolk et al., 1989; Wilson, Smith, & Johnson, 1985). Indeed, one study went so far as to conclude that the presence of dissociation could be a valid diagnostic discriminator between sexually abused and nonabused college women (Briere, 1988; Briere & Runtz, 1988).

Only recently, with the renewed interest in the long-term effects of childhood abuse, has the concept of dissociation found its way back into the psychoanalytic literature. Although it has been occasionally mentioned in the past (Dickes, 1965; Fairbairn, 1954; Fliess, 1953; Sullivan, 1956), its complete integration into our understanding of psychic regulatory processes appears to have been enjoined along with any serious consideration of the influences of real events on psychic structuralization. When the concept does make an appearance, both in the intervening years and in the present, it appears to have survived, more or less intact and unaltered by time. Like the process it describes, dissociation was for a long time forgotten, occasionally popping up, but essentially unmodified or elaborated over time. Bromberg's moving description (1991), although cast within a more interpersonal framework, puts forth a contemporary psychoanalytic perspective entirely compatible with Janet's initial descriptions. Bromberg states: "Dissociated experience thus tends to remain unsymbolized by thought and language, exists as a separate reality outside of self-expression, and is cut off from authentic human relatedness and deadened to full participation in the life of the rest of the personality. . . . Meaningful existence in the present is preempted by the repetitive, timeless, traumatic past, and the present is little more than a medium through which this unprocessed past may be known" (pp. 405–406). The clinical relevance of these processes with adult survivors of childhood abuse (as well as with others) remains, with few exceptions (Davies & Frawley, 1992a;

Dickes, 1965; Ferenczi, 1932; Fleiss, 1953; Shengold, 1989) virtually unexplored. It is to a fuller exposition of this clinical process and to its centrality to that particular patient population that we now turn.

Dissociation and Childhood Sexual Abuse

Our own concept of dissociation, though encompassing all the characteristics mentioned, goes one step further in articulating a fundamental clinical assumption. We understand the internalization of childhood sexual abuse to occur within a relational-developmental model similar to that described by Fast's event theory (1985). We believe that events become incorporated and ultimately understood vis à vis the particular matrices of self and object experience within which they are ensconced and that they are bound together and organized with particular regard to the intense emotional experiences that accompany them. Therefore, it is not the traumatic event alone that becomes significant but of equal importance is the traumatized individual's experience and representation of self within the abusive events and her experience and internalization of the others in his or her world as they are represented at such abusive moments. Here the clinical implications are most important. The trauma and sex abuse literature—indeed even the relevant psychoanalytic literature—tends to stress the patient's need to recover dissociated memories of *pathogenic events* and to express these with full affective discharge. We believe that it is the oversimplification of the treatment process that has in part contributed to the growing controversy over the reliability of traumatic memory that now floods the popular media (see also chapter 6).

Recovery of the traumatic event(s) is merely one aspect of the clinical work that must be accomplished. Because we view these traumatic experiences as embedded in the entire constellation of the patients' internal object world and concommitant aspects of self experience, we view the emergence, containment, encoding, and integration of this entire split-off aspect of experience to represent the overriding therapeutic goal.

Included, then, in our understanding of the dissociated "child self" to which we refer, is a completely separate organization of self and object representations; the memories of traumatic events that bind these representations to each other; intense and unmodulated affect states specific to the trauma; and a level of ego organization specific to the developmental stage at which the traumatic event and pathogenic ego dissociation occurred. One can expect fantasied elaborations of these experiences to have been foreclosed by the trauma reaction but to emerge, in accord with the developmental fixation, during the integration that occurs as a part of the treatment process. We stress here that our concept of "the dissociated child self" bears no resemblance to the now popularized concept of the "inner child." The inner child as we understand her is a whole being with a multitude of integrated experiences, perhaps more in line with Winnicott's "true self." Our "dissociated child self" is a specific organization of self and object representation unique to the abusive set of events and containing the affective, cognitive, physiological, and fantasied elaborations of those events in a cordoned-off ego state associatively unavailable to the remainder of the personality.

To understand the centrality of dissociative processes in the lives of adults who were sexually abused as children (Davies & Frawley, 1992a, 1992b), it is important to understand the differences between the concept of dissociation and the more familiar notion of repression. Repression is an active process through which the ego attains mastery over conflictual material. Dissociation, on the other hand, is the last ditch effort of an overwhelmed ego to salvage some semblance of adequate mental functioning. Here our views are consistent with those of Fairbairn (1954), who sees dissociation as the result of ego disintegration "a passive process—a process of disintegration due to a failure on the part of the cohesive function normally exercised by the ego . . . it thus stands in marked contrast to the concept of repression formulated somewhat later by Freud" (p. 105). Repression brings about the forgetting of once familiar mental contents (i.e., events, affects, identifications, etc.). Dissociation on the other hand, leads to severing the connection between one set of mental contents and another. Dissociation can occur between categories of mental events, for example, good and bad experiences with the same object, between certain events and their affective representation (Krystal's alexithymia, 1988); between events and the meaning of those events (Grotstein, personal communication, 1992); perhaps even between events and the words that symbolically represent them. Therefore, a patient can be aware of an abusive trauma in one state and completely unaware of its existence in another. Likewise, a patient can retain memories of an event but have absolutely no access to their emotional impact except within an alternate state of consciousness. Therefore, the working-through of repressed contents involves the process of remembering. Working through dissociative states involves an ongoing effort at integrating mental contents severed by traumatic regression and maintained in disparate ego states that alternate in accessability.

Repression leaves the individual with the experience of being more masterfully in control of his environment; dissociation is experienced as an inadequate response, a submission and resignation to the inevitability of overwhelming, even psychically deadening danger. Repression creates a context for signal anxiety or symptom formation that maintains disavowed mental contents from awareness. Dissociation, in contrast, represents the failure of such signal functions to call into effect any of a number of defenses capable of preventing the bifurcation of reality and the constriction of experience and emotional life inherent in dissociative pathology. In Harry Stack Sullivan's words, "the dissociated personality has to prepare for almost any conceivable emergency that would startle one into becoming aware of the dissociated system." (1956, p. 203).

A further distinction can be made between repression and dissociation. Repression is a mental operation performed on (depending on one's theoretical orientation) wishes, thoughts, aspects of identifications, events, *known to the patient*. Recovered via psychoanalytic work, repressed materials are experienced as once familiar, rediscovered aspects of mental life; the patient's experience here is one of recognition. The experiences that reemerge, either verbally or via transference-countertransference reenactments or manifestations, have been previously experienced, psychologically digested, encoded, and then forgotten. In the treatment situation, repressed contents can be psychologically operated on by the patient; they can be maintained out of awareness, distorted, and psychically elaborated via fantasy, their derivatives finding verbal expression within the analytic hour. Despite the occasional intractability of repressed experiences, they reemerge in a more or less linear fashion, are subject to interpretation, and, once recalled, are usually accessible for the remainder of the analytic work.

Dissociation, in contrast to repression, involves the foreclosure, not the elaboration of psychic contents. Because no internal psychic work has modulated the terrifying, pathogenic experience for the patient, their reemergence is, essentially, a repetition of the original traumatic state. There is no verbal encoding via which meaning can be attributed to the mental representation of these experiences. Therefore, they tend to reemerge as fragmented, meaningless, visual images; rapidly shifting physiological states; nightmares; intrusive thoughts, and so on. For most patients, the experience is terrifying, again beyond words; and analysts unfamiliar with the manifestations of such traumatic revival in clinical work are all too often cast adrift, caught up and controlled by a process that seems to have a life of its own.

It is not uncommon for analysts to feel that such patients are on the verge of a psychotic decompensation and to inadvertently resort to heroic rescue measures—inappropriate overmedication, hospitalization, even shock treatments—in an effort to stem the tide of what looks like a burgeoning psychosis. Unfortunately, such measures all too often reestablish the psychic foreclosure that created the patient's problems in the first place and communicate to the patient the analyst's inability to understand the material that is emerging and the patient's fearful reaction to it. Although medication and hospitalization are needed on occasion to support the patient through the reemergence of such chaotic experiences (see chapter 11), it is important that the analyst not overreact. Such recommendations, meant to help the therapeutic pair to contain the traumatic reenactments long enough to organize and give meaning to them, must be understood as temporary supportive measures, not as adequate long-term solutions. Indeed, the analyst's understanding that such disorganizing experiences do not represent the psychotic ravings of a decompensating patient but, rather, the courageous attempts of a previously traumatized patient to make sense of her dissociated states, will go a long way, in and of itself, toward establishing the kind of psychic meaning that will help to contain such episodes in treatment. Such supportive measures, when necessary, will be viewed by the patient as adjuncts toward helping her accomplish the necessary psychic work, not as attempts to shut down a process that threatens to overwhelm and frighten the analyst. Here the analyst's familiarity with and understanding of dissociative processes and the differences inherent in the distinctions between "the return of the repressed" and "the return of the dissociated," particularly as they shape transference-countertransference configurations, is of the utmost importance.

The Emergence of Dissociative States

Most survivors of childhood abuse are faced with the dilemma of having to negotiate the external, interpersonal worlds of friendship, school, authority, career, and so on in spite of the fact that they have, relatively early on, been betrayed by a person with whom they share one of the most intimate relationships of their lives. It is remarkable to observe the degree to which most survivors can, via dissociative processes, painstakingly erect the semblance of a functioning, adaptive, interpersonally related self around the screaming core of a wounded and abandoned child. This adult self has a dual function; it allows the individual to move through the world of others with relative success, at the same time protecting and preserving the abused child who lives on, searching still for acknowledgment, validation, and compensation. It is the impact of this essential splitting and dissociation at the core of the personality and its effects on all later personality development to which we now turn our attention.

To integrate the extensive trauma literature with psychoanalytic theory and technique, we have attempted to demonstrate a critically important point. The patient who was sexually abused as a child is not an adult patient with particularly vivid memories of painful childhood experiences existing in the context of other, happier, more loving times. This child is a fully developed, dissociated, rather primitively organized alternative self. It is imperative that the therapist who begins working with an adult survivor of significant childhood sexual abuse understands that he/she is, in fact, undertaking the treatment of two people: an adult who struggles to succeed, relate, gain acceptance, and ultimately to forget, and a child who, as treatment progresses, strives to remember and to find a voice with which to scream out her outrage at the world.

The dissociated child self has a different ego structure, a more primitive and brittle system of defenses, a fuller and more affect-laden set of memories and has clearly become the repository for the patient's intense, often overwhelming rage, shame, and guilt. We often find the child with a different wardrobe, different facial expressions, body postures, voice quality, set of linguistic expressions. "She" takes on the persona of a timid little girl; "he" assumes the air of an awkward preadolescent whose emergent sexuality has lagged behind that of his chums.

It should be noted that dissociation exists along a broad continuum with coexistent, alternative ego states moving in ever-shifting patterns of mutual self-recognition and alienation. It is not uncommon for the child-self to contain several different personas, often with different access to historical information and memory. Common among these personas are the good-perfect child; the naughty-omnipotent child; and, ultimately, the terrified-abused child. Given the frequent coexistence of these alternative states, it does not seem that they represent true multiple personality organizations, the occasional presence of which is addressed more specifically later in this chapter. In most instances, the adult and child are at least partially aware of each other's existence; it is the child's incestuous secret and overwhelming rage about which the adult is often completely ignorant.

Although the adult and child are, in most situations, aware of each other, they are not friends. They have entirely different emotional agendas and live in a constant state of warfare over whose needs will take priority at any given time. Each feels entirely abandoned by the other. The child believes that the adult has "sold out" by progressing with life as a grown-up. After all, grown-ups are bad and do bad things. To become one of them is the ultimate betrayal. The child takes every opportunity, therefore, to subvert the adult's attempts to separate from the past and her identity as a victim to become a part of the outside world. She uses the techniques she was taught by her abusive parent (other) to undermine the confidence of her other self: seduction; cajoling; manipulation; and threat of abuse (in this case self-inflicted). As she herself felt invaded, she often invades the unexpecting conscious sensorium of the adult in inappropriate and disruptive ways, causing great confusion and disorientation, at times bringing to a halt whatever activity the adult was engaged in at that moment. She stands in relation to her adult self; a provocateur, with a terrorist's commitment to a program of unrelenting insurgence.

On her end, the adult persona "hates" the sadistic and disruptive child with bitter intensity. On the most conscious level, the adult views the child as a demanding, entitled, rebellious, and petulant pain in the neck. If she remembers being sexually abused in childhood, she blames her child self for it, thereby refortifying her insistence on the child's thorough and complete badness. She was "the seductress" and as one patient announced, with burning rancor, in her first session, "she got what she deserved . . . it was coming to her." It is almost incomprehensible to us that here the patient is talking about herself; the part of herself that was rather sadistically abused as a child, abused by her own father. We see, though, the effectiveness of the dissociation that spares both the adult persona and the father from the full impact of the child's rage. The hate is turned back upon the child who has, after all, been well trained in the art of self-victimization.

In situations where the patient has not yet recovered actual memories of childhood sexual abuse, she stands in relation to her demanding and disruptive child self, a passive and mystified player; she who gives voice to the child's tantrums, mood swings, and demands without exactly understanding why. "It's as if a voice rises up in me," reported one patient. "I know it's my voice . . . I recognize the sound of it . . . but it's so odd, I have no idea what the voice is going to say. All I know is that usually it says something to get me into trouble."

If the disparity between the intensity of the child's rage and shame, and the content of her thoughts becomes severe enough, the patient may experience full dissociative episodes, where the child is given full reign to express, remember, reenact, without any conscious recollection of the experience. As is the case with true multiple personalities, patients report losing time, suddenly finding themselves in the middle of a situation but not remembering how they got there, and so on. One patient would report, with some regularity, sitting down to write business reports only to find that they had already been done—and to perfection! "It's like the shoemaker and the elves," she would say. "I go to sleep and when I wake up there it is!" This particular patient entered treatment because of persistent problems on her job. Although it was immediately clear that her personal life was also extremely restricted, she kept these issues out of the early phase of her treatment by insisting that a social life was completely unimportant to her.

On her job, the patient was considered a truly brilliant and incisive thinker whose written analyses supported and gave direction to much of her firm's ongoing work. However, she was completely incapable of presenting her written work, either within her office or to clients. She was terrified of being looked at, exposed, and penetrated by the stares of others. A severe inhibition, based in large measure on dissociated exhibitionistic urges, would give rise to the most paralyzing experiences of humiliation and shame in these situations. The inhibition was so complete that often others would be called upon to present the patient's work to clients. To make matters worse, the patient was considered moody and demanding, with a reputation among colleagues for being "entitled and difficult to get along with."

Although she had no conscious recollection of the ongoing sexual abuse by her father between the ages of 7 and 12, the patient had perfectly recreated the emotional climate of these confusing early years in her present work life. She was gifted, special, and favored in some way that remained quite a mystery to her. Because she had no memory of writing her "brilliant" reports, she could hardly value herself for writing them, as others valued her. Despite her vague sense of specialness, she also felt despised and abused by her colleagues. She felt deserving of this abuse because she agreed that her behavior was often demanding and unpredictable. The patient herself experienced these abrupt mood swings and outbursts of demanding entitled behavior as ego-alien intrusions; and, on occasion, when the affect was most intense, she had no recollection of them at all. Without the memories that would spur compassion for this "other self," the patient was filled with fear and self-loathing.

> PATIENT: "It's like there's this baby part of me . . . she's scared and pitiful sometimes, and I hate her for that . . . but then she turns hateful and demanding . . . she won't be satisfied . . . I try, but I can't. She wants more and more, but I don't know of what. She won't leave me alone, and she won't grow up. Sometimes I think she takes over completely, and part of me gets scared of what she'll do. I go away I think . . . I just can't bear to listen."
>
> THERAPIST: It seems to me she's likely to stay around until someone hears what she's trying to say.
>
> PATIENT: The less attention she gets, the better. The only thing I can do is ignore her . . . starve her out . . . otherwise, she'll never leave. If I give her nothing at all, maybe she'll go away and leave me alone. [Quietly] . . . Maybe she'll die . . . I really want her to die.

Here again, the hatred and death wish for the child self. This is not the omnipotent seductress who is blamed by the adult for her own abuse, but the raging and entitled child, who makes her pain clear but keeps its source a mystery to all, including herself. Not yet on the analytic scene, but struggling to emerge, is the terrified child; living in a dissociated world of perpetual abuse, terrorized not only by the actions of another, but by the prospect of speaking her own words and knowing her own mind.

It is almost always the adult self who presents herself for treatment. She is either struggling with overt nightmarish memories of childhood, or in her amnesia, she is plagued with one or many of a list of vague, debilitating complaints: sexual dysfunction; depression; intense guilt; poor self-esteem; self-destructive impulses; drug and alcohol abuse, and the like (Gelinas, 1983). It is only slowly—and after much careful testing—that the child persona begins to make her presence known. She may step forth boldly and dramatically, as in the development of sudden panic attacks or in the eruption of painful and frightening somatic complaints. The child may also enter quietly, almost imperceptibly. The therapist may first become aware of her presence by an oddly childish mannerism; a way of wiping away tears or twisting a lock of hair. At other times, he or she may signal his arrival with a subtle change in vocabulary, grammar, body postures and movements, different styles of clothing, a particular voice or facial expression. Many times, the therapist's first awareness of change has to do with a perceived shift in the nature of the transference or in his or her own experience of the counter-transference. Regardless, however, of the specific manner of entrance, it is most often the case that the child enters the analytic scene sometime before the recovery or disclosure of specific memories of past abuse begins.

The reasons here are clear. From the child's perspective, the analyst is, as yet, an unknown quantity, a stranger. True, she has been listening, but what she has heard has been limited by the nature of the adult-analyst interaction. From the child's point of view, it is the analyst and the adult who interviewed and chose each other. It is they who have evolved a relationship, have begun to define the limits of their trust and to deal with painful and intimate issues. As a dissociated self system with a separate object world and ego structure, the child has been kept very far away from the analytic field. The child has had little or no impact on the analytic relationship, and the relationship has affected her only insofar as she has perceived enough trust between the analyst and the adult to encourage her participation. To be sure, the emergence of the child in the treatment signifies that the early work has proceeded well and that the heart of the treatment is about to begin.

There are now two different patients on the analytic scene. An adult self, whom the analyst has already begun to know, and an illusive child self, who appears and disappears at will, introducing endless confusion into the analytic process. It behooves us to pause here and take a closer look at this child self system and at the ways in which he or she attempts to engage the analyst in playing out unconscious wishes, dreams, and fears.

Without question, the most singularly important thing to understand about the child is that she exists only in the context of a perpetually abusive internalized object relationship. It is this aspect of the self and this aspect of the object that have been, literally, ejected from the patient's more integrated personality functioning and allowed to set up an independent existence for the sake of pursuing their separate needs. Mature personality organization is an amalgam and integration of a multitude of widely varying self experiences and object experiences, each with its own unique affective-ideational-instinctual charge (Kernberg, 1976; Ogden, 1986; Volkan, 1976). Ideally, this integration leads to wide-ranging, internal representations of the self and object that are at times contradictory but not mutually exclusive. Love and hate coexist, are modulated, each by the other, and give rise to the potential for ambivalence and mourning, as well as intense passion and ambition.

In the patient who has been sexually abused, the child aspect of the self representation, along with that of the abusing other and their complex system of emotional connection and exchange, is cordoned off and isolated from the rest of the personality. It remains virtually frozen in time, the images unmodulated by any others of a different, perhaps gentler nature. These images become the embodiment of the murderous rage and pernicious self-loathing that drive the child in her relationships with others. In their intensity, they fuel the psychotic-level terrors of annihilation and world destruction that so infuse the patient's internal experience. The child cannot grow. Her anger and self-hatred go untempered—therefore unintegrated. Her world is a world of betrayal, terror, and continued emotional flooding. Her reality has been penetrated by a hostile, invasive force and her perceptions tragically distorted by her abusive experiences. What is bad she is told is good; what hurts is something she has been told she secretly wants and asks for. Her body aches. Her mind is in a constant state of upheaval and confusion. When, as a child, she turned to those around her for a way out, she was confronted either with threats and further abuse or neglect and formidable denial. The child is incapable of expecting anything different from the analyst. She experiences herself as terrified, completely alone, and helpless. Only the adult persona can ask for and receive help. The child cannot ask; and it is, indeed, a long while before the analyst's "help" begins to penetrate the formidable dissociative barriers.

The extreme dissociation of the abused child into a separate self and object system is, essentially, an attempt by the patient at damage control. As physicians attempt to isolate and remove a potentially invasive malignancy before it can affect healthy tissue, the adult survivor of childhood sexual abuse attempts to isolate and eject the toxic introject and accompanying self-representation before the capacity to trust oneself and others is entirely destroyed. The child self may be condemned to a world of unrelenting paranoia, but the adult persona, having ejected these toxic experiences, attempts a rudimentary integration, where self and object representations coalesce at a higher level of development. Indeed, the adult persona of many of our patients is marked by a rather hypomanic defensive style, where aggression is routinely projected and then denied. The adult in these instances takes on an air of uncanny innocence. He or she is often eager, if not compulsively driven, to help others. The consummate self-denier, the patient is unaware of the ways in which others take advantage of her well-intentioned need to help and are equally unaware of her own resentment at often being taken advantage of. She struggles but fails to make sense of her complete inability to say "no." Others seem to be capable of possessing her completely.

Clearly, the balance attained here between adult and child is tenuous at best, with a codetermined impairment of ego functioning that makes successful adaptation virtually impossible. Secondary-process thinking is subject to the constant intrusion of more primitive ideational strains. Reality testing is impaired by the pathological defensive patterns and the dissociative trends that give rise to a confusing duality in functioning. Somatic complaints are rampant, and the struggle against self-abusive urges is constant and unrelenting. Unlike diseased tissue that can be rendered harmless, once removed, the child self is fully aware of her extradition and can wage an insidious campaign against the adult, thus making any successful adaptation even more unlikely. It is not uncommon for an adult survivor in treatment to arrive at the point where she can articulate the ongoing struggle between that aspect of her personality that wants to function independently and successfully, and those more childlike aspects that feel such an adaptation to represent a "sellout" and betrayal of the child who suffered so unmercifully.

It is often at this precise moment of crisis, as adult and child are beginning to come together, when memory of childhood abuse threatens to emerge and overwhelm the adult sensorium, that a third persona can appear, the adolescent protector-self aspect of the personality, who conveys a tough, streetwise, intensely cynical view of the world. She comes equipped with a truly dazzling array of impulsive, acting-out, self-abusive symptomatology designed to preoccupy the adult, befuddle and distract the therapist, and above and beyond all else, obfuscate the threatening emergence of the child self and her traumatogenic memories. The compendium of delinquent and self-abusive behavior includes stealing, truancy, pathological lying, burning, cutting, and the entire spectrum of anorexic-bulimic symptomatology.

The adolescent persona has no memories of specific childhood abuse, and, rather than understanding her delinquent, self-abusive behavior as symptomatic of an earlier trauma, her own abusiveness is often used to excuse a general attitude of parental neglect, indifference, or hurtfulness. The adolescent must at all cost contain the child; but the only methods of containment and control available to her are the cruel and sadistic methods she had experienced as a child. The adolescent persona is, in essence, the clinical manifestation of the sadistic introject in its dissociated adult form. Certainly this extreme resolution cannot work indefinitely, and the adult, at great unconscious risk, enters psychoanalytic treatment.

Once the participation of all the psychic players has been ensured, analytic work can proceed. Of tantamount importance is the integration of the adult and child personas' experiences. This involves, above all else, the recovery and disclosure of as many memories of early sexual abuse as is possible. This includes, of course, the actual memories as they emerge for the patient; the fantasies and secondary elaborations that arise in the patient's associations, dreams, or memories; and a full affectively integrated reliving and working-through within the transference-countertransference of the traumatic overstimulation, terror, and dissociation. It is only when the patient witnesses the dissociation during the course of treatment that she becomes truly convinced of its existence and can begin to anticipate and circumvent the experience, thus precluding it from intruding at times of heightened emotionality and excitement. As the adult listens to the child's words and slowly begins to understand their significance, new meaning is given to previously inexplicable symptoms. The acceptance and integration proceed slowly, but ideally the interpenetration of these two personas each provides some compensation for this intensely painful process.

The adult, no longer terrified of the child's experiences, comes to appreciate the reasons for her rage and to acknowledge its justification. There is a new compassion for this former enemy and a wish to heal her wounds. Because the adult comes to slowly allow the child back into a shared consciousness, she can also provide the child with some sorely needed parenting. In providing understanding and acceptance for her child self, the adult can go a long way toward gratifying a painfully frustrated developmental need.

The child, on the other hand, is no longer driven to undermine the adult's successes. Her program of insurgence can, at last, come to an end. The adult's thought processes are no longer subject to constant invasion and disruption. In addition, the adult is revivified by once again integrating the child into her inner world. In excising the dangerous child persona, many other important childlike capacities have been lost. The child, now freed from her painful and all-consuming burden, is released to discover, perhaps for the first time, these other capacities and to bring them back to the adult, who also experiences them anew. Vitality and the shameless passion known only to children can reinfuse the adult's interpersonal world. Play and fantasy—for so long dangerous regressive forces—will enrich her internal life and breathe creativity into her practical, survival-oriented mind. Ambition, always too close to aggression and exhibitionism, either dissociated or inappropriately acted out, can assume a more readily modulated position and spur the adult to a greater enjoyment of her successes.

One patient, for example, presented her dysphoric, anhedonic, rigid adult self for treatment. Some time later, after she had made considerable progress in integrating the dissociated child self, she reported to her analyst a day spent at an amusement park. She had ridden the fastest rides, eaten cotton candy, flown a balloon, and reveled with delight in all of it. In her next session, she began to muse about returning to school for a master's degree in her field.

Her progress demonstrated the force and the consequences of integration. But during this intensely painful phase of treatment, the forces of integration exist in a constant battle with the ever-ready tendencies toward dissociation and disorganization. For it is during this phase that adult and child together must come to terms with the two most deadening realities. The first, the realities of the abuse that occurred; and the second—and perhaps more difficult fact—a childhood that was destroyed and won't ever be reclaimed.

It is a universal fantasy among all adult survivors of childhood sexual abuse that once the horrible facts of the abuse become known, the world will be moved to provide a new and idealized, compensatory childhood. This had always been the antidote; the daily pain-killing drug that became an addiction for the tortured child. She fed herself, in one patient's words, "daily doses, prn for pain," in order to go on living. It is often the renunciation of this wish that proves to be even more unimaginable for the child than accepting the realities of her abuse. Acknowledging the impossibility of bringing this fantasy to realization represents a betrayal of her most sacred inner self.

It is often this issue that gives rise to the most serious suicidal ideation, a threat that must, particularly in this context, be taken seriously. However, even when suicide is not an issue, renunciation of this idealized, compensatory childhood almost always results in a refortification of dissociative defenses and hatred for the child self. Through a purely childlike piece of logic, the dissociated self believes some form of these words uttered by one patient: "If what happened to me was unfair . . . if I did not deserve it, then I would get what I did deserve . . . what all the other children had. If people only knew, they would make sure that I got it. If I am not going to get it, even now when they know the truth . . . then I must have deserved what happened to me after all. I must be bad."

Another patient said:

This is too much. I can deal with the abuse . . . I think . . . maybe, I can. But the idea that this is all there will ever be. That when I think of being little, all I will feel is pain and terror . . . that's too much . . . I can't live with that. I want to feel what I see in the eyes of little children. You (therapist) say I deserve this . . . so why can't I? The sense of safety, I want a place that's safe. I want to get into trouble and be mischievous . . . safe trouble . . . usual trouble. I want someone else to do the worrying and the punishing. I'm tired. You say I can feel some of these things as a grown-up . . . you tell me about them. But how can I feel them when I'm not sure what they are . . . words. It's like trying to describe a color to someone who was born blind.

This underlying theme, which runs throughout treatment, does call forth periods of the most profound and intractable mourning. It tests a patient's determination to survive the threat of overwhelming disorganization, and it challenges the analyst's capacities to withstand her patients' despair and the limitations of her own abilities to alleviate suffering. Above all else, the analyst must allow the patient to experience and express his grief in full measure. This expression must be unencumbered by a need to appear better for the analyst's sake.

The patient must recognize and come to terms with the finality and irreversibility of the traumatic loss. This is a long and arduous process of working through intense rage and profound pain. Every resistance possible will be called up by the patient to avoid this mourning process; and the analyst will inevitably be swept up into a maddening conundrum of illusively shifting transference-countertransference enactments. The child will hold on, first to her denial, then to her expectation of compensation, with a ferocity that the analyst may not have experienced previously. In addition, the analyst may experience some trepidation about allowing such primitive transference paradigms to play themselves out and about tolerating such extreme regressive disorganization in a previously functional patient. However, this regressive process is unavoidable; only by allowing the child self to emerge, speak, and mourn will the emotional trauma be healed and the structural insufficiencies mended.

Inevitably, such a formulation, which stresses the inextricable linkage between trauma and dissociation, will call forth questions about the presence and diagnostic differentiation of the processes we describe from those inherent in the development of multiple personality disorders. In accordance with what we regard to be the best psychiatric literature on the subject (Putnam, 1989; Ross, 1989; Ross & Lowenstein, 1992), we believe that dissociation and dissociative disorders exist on a continuum, with multiple personality disorders representing the most extreme form of the kind of process we have described. The earlier, the more chronic, the more sadistic the abuse, and the closer the object relationship between abuser and victim, the more likely will be the development of multiple personality disorder. So, although all adult survivors of childhood sexual abuse do not show multiple personality structures, it seems that the best current estimate is that between 88% and 97% of all multiple personalities have experienced significant sexual and/or physical abuse in childhood (Putnam, 1989; Ross, 1989).

It is our belief that an approach that views dissociative barriers as boundaries drawn around particular organizations of self and object representation (as opposed to a view that stresses only the dissociation of specific memories) provides a clearer way of seeing entitites within the entire spectrum of dissociative pathology from a more theoretically continuous perspective. Such an understanding facilitates the capacity of a psychoanalytically trained clinician who finds him or herself confronted, perhaps for the first time, with a patient suffering from a true multiple personality disorder.

We also believe that a relationally oriented conceptualization of dissociation sheds some light on one of the continuing controversies in the multiple personality disorder literature, particularly that written from a psychoanalytic perspective. Some analysts have expressed their concerns that the emergence of "alter personalities" appears to intensify in the treatment setting, thus raising the possibility that such splits are iatrogenic, specifically as they relate to transferential reenactments. Often, an analyst "covering" a colleague's practice because of illness or vacation claims to see no evidence of the multiplicity that has been described and thus remains mystified by the diagnosis or attributes it to a countertransferential overinvolvement on the part of the treating therapist. Within our conceptual frame, however, such seemingly different experiences on the part of these two hypothetical analysts suggest no inherent internal contradictions.

It is our view that dissociation, because it is traumatogenically rendered, exists, fundamentally, within a relational context. Such mutually exclusive, alternating states are constellations of self and object representations with the traumatic memories themselves, providing both the glue that binds these representations together and the terror that divides such memory groupings from others of a more benign and tolerable nature. It should not be surprising, therefore, that such fundamental divisions will be most likely to manifest themselves around the re-evocation of experience specific to intense transference-countertransference emergence within an ongoing analysis. That such experiences are called forth only within the treatment setting by no means implies that they are created by that setting. If such a view prevails, than all transference manifestations would fall prey to the same dubious speculation.

Although a thorough review of diagnostic criteria and treatment procedures specific to instances of multiple personality disorder are clearly not within the scope of this book, the reader working with adults who were seriously abused as children should be alert to the overlap in these two areas of clinical work. Enhanced sensitivity to the presence of such phenomena will enable the analyst to seek out appropriate reading, didactic work, and supervisory consultation when such a clinical eventuality occurs.

Clinical Implications

In presenting our thoughts on the psychoanalytic treatment of adult survivors of childhood sexual abuse we are asked again and again about the level of regression described in our clinical work and exemplified in treatment vignettes. Is such regression necessary for the working-through of early traumatic abuse, or is it an iatrogenic artifact of an unnecessarily regressive analytic style? Is the dissociated child persona a structural and clinical inevitability of chronic trauma, or is it merely the patient's accommodation to a particular point of view held by the analyst? We have found ourselves—and have had confirmed by numerous colleagues, students, and supervisees—that speaking directly to the child persona and understanding tenaciously entrenched therapeutic stalemates from the child's perspective—that is, taking into account her own unique ego organization and system of internalized object relations—changes profoundly the nature of the analytic work.

With this formulation in mind we make the following clinical recommendations:

1) Speaking directly to the child persona in the adult survivor is the most effective way of recovering all of the traumatogenic memories. This is particularly important, because it is the more severe end of the spectrum that exists outside of conscious awareness.

2) Speaking directly to the child persona is also the most effective way to work through via the transference-countertransference a more pathological internal system of self and object representations and reality-distorting defenses. Such an internalized structure seriously impinges on the patient's current interpersonal relationships, and, in many cases, sets up these relationships along sadomasochistic lines that make the patient an ongoing victim of real or perceived abuse. Here the real experiences interact synergistically with the cordoned-off internal object world of the abused child persona to further confirm her intrinsic badness and, therefore, to indirectly intensify dissociative barriers.

3) The establishment of an alliance between the child persona and the analyst has the effect of symbolically changing the original traumatic experience of isolation and despair by bringing about the internalization of a new therapeutic object relationship that produces a permanent change in internal structure.

Although we stress the importance of working with dissociative states in the treatment of adult survivors, we are nonetheless aware that carrying out such tasks can become a complex and problematic clinical process. Two particular areas where the progress of the clinical work is particularly vulnerable to breakdown are illustrated with the following specific case examples.

Repetitive Reenactment of Abusive Memories

In cases where the dissociative barrier is particularly strong (usually implying a more sadistic or earlier experience of abuse), memories can emerge and be verbalized by the patient and analyst, without integration proceeding in the more usual fashion. In such a case, the patient is *extremely* upset, crying, shaking, and trembling, usually curled up with her head buried and not looking at the analyst. Although the patient can tell the story of her abuse while in such a frenzied state and the analyst can obtain *knowledge*, perhaps for the first time, about the specifics of the patient's abuse, integration between the child and the adult states within the patient is *not* occuring.

Here, the essential nature of the transference-countertransference configuration evokes the regressive reenactment of a piece of previously dissociated experience in the treatment setting. In such a case, the reenactment may involve a dialog between the patient and her abuser. In such a situation, the analyst merely bears witness to the conversation that went on between the victim and perpetrator during the abuse, with the patient reenacting both roles within the therapy hour. Nothing is addressed to the therapist; in fact, in such a situation, the patient appears to be oblivious to the therapist's presence.

In the second situation, the patient reenacts in the therapy hour a dialog that went on between dissociated aspects of herself during the actual experience of abuse. In this case, the dialog has a repetitive chantlike quality—hypnotic and trancelike in itself. It may be a particular song or a recognizable nursery rhyme, repeated again and again in an obvious effort to block everything else from awareness. In both of these scenarios the patient is oblivious to the analyst's presence; he or she exists only as an observer to this dissociated reenactment. Via projective identification, the analyst, in this context, is often left with the same sense of helplessness and loss of control in the face of overwhelming traumatic regression once experienced by the abused child.

Although the analyst observes, she does not participate in this reenactment. Although the particulars of the transference and countertransference are necessary for and essential to the evocation of the experience, the dissociation is, in this case, a defense against working through the particulars of the relationship, real and fantasied, to the analyst, in the immediacy and mutuality of the treatment setting. When such defenses against working through within the transference become rigidified, these patterns of dissociated reenactment often become repetitive and nonproductive aspects of the therapeutic work. Here a clinical example may help to clarify why such patterns become established and how they might become unfixed.

A talented and experienced analyst recently requested a series of consultations regarding her work with an adult incest survivor with whom she believed that she had "let the regression go too far." The patient was a 27-year-old survivor of father-daughter incest that had begun when she was 5 and continued until the start of menses. The patient's father was alcoholic, and the sexual abuse often included violent physical assaults as well. The patient had had no conscious memories of abuse at the time she began her treatment, but the peculiar juxtaposition of a highly successful external adaptation and more intensely primitive masochistic and overtly self-abusive symptomatology alerted the analyst, who had recently become aware of the growing psychoanalytic literature in this area, to the possibilities of such a history.

This particular therapist had done her homework well, familiarizing herself with much of the literature on trauma, sexual abuse, and psychoanalytic work with this patient population. She had thus gained a familiarity and comfort in working with the return of dissociated material and had, with such knowledge, facilitated the emergence of the child persona and her catalog of previously inexpressible memories within the treatment. Although the analyst now had a working familiarity with many of the significant events in her patient's past, the analysis had assumed a pattern with which she was uncomfortable. We present this consultation because we believe it to be typical of many cases of work with dissociated material that can be allowed to become perseverative and unrelenting. This common problem for clinicians grows out of the exclusive emphasis placed on "full, affectively charged, abreaction" of pathogenic events found in the trauma literature and the relative lack of emphasis placed on the notion that such abreaction, although essential, is only a means toward the ultimate integration of such experiences.

In the present case example, memories of incest experience between the patient and her father began to emerge in much the way we have grown used to hearing. The patient would curl up on the couch and begin to speak in the voice of a younger child. At some point in the session, the retelling of the experience became a reliving, and the patient was essentially unaware of the distinction between these past events and the present context. The analyst was both fascinated and alarmed by the intensity, physicality, and regressive pull of this reenactment. The patient could "end up hiding in a corner of my office, speaking from behind a bookcase or literally writhing in sexually suggestive ways on the couch." At times, the patient was capable of hearing the analyst's interventions, but at many times she was not. These experiences in the session were initially helpful to analyst and patient in convincing them both of the powerful reality of what they had only vaguely suspected to be true and in providing the analyst with many of the details of specific events that would prove to be helpful in formulating interpretations later on in the work.

Over time, however, an interesting transformation, first noticeable in the countertransference, began to infuse the therapeutic relationship. The analyst, who was at first "riveted" by the unfolding drama and raw intensity of the dissociated material, began to feel impatient, almost bored, with regressive reenactments that had started to feel inevitable and repetitive. Speaking almost in a whisper, herself, the analyst guiltily confessed, "It's awful to say this, and I know something is wrong that I'm reacting this way . . . it's one of the reasons I'm here. But last week when she (the patient) was reliving one of her worst memories—something that initially moved me to tears in the session—I actually thought—oh this is so awful—I actually thought, 'so . . . what else is new?'"

This is not an unusual reaction for therapists working with adult survivors, although it is always one that engenders intense guilt. The experience resembles that of a parent who at one time is entranced by the surging power of the imperious and commanding 2-year-old but finds such peremptory edicts much less endearing in the child several years older (Mitchell, 1990). As children mature, we come to expect more of them. As the patient proceeds in treatment, therapists hold to certain notions of developmental progress and therapeutic change, maintaining an empathic identification with the patient's wish to grow. Here, of course, we are on dangerous ground: transference or countertransference? Sadistic frustration by the patient of the analyst's perceived goals for her? Or retaliatory anger on the part of the analyst who wishes to save and cure this troubled soul?

Within a relational model that stresses the belief that together analyst and patient cocreate the paradigms that need to be analyzed, we are spared the need to resolve such conundrums. We assume both of these possibilities, along with many others to be true, signaling not the moral disintegration of this once-empathic analyst but a definitive shift in the intrapsychic meaning of this particular reenactment, that is, the reliving of this specific dissociated event. Signaled by the growing change in the countertransference, that is, the feeling that it is time for the patient to "move on," the therapist must assume a shift in the pertinent relational matrices is being played out in the analytic sessions. He or she is no longer working with the terrified, out of control, traumatically overstimulated child but with that aspect of the sadistic introject, the internalized abuser who seeks active gratification via transference reenactments of past trauma and, in so doing, renders the analyst-victim helpless and guilt-ridden.

Here the counteretransferential change helps to illuminate a reconfiguration in the transference-countertransference interaction, active interpretation of which relocates the once dissociated experience, well into the heart and soul of the analytic relationship. Thus, the potential for reintegration of these experiences, now transpiring under the watchful eye of an observing ego/adult persona, can be maximized. Such is the case with each aspect of the internalized paradigms of self and object representation that inhabit the inner world of the dissociated abused child. As they play themselves out in the relationship to the analyst, they can be witnessed by patient and analyst together, then verbalized, interpreted, and integrated with other aspects of adult functioning. This process of active integration beginning in the patient-analyst interaction should contribute in large measure to a reduction in the type of perseverative reenactments of dissociative states of which the analyst in our case example grew tired.

There are several other technical suggestions that may help to facilitate the integration of such dissociated reenactments, when it feels as if their repetition has become overly gratifying in and of itself, and is no longer useful in recovering new memories. We often ask patients in a dissociated state if they can sit up and talk of the same experiences while maintaining eye contact with the therapist. One patient described the effects of this request far more eloquently than we can. She said, "When I look into your eyes, I see the horrors of my own life reflected there. You look sadder and angrier for me than I can yet feel for myself. . . . Your eyes look loving, but there is still danger hidden there." This patient is struggling to integrate abusive experiences within the context of a new, nonabusive object relationship, a relationship that allows for her perception of the analyst's emotional reactions as well as for the integration of those reactions with her own. We find that simply ask-

ing patients to sit up and look at the analyst can have a major effect upon re-
locating the "scene of the crime" within the analytic dyad. We can understand the "danger" that the patient sees in the analyst's eyes and work with
it far more effectively than we can with a disembodied danger that exists
somewhere "out there."

Some other suggestions may be helpful, such as asking patients, much as
one might with a true multiple personality disorder patient, "Is the grown-
up part of you listening to what you're saying . . . it's so important that she
knows and understands what you are describing." Here one invokes the observing ego of the adult persona to bear witness to her "other self" and its internalized system of more primitive and sadomasochistically organized object relationships. As one patient aptly put it, "You speak not only to the
child, you also speak to the adult about the child." In so doing, one seeks to
encourage an identification between the adult persona and the analyst, as
the latter attempts to engage, regulate, contain, and essentially parent the
abused and dissociated child.

Maintaining the Analytic Frame

Although much of what we have written stresses the centrality of evoking the
dissociated child persona and her related system of self and object representations specific to episodes of abuse, it is equally imperative that the clinician
never lose sight of the adult self and object organization within this relational
matrix. Ultimately, it is the adult persona who bears responsibility for maintaining the analytic frame (i.e., conforming to certain time constraints, paying
bills, respecting the analyst's needs for privacy, time off, sleep, etc.) Any treatment, abuse-related or not, that encompasses certain regressive reenactments
in the transference, must navigate a veritable minefield of potentially treatment-destroying interactions tacitly encouraged by such regression.

Under the sway of regressive reenactments, often outrageous demands
can be made of the analyst by the patient. Although we become used to hearing about the perceived needs of our patients and of struggling ourselves
with the constant tension between symbolic gratifications, frustrations, and
interpretations, such requests, when made by patients with histories of severe abuse, exert particularly powerful and influential countertransferential
pressure. Requests that are contextually embedded in a history of abuse and
neglect, plaintively echoed by the very child who endured such maltreat-
ment, can move the most resolute believer in the powers of abstinence and
neutrality to inappropriate acts of attempted heroic salvation.

However, no sooner does the idealized savior-therapist make contact with
the abused child persona than the operative relational matrix shifts and we
are simultaneously dealing with enactments of the omnipotent, counterabu-

sive child, that aspect of the child that is identified with her abusive parent or other. The analyst must be prepared for the reality that, in a split second, the central organizing transference-countertransference paradigm can shift from that between a nurturing parent-therapist and a needy, damaged, yearning, and ultimately grateful child-patient to that between a weary, depleted, guilt-ridden, helpless child-therapist, and an entitled, omnipotent, raging and out-of-control abuser-patient. Therapists shift, shift back, and shift again, as each paradigm takes its turn at center stage in the analytic relationship.

The emergence and resolution of this particular transference-counter-transference reenactment is addressed in chapter 8, but it should be mentioned here in order to emphasize the point that, although we welcome the emergence of a dissociated child persona and listen to her memories, experiences, and perceived needs, we at all times hold the adult patient responsible for maintaining herself and the ability to continue the treatment. This provides a necessary balance and counterpoint to the regressive pull of such a treatment. It is the therapist's role to enable the child to mourn the childhood that cannot be, not to live it out in the transference relationship. It is, therefore, disturbing to hear the many stories of therapists actively engaging in parent-child type of activities, such as reading children's books to their patients, playing children's games during sessions, and so on, as if this somehow provides recompense for the horrific abuse that has been perpetrated. Far from not helping, such excesses can be counterproductive, interfering with the necessary mourning that must be done, by communicating the therapist's willingness to attempt such "reparenting." We believe that a thorough understanding of the internal object world of such patients will make clear the doomed resolution of such attempts. On the contrary, it is the patient's continued ability to function, that is, to maintain the necessary obligations inherent in her participation in the adult world, that will ultimately convince her of her ability to deal with traumatic memories and reenactments without becoming overwhelmed and retraumatized. We therefore encourage our patients to continue working, to maintain a modicum of social interaction with the outside world. We insist that sessions be fully paid for, that time limits be adhered to, and that reasonable understanding of the therapist's needs in such a therapeutic relationship be maintained. Of course, adhering to such a treatment frame is enormously difficult, and the analyst should always be willing to negotiate with the adult patient the particular therapeutic modifications that may be necessary in order to enable the child counterpart to proceed with the therapeutic work.

Ms. P. was a 32-year-old survivor of repetitive sexual abuse at the hands of an alcoholic and sadistic father. The following excerpt is taken from a session during the third year of a three-time-a-week analysis, occurring at the time the patient was beginning to recover memories of having been forcibly sodomized.

PATIENT: I can't possibly leave now; I know you wouldn't make me do that. I'm all over the place . . . a mess . . . I can't go out there (escalating panic). I know you see somebody after me, but just this once, you'll make that person go away, you must, because I can't, I really can't stop. I'm begging you!

Here the analyst is faced with a seemingly no-win proposition. To "force" the patient to leave reenacts an abusive scenario with the therapist as abuser and patient as the begging, pleading victim. Perhaps less available, counter-transferentially, however, is the therapist and her next patient as the victim of an infantile and out-of-control abuser who just "can't stop" herself.

THERAPIST: I know how much pain you're in, because I've been here with you through this session. And I wish I could do that for you, now . . . to make the whole rest of the world and all my other patients disappear . . . to say to you that, because your father did this to you, you deserve this time to be the only person in the world who matters. I think it's really okay to wish for that . . . I even want you to wish for that. . . . But I can't make it come true.

PATIENT: But why not . . . why can't you just this once. I've never asked before. I even bet your other patient would understand. Crises happen, everyone knows that. I would understand if you had to cancel my session one time because of a crisis with someone else. I may not like it, but I would understand.

The therapist becomes aware that under the countertransferential pressure to empathize with the abused child, the patient is beginning to sound reasonable. She even considers, momentarily, acceding to the patient's demands.

THERAPIST: You make it sound so reasonable, and I suppose from one point of view it is. But it seems to me that there's another point of view that is equally important. If I say okay to you, that it's all right to stay and use somebody else's time . . . I'm really saying that all of the terrible things you've suffered entitle you to be so out of control that you impinge on the rights of that person out there (the next patient). That having been abused gives you the right to ignore the rights and boundaries of another, to identify with your father and turn that patient out there into yourself.

PATIENT: I don't care!

THERAPIST: I know that the little kid in you who has been so terribly hurt doesn't much care about that stranger, and, at this moment I wouldn't expect her to. But the only way I know to make it really safe for that little girl inside to feel all the angry wishes she can possibly imagine is to be very clear that all those angry wishes won't really hurt someone else.

PATIENT: I can't care about other people right now.

THERAPIST: I understand that.

PATIENT: [Crying] I don't even think I care about you.

THERAPIST: That's okay. I'll try to protect myself, too. Then, you can feel all of the hate without having to worry about anyone but yourself.

PATIENT: Okay, so you do that for me; I understand what you're saying, but I still just don't think I can do it. I'm too upset to get up and face the world. I'm out of control.

THERAPIST: I don't think you are. I think you would like the freedom to be out of control, to be free of the burden of having to control yourself. After all, your father didn't worry about staying in control . . . did he? Why should you have to?

PATIENT: I know that you want me say okay to that, that I understand and now I will go nicely. But I still can't do it [panic rising again].

THERAPIST: I have to believe that you can do it, because we are going to stop now. We must do that so that we can go on working in this way. You know that if you have trouble, you can reach me later on this evening.

The patient being described here was able to leave this session and to function quite well until her next analytic hour. However, many patients, despite the best interpretive efforts, will still leave such a session utterly enraged at what they experience as the analyst's brutality. By way of reassurance we can only stress here the belief that our work involves the constant, delicate negotiation of regressive reenactment and progressive working-through and unfolding. The "brutal and heartless therapist" is not a therapeutic failure but a central aspect of the internal organizing matrices of self and object that must be worked through during the analytic encounter. However, together, the functioning, adult patient and the analyst must protect the structure and direction of the treatment from the seductive encroachment of regressive therapeutic enactments that threaten the continuity of treatment.

Here the analyst tries to steer a course through the storm, knowing that all involved will be tossed around unmercifully and that there will be periods when all sense of direction and purpose will be lost. Here, we hold the final destination in mind but know that the ultimate success of our ability to navigate and survive will rest with our ability to pick significant landmarks and milestones out of the encroaching mist. As we become familiarized with the kinds of dissociative processes described, we enhance our ability to react quickly and assuredly without at the same time oversteering the boundaries of the often enshrouded course.

CHAPTER 5

Disclosure and the Recovery of Memories

T HE SEXUAL ABUSE of children is enshrouded in secrecy and denial. Secrecy is imposed by the perpetrator with a variety of intimidations that range from the subtle to the viciously sadistic. Frequently, the silence obtained from the child is so deeply internalized that the victim reaches adulthood with the secret of her violations intact. At more extreme levels of preservation, the sexual abuse remains dissociated from the everyday consciousness of the patient, thus constituting a secret even from the victim herself. If, on the other hand, the child does disclose the abuse while it is occurring, she is often ignored, disbelieved, vilified, or further abused rather than validated and supported.

Given the extent to which the abused child and adult survivor relegate their sexual victimizations to a realm of shadowed secrecy, it is not surprising to find that many women with abuse histories undertake and even "complete" therapy without ever mentioning their abusive experiences. Treatment may bog down and eventually grind to a halt because of a myriad of resistances and seemingly inexplicable, yet powerfully unsettling, transference and countertransference constellations that confuse and frustrate both patient and therapist.

If secrecy is the mainstay of childhood sexual abuse, disclosure to a validating, believing other is the first step in a process of healing the devastating wounds of early sexual victimization. It is therefore crucial that clinicians know how and when to facilitate disclosure, so that they can become that, often first, validating and believing other.

Disclosure of Abuse in Childhood: What Happens?

Some patients, as children, divulged the secret of their abuse early on. Unfortunately, many of these patients met with negative responses from disclosure targets; they were often ignored, blamed, or vilified for the abuse by the person to whom they disclosed.

When, as a child, a patient disclosed her secret to an adult who then failed to intervene or protect her, she, of course, was abused once again. Furthermore, the fantasy that someone would protect her if only she told was dismantled, leaving her even more alienated and bereft. Barbara, who was sexually molested by her father, told her mother about the abuse when she was 12 years old, 4 years after the nearly nightly victimizations began. Barbara's mother was hanging laundry in the backyard when Barbara blurted out, "Mommy, Daddy puts his penis between my legs at night, and I don't like it." Her mother just continued to hang clothes and, when Barbara summoned her courage to begin again, her mother responded, "Barbara, you're in my way. Go in the house, and see if your father is awake yet." The message to this child could not have been clearer; her role was to attend to her father in every way while her mother remained emotionally detached from both husband and daughter. The hostile neglect inherent in this interchange was yet another abusive thread running through the tapestry of Barbara's childhood.

Clearly, the child who disclosed her sexual abuse when she was young and met with a negative response often becomes an adult patient, who, even if she remembers the sexual traumas, is terrified of disclosing again only to be rejected once more. It is the therapist's sensitivity to and comfort with derivatives and symptoms suggestive of a history of sexual trauma that can lead to disclosure and the beginning of healing.

Facilitating Disclosure of Sexual Abuse in Treatment

Psychotherapy, from its inception, has been dedicated to the belief that talking about one's life within the context of a therapeutic relationship is mutative. Since Anna O's discovery of the "talking cure," therapists have been urging people to talk. Because, however, a patient's sexually traumatic history is frequently beclouded by long-held secrecy, it is imperative that the therapist take an active position in eliciting information about past abusive experiences. Before delineating ways in which disclosure can be facilitated, we examine resistances to this process that are sometimes mentioned by clinicians.

Resistance to Asking

Therapists may be reluctant to ask about a history of abuse for a number of reasons. First, they may feel that patients will divulge important aspects of their histories when they are ready. Asking, in this case, is experienced as premature or intrusive. Clinicians may also hold that a history of sexual abuse, if present, is just one more part of a patient's narrative and does not represent something especially to seek after. In this case, asking is judged to be irrelevant. A third concern raised by therapists involves the believability of sexual abuse disclosed in response to questioning during history taking, particularly sex abuse disclosed by psychotic and borderline patients. This argument echos Freud's in questioning the reliability of the data presented by more disturbed patients. Finally, therapists doubt disclosures of childhood sexual abuse and attribute these reports to unresolved oedipal conflicts and fantasies.

Each of these arguments against asking a patient about sexual abuse often represents countertransference resistance on the part of the therapist. Psychological trauma, especially sexual abuse, raises anxiety and discomfort within the clinician. Like society at large, a victim's family and, frequently enough, patients themselves, therapists do not want to know that patients sitting before them were violated sexually, often repeatedly, perhaps sadistically, maybe at very young ages. We want to recoil and close our eyes to the commonness and viciousness with which children are sexually victimized. And so, too often, we do not ask, citing the potential intrusiveness or irrelevance of such questions, or we find reasons to disbelieve what we hear, invoking the reported tendency of more disturbed patients to distort, or relying on the centrality of oedipal theory to recast what we are told. The latter two potential therapist resistances may be particularly devastating to patients who have been invalidated earlier in their lives when they talked about their abusive experiences.

The literature linking early actual trauma and borderline pathology suggests that, indeed, the borderline patient's presentation of her childhood may be quite distorted. In contradistinction to traditional conceptualizations of the borderline (Kernberg, 1984), however, this literature suggests that the way in which borderline patients distort often is to present their histories as far rosier than they really were in an attempt to preserve positive images of much-needed and loved parental objects.

Our clinical experience is certainly more in keeping with this emerging paradigm of borderline pathology. Adult sexual abuse survivors tend to be enormously and poignantly supportive of their abusers, particularly parental perpetrators, and often for years deny or minimize the extent of their past victimizations. We thus find it more difficult to help patients to accept full cognitive and affective remembrance of their abuse than to validate the reality that abuse in fact occurred. In other words, the fantasy among our patients is that their childhoods were better than they really were.

As to mislabeling as oedipal fantasies reports of actual childhood sexual abuse, we stress the phenomenological differences between patients presenting with oedipal fantasies and those holding memories of actual early sexual trauma.

First of all, the patient struggling with psychological problems primarily related to unresolved oedipal conflicts is unlikely to present with the severe symptomatology and ego fragmentation found among adult survivors of childhood sexual abuse. Next, the phenomenological presentation of oedipal material is markedly different from sexual abuse memories. Oedipal fantasies, although frequently disturbing to the patient, do not carry the imagistic or affective wallop of sexual abuse memories. Furthermore, the anxiety surrounding oedipal material is usually a response to the murderous rage felt toward the same-sex parent; it is not evoked by the explicitly sexual aspects of the oedipal conflict. Finally, oedipally driven anxiety is usually warded off from direct subjective experience; it is manifested instead in symptoms such as phobias or physical complaints. When patients discuss their oedipal conflicts in treatment, their ego functioning most often will remain intact.

The anxiety connected to sexual abuse memories, on the other hand, is directly connected to sexual aspects of the survivor's relationship with the abuser. Most often, it is not successfully warded off through symptom formation but is experienced subjectively and, in fact, frequently floods the patient, resulting in dissociation, severe impairments in ego functioning, and flashbacks or intrusive thoughts about the abuse. Thus, although sexual abuse memories and the consequences of early trauma can, and often do, coincide with oedipal conflicts and fantasies, the presentation of one differs sufficiently from the other to enable clinicians to trace the roots of what they are hearing in the consultation room.

The Importance of Asking

Given what is known now about the prevalence of childhood sexual abuse in general and among a patient population, especially an apparently borderline population, and given the secrecy usually surrounding an adult survivor's childhood victimizations, it is incumbent on therapists to ask about sexual abuse just as they routinely query about any other potentially meaningful childhood experiences.

During history taking with every patient, we explore for possible past abuse. As patients discuss with us their past and present sexual experiences, we routinely inquire about sexual abuse, saying something like, "I wonder if you could tell me about any uncomfortable or distressing sexual experiences you may have had as a child or teenager?"

There are subgroups of patients to consider when asking these questions, ranging from the nonabused patient to one who has completely dissociated the memories and affects associated with early actual traumas. It is therefore important to evaluate responses to these questions in terms of both verbal content and nonverbal process. Most nonabused patients, for instance, handle these questions routinely; matter-of-fact negative verbal responses are complemented by equally matter-of-fact body positions, facial expressions, affect, voice inflection. Patients who were, in fact, abused will also range along a continuum.

Some adult survivors enter treatment desperately hoping just to be asked about their abuse so that they might begin to speak (Herman, 1981). These are patients with conscious memories of their childhood traumas who want to speak but may not unless and until they know the therapist is willing and able to hear their stories. Just asking about a history of sexual abuse is frequently enough to facilitate disclosure from these patients.

There is now empirical data supporting the efficacy of simply asking new patients about sexual abuse. For instance, Briere and Zaidi (1988) conducted a study in which 100 intake reports on nonpsychotic women presenting to an urban psychiatric emergency room were reviewed in two phases. In the first review, 50 charts were randomly selected and the intake report was checked for a history of sexual abuse; 6% of the charts reflected such data. Clinicians were then instructed to question intake patients for previous sexual victimizations. Another 50 postinstruction intake reports were randomly reviewed, and, this time, 70% of the women interviewed reported having been sexually abused at some point in their lives. These researchers and others (Cole, 1988) emphasize that many of these women had previous encounters with mental health facilities during which their abusive histories were not disclosed. We thus stress the imperative need to ask every patient about any abuse in her past. Asking often facilitates disclosure, and disclosure is necessary for healing to occur.

Sometimes, of course, just asking does not result in disclosure. This can happen when the patient has dissociated all memories of the traumas. It can also occur when the patient has conscious abuse memories but bears allegiance to an internalized silencing or much-needed object. Finally, it can be associated with the patient's fear that the therapist will ignore or disbelieve disclosed abuse. Having conscious but as yet unspeakable memories places this patient at the next point on a continuum.

A patient who clearly remembers her abuse may have carried her secret for many years and is still tenaciously attached to an internalized silencing, shaming object. Disclosure of past abuse evokes whatever threats or promises the perpetrator used to obtain silence and also endangers the internalized relationship; disclosure is thus threatening to the patient's organization of self and objects. Disclosure also may be experienced as dangerously risky because it raises the spectre that the therapist, perhaps like others before, will ignore, disbelieve, or in some way invalidate the importance of the early trauma.

This patient probably will not disclose her sexual abuse during history taking but is likely to offer positive nonverbal responses to the therapist's queries. Often, this patient tenses up at questions regarding sexual abuse, quickly glances away as she verbally denies her own history, or provides overly intense and elaborate protestations that she was never abused. Even if the sexually abused woman who remembers her victimizations is not prepared to disclose during history taking, the therapist's questions inform her that he knows and believes that children are sexually abused, that those violations are important clinical material, and that he is prepared to join the former victim in working through the memories and affects linked with any such abuse.

Who Speaks First?

Even when the therapist presents as willing and ready to work with a patient's abuse history, it is frequently a tremendous struggle for the patient actually to verbalize the truth of her abuse, even when both she and the therapist have been circling around it, like an airplane seeking the right approach path for landing, for many weeks or many months. Initially, the therapist who suspects a history of sexual abuse in her patient can wonder with the patient at the meaning of derivatives of betrayal, intrusion, unwanted penetration, lack of validation. Patient and therapist can seek the meaning of transference and countertransference paradigms that replicate aspects of abuse, such as the patient's experience of the clinician as a dangerous penetrator of the patient's mind. Therapist and patient can sort out the significance of such dramatic symptoms as cutting, substance abuse, repeated involvement in abusive relationships, or amnesia for all or part of childhood. At some point, however, someone has to land the plane by actually putting into words the reality of the patient's previous sexual trauma.

Who will land the plane and when and how becomes a dilemma of timing and technique for the clinician working with a patient who knows about her abuse, who knows the therapist knows, who knows the therapist knows the patient knows, but who still resists the ultimate verbalization of the unspeakable trauma. For the therapist to name the unnameable first may feel abusive to the patient who struggles to maintain denial, secrecy, and allegiance to important childhood figures. On the other hand, for the therapist to collude with not knowing ad infinitum may too closely replicate the patient's experience with an unseeing, unhearing, unavailable, nonabusing parent; a parent who knew about the sexual violations but who failed to validate and support the patient when she was a little girl. In addition, the therapist's participation in ongoing avoidance of the known may be perceived by the patient as the clinician's reluctance to process the abuse with the patient. In this case, the survivor feels that the therapist views her the way she sees herself—a shameful, disgusting, unacceptable being. At an even deeper level, the process of endlessly circling the abuse secret without ever quite landing on a verbalization becomes a way for the patient to tantalize the therapist much as she once was teased and overstimulated by the sexual abuser.

It is often appropriate and even crucial for the therapist to speak first; to put a name to the unnameable; to begin to symbolize that which has remained unorganized and raw within the patient's psyche. If therapist and patient have engaged in a reasonably full process of examining symptoms, dreams, derivatives, transference and countertransference phenomena, all of which lead to a conclusion that the patient experienced childhood sexual abuse and, if the therapist senses that he and the patient are, in fact, endlessly circling an unspoken known, it is then therapeutically indicated for the clinician to speak first. To do so is to validate the patient's inner reality in a way that establishes the therapist as a powerful counterpoint to the patient's internalized silencing/abusive objects. It is setting out a claim that past abuse is an important clinical issue that the therapist can stand discussing with the patient. It also demonstrates that the therapist can set limits on unending tantalizing and overstimulation. The following vignette between Lisette, a patient who was sexually abused by her father, and the therapist illustrates how the therapist might go about speaking the secret first:

THERAPIST: You know, it seems to me, that you and I have been dancing around an important secret. I think that, at this point, we both know there's a secret, we both know what the secrect is, and each of knows that the other knows. But, so far, we haven't put it into words.

LISETTE: I don't know what you mean.

THERAPIST: Well, we've talked about a number of issues that are powerful and painful for you. We've talked about how much you hate your body. We've talked about the possibility that you're reliving something when you "see" a man standing beside your bed when you fall asleep at night. We've talked about how scared you get whenever your husband wants to make love. We've notice how you "space out" every time we talk about your childhood relationship with your father. We've wondered why you have very clear memories of life up until age 7 and then no memories of life between ages 7 and 15. We've talked about all this and more and we've wondered about the reasons for all this, but we don't ever seem to be able to land on, to put into words, a reason for many of your symptoms and conflicts.

LISETTE: Do you think you know the reason?

THERAPIST: Well, I actually think we both have been entertaining similar thoughts. But it sounds to me as if just thinking these thoughts seems dangerous to you, and so you may wish that I would put them into words first.

LISETTE: I'm confused; I don't know what's going on.

THERAPIST: Well, it seems odd to me that, given all we have discussed about your life past and present, that the one thing we've never openly talked about is the possibility that you were abused sexually as a child.

LISETTE: Oh, I don't think that could be.

THERAPIST: It doesn't seem to me that we have to decide *if* it happened right now. I wonder, though, why it is that we can't even explore this possibility.

LISETTE: You *do* know. You *know* I think it happened. But I hate that it happened, and I don't *want* to know, I don't *want* to.

THERAPIST: These thoughts—this possibility that you were abused—are awful to grapple with. My experience, though, is that struggling with this awful possibility is bearable when you feel you can do it with someone else. So I think it can be bearable for you if we do it together.

The patient and therapist in this vignette had been exploring a myriad of derivatives of sexual abuse for months—dreams, symptoms, transference and countertransference paradigms, repeated relational configurations in the patient's life. In addition, the patient had provided derivatives suggesting her awareness that she and the therapist shared an unspoken secret. Furthermore, the derivatives implied that the secret was experienced as detrimental to the therapeutic relationship. Finally, there were indications that the patient wanted the therapist to speak first. For instance, the patient offered a dream about a childhood friend who, in the dream, knew a secret about the patient. In the dream, the patient yearned for the friend to tell the secret so that it was open between them.

The clinical dilemma in this situation is delicate. By not speaking first, the therapist attempted to avoid too close a replication of the sexual abuser who psychologically and physically penetrated the patient long before she was emotionally ready to cope with that stimulation and knowledge. At the same time, not speaking first may have instead too closely duplicated the position of the nonabusing parent who for too long knew the secret of the patient's abuse but said and did nothing. In this case, the clinician decided to present herself as an object significantly different from the patient's mother who seemed to have known about the abuse but did nothing; the therapist named the unnameable first. It is important to note here the patient's great reluctance to put her abuse into words; far from embracing an identity of an incest survivor, the patient struggled to protect her parents, real and internalized, from the truth of her childhood molestations.

Although we advocate great caution in preempting the patient's intiation of disclosure, there are instances such as the one presented in this vignette in which it is not only acceptable but perhaps vital for the therapist to speak first. This kind of clinical dilemma can be trying for both patient and therapist. Even more challenging, however, is disclosure work with the patient who has dissociated all memories of her childhood abuse.

Disclosure in a Dissociated State

During history taking, the survivor who has dissociated the memories of her abuse will truthfully deny any history of sexual trauma. The therapist, however, is likely to note a look of vague discomfort, a slight shift in body position, as if the question disturbed something far within the patient. It may also happen that this patient will dissociate at the therapist's inquiry about past sexual trauma, briefly—or not so briefly—"spacing out." These nonverbal responses alert the clinician to the possibility of an abusive past. Combined with careful assessment of the signs and symptoms of childhood sexual abuse discussed in Chapter 2, these nonverbal cues allow the therapist to prepare for the possible disclosure of the dissociated trauma.

In work with a patient who has dissociated her childhood traumas, disclosure of the abuse occurs when the abused child part of the person, holder of abuse memories, emerges to share her story with the clinician. For this to happen, the therapist must accept, work with, and even encourage the dissociated states into which the patient enters during treatment. It is through these states that the truth unfolds, first to be spoken to the therapist.

A patient with dissociated traumatic material begins to "space out" during sessions or describes dissociative experiences that occur between sessions. The therapist notes that the dissociation happens most frequently when certain subjects are raised in session. For example, Lorna, whose father abused her for 9 years, presented to treatment with no conscious memories of her sexual abuse. After a few months of therapy, she began to dissociate during session. As time went on, the therapist realized that Lorna consistently dissociated after she mentioned her childhood relationship with her father, her own sexuality, or her current relationships with men. During a dissociation, Lorna's eyes glazed over, she sat stiffly in the chair, and she was unresponsive to questions from the therapist. When she "came back," Lorna had no memory of what she had been saying before she dissociated, nor could she describe what happened internally during the period of dissociation.

The therapist began to remind Lorna of what she had been discussing before the dissociations and asked the patient what about the subject, her girlhood relationship with her father, was so upsetting that Lorna had to distance herself by "spacing out." Eventually, the therapist interpreted to Lorna that it seemed that talking about her father, other men, or sex triggered feelings Lorna wanted to avoid. After some months and during a dissociative episode, Lorna relived and described her father raping her at age 6. At that time, Lorna's voice, facial expression, and body posture were consistent with the presentation of a 6-year-old child. Similar episodes occurred over a period of many months, during which the dissociated child part of Lorna recalled and relived her sexual traumas.

It is important to note that disclosure of Lorna's sexual abuse occurred when the therapist accepted and worked with the patient's dissociations. Focusing on dissociation as a mode of communication as well as a defense against knowing enables the clinician to facilitate disclosure of dissociated traumatic material.

Disclosure of abusive memories, affects, and associated fantasies is essential to the successful treatment of adult survivors of childhood sexual abuse. If the therapeutic road eventually leads to the disclosure of sexual trauma, the therapist must be prepared for a range of possible effects of disclosure.

Effects of Disclosure

Although there are many positive outcomes of disclosure, initially breaking the abuse secret may engender increased disorganization and symptom exacerbation, such as disturbing flashbacks, reenactments of some aspect of the trauma, or self-punitive behavior evoked by the betrayal of and disloyalty to the family represented by the very act of disclosure. These consequences of disclosure reflect the return of bad objects to whom the adult survivor remains unconsciously and tenaciously attached (Fairbairn, 1943).

A group at greater risk for suicide than women without histories of sexual victimization (Bagley & Ramsay, 1986; Briere & Runtz, 1986), survivors may attempt or complete suicide when disclosure evokes very painful, very rageful previously dissociated memories and affects associated with their abuse (Courtois, 1988). In these cases, attempted or successful suicides can be viewed as vicious attacks on and by the patient's introjects, as well as an expression of rage toward the therapist for colluding with, even encouraging, the disclosure. Consider a clinical example of one patient's reaction to her disclosure of her father's particularly sadistic sexual abuse.

Vera's incest ended only when, at age 20, her father tried to murder her one night when she struggled to escape. For years, years that included a number of psychiatric hospitalizations, Vera told no one about the incest. The first time she did disclose, she became acutely suicidal. Violently resisting hospitalization, she required four male paramedics to restrain her. For some time, subsequent disclosure of material related to her incest evoked a similar response. Eventually, through repeated interpretation of the repetition of the trauma invoked through her actions, Vera was able to see that after she revealed memories or affects associated with her incest experiences, she behaved in a way that resulted in a terrifying reenactment of her father pinning her down on the floor to rape her. In a convoluted and self-destructive way, Vera was enacting loyal preservation of her internalized relationship with her father.

Although this is an extreme example of the negative consequences of disclosure, it dramatically illustrates the point that revelation of the abuse secret may sometimes result in temporary deterioration of the patient's functioning with a concomitant increase in symptomatology. After exploring a patient's reactions in session to any disclosures of traumatic material, we find it helpful to predict to the patient that she may experience more frequent memories, flashbacks, intrusive thoughts about the abuse, along with intensified affective reactions of rage and terror. Depending on a patient's symptom history, we suggest that she may feel fragmented, depressed, suicidal, or that she may want to engage in self-destructive actions, such as self-mutilation, drinking, or driving recklessly. We stress to the patient that, although this exacerbated symptom picture can extend for some time, it is temporary. We educate the patient about the improved functioning that results from talking about and integrating her traumatic experiences in therapy. Predicting some of the possible negative consequences of disclosure can sometimes, although not always, help patients to tolerate disorganizing affects and self experiences without engaging in impulsive enactments.

Despite the turbulence that sometimes follows an adult survivor's disclosure of her childhood sexual abuse, the opportunity to reveal the secret and to discuss her abusive experiences with a validating other more usually signifies the beginning of healing for former victims.

Because, by definition, women who have not disclosed their abuse secrets are unavailable to researchers, it is difficult to validate empirically the ameliorative effects of disclosure. However, research studies (Brunngraber, 1986; Courtois, 1980; Frawley, 1988) suggest that disclosure of childhood sexual abuse is experienced by the patient as ultimately immensely relieving and that it is crucial to reopening intrapersonal and interpersonal relational channels. Disclosure initiates a process of remembering and relating that eventually results in structural integration and improved functioning, although remembering is itself a complicated process.

The Recovery of Traumatic Memories

One of the most important therapeutic processes that occurs during treatment with a survivor of childhood sexual abuse is the remembering, speaking aloud, and integration of often long warded-off traumatic memories. This is conceptualized best as speaking the unspeakable and naming the unnameable. Even if patients have shared the fact that abuse occurred with someone before entering therapy, seldom have they talked about what was done to them and what they felt like at the time.

Complicating the process of remembering is the fact that specific traumatic memories are frequently state-dependent (van der Kolk, 1989). They were encoded in trauma-related states of helpless terror and wordless rage and are accessible only when the patient reenters those affective states, something that occurs only when transference and countertransference reaches a level of intensity that triggers evocation of these states. Further complicating the recovery of memories is the fact that traumatic memories were often not encoded semantically but were processed only on a sensorimotor level of cognition. Unsymbolized and unspoken, the abuse remains unorganized and vast within the patient's psyche, where, alive and encased in wordless terror and rage, it works on her from outside her control. To symbolize the experiences for the first time, to put words to what happened to her, is eventually to contain the vastness of the abuse, to shrink it from the size and shape of a monstrous bogeyman from childhood to a still painful but more manageable narrative about truly past events.

In discussing the encoding and retrieval of traumatic memories, we enter an area of fierce controversy. Psychoanalytically oriented clinicians, aware of the organizing role of fantasy in a child's life, frequently question the accuracy of childhood memories, traumatic or not, reported by patients. Memories of sexual encounters have been considered particularly suspect because of the perceived central influence of oedipal fantasies. More recently, some experimental psychologists (Loftus, 1992) have joined the fray, insisting that memories of sexual abuse reported in therapy may result from suggestions made by the clinician. Trauma research, however, indicates that traumatic memories are indeed retrievable and are essentially accurate.

Lenore Terr (1991), in her work with traumatized children, reports that children who were abused as infants or toddlers and who, at the time of treatment, were amnesic of their ordeals repetitively drew, played out, or reported "seeing" accurate portrayals of their original traumas. Terr gives an example of a 5-year-old child who was sexually and pornographically abused in a daycare center between the ages of 15 and 18 months. Amnesic of these events, the child reported a "funny feeling" in her "tummy" whenever a finger was pointed at her; photographs confiscated by authorities investigating the daycare home showed an erect penis pointed at the same place on the victim's stomach that she herself identified when describing "funny feelings" (p. 13).

Adult patients' stereotypic behaviors, dreams, seemingly inexplicable fears, or recurrent, intrusive thoughts often accurately convey details of previous trauma. We say accurately because, in more than a few cases, the validity of the memories have been corroborated by third parties who were aware of the sexual abuse when it occurred.

Although recoverable, traumatic memories range along a continuum from those wholly dissociated and out of awareness to those organized and integrated into the consciousness of the patient. Patients arrive in treatment at different points of remembering; some start therapy with very clear, integrated memories, and others begin their healing at some place on the continuum. The road to remembering is thus marked by unexpected and, for the patient, frightening turns.

Many adult survivors of childhood sexual abuse arrive in treatment with only hazy impressions, if any, of their abuse. Their memories are not semantically encoded but reside within their psyche in unsymbolized, unorganized formlessness. Once these patients are in treatment and the therapeutic relationship reaches a critical point of intensity, they may begin to experience what to them are inexplicably powerful reactions to seemingly benign environmental stimuli. Consider two clinical examples.

Maria had a violent reaction every time she saw a certain shade of blue—her throat constricted, her heart palpitated, and she felt nauseous and dizzy. Frightened, she felt she must be crazy because of this disorganizing response to a shade of color. Finally, Maria remembered that the room in which her uncle sodomized her was this very shade of blue, as was the coverlet on which the abuse took place. Having recovered the memory, her reaction to this color became much less intense.

Lizzie, who had been viciously abused by multiple perpetrators, was so unable to verbalize her experiences that she called all terms associated with the victimizations "yuck" words and "yuck" things. To say or even hear the "real" words—rape, penis, vagina—was tantamount to reexperiencing the abuse, right then in the present. At hearing these words, this patient dissociated and literally relived abuse, often writhing and crying out in pain. When she "came back," she remembered nothing of the dissociative episode. Only gradually was she able to tolerate and then finally say words associated with the abuse. This growing tolerance coincided with remembering and relating the details of her violations.

These survivors remembered before they knew they did. They "remembered" first in unsymbolized ways that were reenactments rather than memories as we usually understand them to be organized and integrated into a well-functioning ego. At this furthest end of the memory continuum, the patients' memories of their abuse were almost wholly dissociated. Split off from consciousness, they retained the affective strength of the original trauma and operated with great power from outside the patients' awareness.

When the therapist is working with a patient who is experiencing unsymbolized memories of abuse, it is important that he join with the patient in exploring the meaning of wordless revivals of trauma. In fact, the first step for the clinician to take is to communicate to the patient that these experiences have meaning that eventually can be understood and symbolized. Then, the therapist can encourage the patient to stay with, and associate to the disturbing stimulus in session. In most cases, the patient will be able to experience the visceral or affective reenactment in the consulting room and, with the therapist's support, retrieve the memory behind the experience.

At the next point on the continuum are memories that are expressed through somatic experiences that symbolically represent some aspect of the original traumas. These usually involve visual or kinesthetic perceptions that some part of the body, or the whole body, is undergoing change. Such body parts as hands, legs, thighs, or buttocks may feel bigger or smaller; numbness or pain may be felt in certain areas; and the survivor may feel that she is becoming smaller, the size of a child. These are very powerful experiences, during which the patient actually feels and sees the supposed somatic changes. Two clinical examples make the point.

Annalee was sexually abused by her grandfather. She began to remember the molestations through somatic events. Specifically, Annalee would partially dissociate and experience her thighs as huge and very heavy. Sometimes, when she looked down, she saw them as enormous, bulging out below her waist. Eventually, Annalee recalled her grandfather lay on top of her after molesting her. The somatic experience symbolized the weight and pressure of her grandfather bearing down on top of her body.

Dorothea, whose father abused her, began to experience a mild form of peripheral neuropathy in her left leg and foot shortly after she first disclosed that her father had molested her from ages 6 through 12. This usually signals the onset of another new memory or the elaboration of an already recalled abuse memory. Later in treatment, Dorothea realized that she always had dangled her left leg and foot off the side of the bed during the abuse; they were parts of her that she was able to keep from her father. The peripheral neuropathy symbolically represented both the abuse and her struggle to protect some part of her body from violation.

These somatic experiences are frightening for the patient, who often feels that she is going crazy. Once again, it is essential that the therapist normalize somatic memories within the context of the ways in which childhood sexual abuse survivors recall their childhood traumas. Assuring the patient that she is not going crazy but is striving to remember an as-yet unsymbolized memory often allows the survivor to join and stay with the experience instead of resisting it. Then, therapist and patient together can explore associations to the somatizations until, at last, the original trauma is recalled to memory.

Moving along the memory continuum are terrifying hypnogogic and hypnopompic events. Hypnogogic events occur in the state between wakefulness and sleep; hynopompic events happen between sleep and wakefulness. At these times, the patient has a hallucinatorylike experience during which she relives some aspect of the sexual trauma. Often, she feels as if the perpetrator is in the room preparing to abuse her. Because a patient's original abuse usually occurred at night and because of the lack of body control associated with these near-sleep psychic states, hypnogogic and hypnopompic events are particularly common and especially frightening for many survivors.

Marianna was sexually abused by her brother for several years of childhood. She was plagued by a recurrent hypnogogic experience that began shortly after she entered treatment. In that space between wakefulness and sleep, she sensed her brother's presence next to the bed and felt his breath in her ear. Terrified, she was unable to move or scream; all she could do was to lay still until she woke up fully and assured herself that she was alone. Not surprisingly, this patient's sleep was disturbed for the months that she was gripped by this hypnogogic threat. She dreaded going to bed at night and often fought off sleep to avoid the experience. The whole process repeated her childhood dread of bedtime and her brother's nocturnal visits to her bed.

As was true for unsymbolized reexperiences of abuse and somatizations, it is crucial that the therapist normalize these hypnogogic and hypnopompic events for the patient, placing them in the context of expectable stops on the journey to fully remembering childhood traumas. When the patient is sure that she is not crazy, she often becomes more tolerant of these events and the work of associating to them in session can proceed until the memories are more fully recovered.

At the next point on the memory continuum are dreams or nightmares that are, in fact, accurate portrayals of original trauma. It is our experience that childhood sexual abuse survivors frequently have dreams that are virtually undisguised depictions of their abuse. Unlike the highly symbolized dreams we are more used to unraveling, these dreams paint pictures that are what they seem to be—dreams, in other words, that have little symbolic overlay.

For example, Nanette, who was abused by her grandfather, presented to treatment with only hazy impressions of her abuse. She reported a recurrent dream in which a distinguished looking, silvery-haired man led a little girl down a long flight of stairs into a darkened basement. Here, the old man pulled the girl's white tights down and digitally penetrated her. The little girl in the dream was paralyzed; she wanted to run, but her legs would not move. When Nanette eventually recalled her abuse in some detail, she realized the "dream" was in reality a very accurate depiction of her grandfather's molestations, which occurred in the basement of his house.

Other memory-dreams are symbolized only slightly more. Casey, for example, also had a recurrent dream. In it, a tall, thin man in a basketball uniform stood above a young girl's bed. When the girl awakened and opened her eyes, the man dropped a basket of slithery snakes into her bed. Casey's brother, a tall, stocky football star, stole into her room at night to abuse her by placing his penis between her legs and rubbing against her. The dream provided an only minimally disguised route to the memories.

It is important for therapists working with sexual abuse survivors or patients thought to be survivors to evaluate dreams reported by the patients as potentially accurate or only slightly masked representations of the childhood traumas. These dreams can be helpful in suggesting avenues of exploration that facilitate evocation of the memories in treatment.

Moving still further along the memory continuum are flashbacks usually triggered by external or internal stimuli that are associationally linked to the abuse. Flashbacks may begin or intensify after initial disclosure of abuse, and they often are terrifying for the patient whose functioning they intrusively interrupt. During a flashback, the patient suddenly reexperiences some aspect of her victimizations. She usually has a vivid visual memory accompanied by powerful affects associated with the original experience. Typically, there is a partial dissociation during the flashback. The patient, however, usually remembers the content and emotional tone of the flashback once it has passed.

Ellen Ann, a father-daughter incest survivor, began to experience flashbacks shortly after she disclosed the abuse secret for the first time in therapy. When she and her husband made love, she suddenly saw her father's face instead of that of her spouse. During the flashback, she experienced herself as very small and relived being raped by her father. When the flashbacks passed, she was able to describe both content and affective components of the experience. Ellen Ann did not remember, however, her behavior during the flashback, nor could she recall her husband's response to her.

Flashbacks occur suddenly and deliver a powerful emotional wallop. Patients beset by flashbacks dread them and may avoid situations, such as sex with a spouse, that are likely to elicit these disorganizing glimpses of the original trauma. It is often helpful for the therapist to put flashbacks into perspective for the patient. Frightening and disorganizing though they are, flashbacks are also part of a process of separating from and gaining mastery over the internalized abuser and the past abusive events. As the patient continues to remember and process her abuse within therapy, flashbacks tend to occur less frequently. When they do, they are experienced increasingly as more cognitive and less affective phenomena. In addition, the patient begins to feel that she has some control over the flashbacks. For example, one patient who was far along in her therapy reported that a flashback began one night as she and her husband began to make love. At this point, she was able to will the image of her father away, insisting to herself that she was a grown woman having sex with someone she loved. The therapist and patient then explored in session the precipitants of the flashback.

At the next point on the continuum are intrusive, obsessive thoughts about the abuse that plague the patient. These tend to occur after considerable working through of dissociated or somatic memories or flashbacks and do not carry the same affective power as those other forms of memory. Intrusive, persistent thoughts can be conceptualized as embedded in a process of gaining mastery over past traumatic past events. Although they certainly represent the insistent return of distressing object relationships, they also afford the patient an opportunity to work these over and gradually gain control of their disorganizing impact. They are often irritating for the patient but usually are not particularly disorganizing or terrifying.

Katie, for example, who was sexually molested by her uncle, complained that thoughts of the abuse would begin at work and that, once they began, she "couldn't think of anything else for hours." She mulled the abuse over and over, analyzing every aspect of the experiences with her uncle and fantasized about ways it might have turned out differently. These intrusive thoughts followed years of treatment during which Katie struggled first with somatic memories and then with flashbacks. The obsessional working over of the incestous victimizations was actually a way of separating from them by gaining mastery over their dominance. Through her obsessive concentration on a memory once it intruded, Katie began to dominate the experiences rather than being dominated by them. Where once she would become disorganized and chaotic at the intrusion of a memory, perhaps having to leave work for a day or more, now she imposed her own thought processes on memories as they came along. After many months of this preoccupation, the memories began to fade in frequency and intensity. Katie one day realized with some relief that she had not thought about her abuse in over 3 weeks.

It can be seen that the recovery of traumatic memories is a long, often complicated process during which a patient moves toward integrating these events into her consciousness. It is a process marked by great disorganization and pain. At the end, the memories of sexual abuse, now more clear and, at the same time, less affectively powerful take their place within the patient's life narrative, where, still painful, they are also truly past. Perhaps Louise Armstrong (1978), an incest survivor and author, puts it best when she says, "So it doesn't go away? It recedes. . . . You don't have to like it. You just have to live with it. Like a small, nasty pet you've had for years" (p. 260).

CHAPTER 6

Reality Testing and the Question of Validation

IN WORK WITH adult survivors of childhood sexual abuse questions about the nature and adequacy of the patient's reality testing assume particular importance in attempts to understand the particular and idiosyncratic patterns of reality distortion and interpersonal difficulties secondary to failures in reality testing. We believe that the early imperative for the patient to subordinate her own perceptions of reality to those of an overwhelming and invasive other represents one of the most insidiously damaging effects of childhood abuse (Slavin, 1992), imposing lasting, long-term weaknesses in ego structuralization and interpersonal processes. These areas of vulnerability come to have a direct impact on a patient's adaptational skills, her capacity for healthy object relationships, and her self-reflective capabilities. They will also figure prominently in the unfolding psychoanalytic drama between patient and therapist.

This chapter seeks to offer a clarification of (1) the nature of reality and reality testing for a child who has been sexually abused; (2) the nature of pathological doubting as it affects adult survivors of childhood sexual abuse; (3) the compromises in integration that must be made to preserve the patient's level of functioning, and the particular patterns of interpersonal behavior and self-reflective awareness that result from this failure to integrate; and (4) specific clinical issues that emerge as a result of these ego deficiencies.

The Nature of Reality

The world of the adult survivor of childhood sexual abuse is a fragmented, discontinuous, and often frightening reality that subsumes a multitude of contradictory experiences, frequently eluding logical cohesion and organization. Caught in the cross currents of partisan perspectives, torn apart by the inability to integrate mutually incompatible experiences of reality, and driven by the opposing needs to both obfuscate actual experience and yet be hypervigilant to the ever-present dangers of repeated abuse, the adult survivor of childhood sexual abuse often feels out of control and crazy.

In the growing child, the developing capacity to accurately perceive reality emerges in part out of the dual survival needs of obtaining gratification and avoiding danger. In most normal childhood situations both of these abilities are enhanced by the adequacy and refinement of such skills; by a heightened sense of all that is possible, and a carefully constructed experience of that which must, for survival's sake, be avoided. For the child growing up in a chronically abusive household, however, the effects of developing ego functions, particularly those that mandate a consolidation and integration of denied or dissociated aspects of sexual abuse, can insidiously threaten a very tenuous psychic balance. Certainly, reality, in such cases, provides little in the way of acceptable gratification; and danger can only be avoided by a retreat into defensive inhibition or omnipotent fantasy.

Melissa's history provides a moving case in point. The patient entered psychoanalysis at the age of 29, speaking of "depression, low self-esteem, and an inability to take her life seriously and feel like a part of the adult world." She had graduated summa cum laude from a prestigious university and gone on to attain several graduate degrees. However, she remained unable to turn any of her many talents into an income-generating career. She therefore remained in a semi-dependent situation, vis à vis her widowed mother, by whom the patient reported being infantalized, manipulated, and emotionally abused. During an extended consultation, the patient also confided in her analyst that she was a compulsive cutter; that rarely a day went by without a deep gash being made somewhere on her body. She also reported complete sexual inhibition, of both action and fantasy. The patient spontaneously reported that her parents had been very socially active in their New England community, regular churchgoers who were heavily involved in several local charities.

The patient could recall no memories of having been abused as a child (though the case history was clearly suggestive) and reported that, on the contrary, she had been the clearly favored of two daughters. As she put it, "I was something of a pampered little pet to both my parents. It was my sister, I fear, who was badly treated by both. I never understood why. She was such a good girl." Melissa could not, at this time, provide any further details of how her sister had been mistreated, claiming only, "you know, the usual kid stuff; she was always in trouble for something, always doing something not quite the right way!" Melissa's story emerged very slowly and then only against a backdrop of increased psychic disorganization and powerful impulses to act out in self-destructive ways.

The story that began to unfold was not atypical. It appeared rather clearly that the patient herself was never sexually molested, but she was for a period of about 5 years forced to witness her father rape and sodomize her older sister. This appears to have happened on a regular basis, "at least once a week," by the patient's account, usually on the night that her father went out drinking with his friends. The patient described what would happen in her own words:

> Our beds were next to each other. He would sit me on my bed and say, "Now watch very carefully. Watch what happens to little girls who think nasty thoughts." Then he would ... he would do these (whispered) horrible things to her. . . . I didn't even know what he was doing then. Now, I know. She would cry out for help. It must have hurt her terribly [crying now]. No one ever came. I never understood where my mother was, why she never came. It didn't feel real. I used to think to myself, if this is real, why doesn't Mommy come. He told me that if I ever told anyone what I saw he would do the same things to me; then he would tell them that I was crazy, and they would come and lock me up in a mental hospital. He said I must never speak about it at all. Of course, I obeyed. For a while.

Here, a young girl is forced to observe unthinkable things being done to her older sister. She is locked into a passive-masochistic position vis à vis her father, whose presentation at these times is so entirely different from the norm that the young child must question her own perceptions. The whole scene is not unlike a recurring nightmare in which the behaviors of each persona are bizarre and terrifying and at times bear little resemblance to the dreamer's conscious, waking, daytime experience of them. Furthermore, any attempt to analyze, integrate, or otherwise make sense of the experience is foreclosed by the injunction against speech. The child must never speak of what she has seen. In the light of day, it will be she who is deemed crazy, she who will be isolated and abandoned.

Here we have an assault on the patient's very ability to trust her own perceptions; to decide what is real and what is not real; what comes from inside the self and what from outside; even what is asleep and what is awake. It should not be surprising that on three different occasions, as the patient struggled to remember and speak of some particularly vivid and overwhelming childhood memories, she fell asleep during her analytic session. The regressive reenactment within the treatment setting was poignant: a little girl whose eyelids had grown too heavy and full, struggling to stay awake, to see what was so clearly laid out before her, rubbing her eyes with clenched fists to clear away the filmy haze, so that she might see more clearly, and yet ultimately succumbing to the wish to retreat to some distant, safe, dreamlike state. Reality could wait.

On each of these occasions, Melissa awoke in a particularly chipper, almost hypomanic mood. She was somewhat flustered and embarrassed by her behavior but showed little interest in exploring its meaning until sometime later in the treatment. Likewise, she had no memories of what she had been discussing at the time she fell asleep, claiming only to remember that it was quite intense and potentially disturbing. Though she was surprised that she could not remember what she had been talking about at the time she fell asleep, the surprise itself had an air of Freud's early "la belle indifference." The patient appeared mildly disconcerted, not deeply disturbed by this unusual and dramatic memory loss. Morning had clearly come, bringing with it a very different reality and taking away those other things that had been so intensely disturbing and even disorienting; those things belonged to the night. Clearly, this experienced discontinuity was not unfamiliar to the patient. In fact, it was the sine qua non of her particular adaptation to reality.

It would be several years further into treatment before Melissa could assign meaning to these events. Ultimately, she remembered how she had escaped the abusive scenes in her bedroom by retreating into sleep.

> There seemed to be no retaliation for this. It was probably a relief to have me out of the way. The odd thing though, was waking up in the morning. It was as if I was waking from a bad dream. Everything was just as it had been the night before when I went to bed. Everyone was normal; my father, my mother . . . just the way they always were; but nothing like the way they were at night. I would think, he couldn't possibly have done such things; she couldn't have allowed such things to go on. They wouldn't look so normal now if they had gone on. Then, I would be sure that I had made the whole thing up. I would think how hideously evil I must be to invent such thoughts about my own loving parents.

Clinically, then, this is a 5-year-old patient whose perception and experience of reality are already split into two mutually exclusive sets of mental events, an object world traumatically torn asunder at precisely the time when integration of disparate part objects is of tantamount importance. Here, good and evil do not come together. They are isolated not only, as with borderline personalities, to preserve and protect the good self and object representations from the envious, murderous, devouring wishes of the bad but, even more fundamentally, to artificially construct and create a core sense of sanity and order, essential to survival, where circumstances have conspired to allow no such haven of predictability and safety to exist. For the self, there is only the threat of annihilation or of insanity—destruction from the outside world of abusive, sadistic others or from the festering, evil, insane world within.

The sad epilogue to this patient's story is, unfortunately, not atypical. At the age of 12, approximately 2 years after the cessation of her father's abusive behavior, and feeling overwhelmed by her own sense of evil and insanity, Melissa finally spoke the forbidden words to both her sister and her mother. Obviously desperate for confirmation, Melissa recalls:

> My sister looked at me with this kind of glazed-over iciness, her eyes were opaque, I couldn't see into them, and she said she hadn't the slightest idea what I was talking about, and she refused to discuss it any more or ever again. I begged her to tell me just this once that she remembered the same things I did . . . but all she said was that I was crazy; she remembered no such things. It was even worse, if possible, with my mother. She got that same odd look in her eyes, but she became agitated and rather frantic, screaming about what a filthy and disgusting mind I had. She said the same thing, though, that maybe I was crazy. That I had always been a little odd, even as a child, and maybe I was really out of my mind. The thing is . . . the important thing now is . . . I think that was the first day . . . [whispered] the first day I cut myself . . . I cut this filthy, crazy, disgusting, thing that I was.

Melissa made one further attempt to disclose the events in her home. She tried confiding in an adored English teacher; and, although the teacher had been gentle and sensitive to Melissa in all other ways, in this instance, she simply told her that young children often imagine frightening scenes that include their parents, and these stories are seldom, if ever, true.

It would be impossible here to chronicle the subsequent years of this patient's treatment, the extraordinary courage she brought to bear in facing the horrors of her early life and the insidiously invasive reality distortions imposed on her by circumstances. However, an unusual denouement seems particularly compelling and apropos.

The patient remained in analytic treatment for approximately 8 years. At the time she terminated treatment, her condition was much improved. She had established her financial independence from her mother in a job that gave her both personal satisfaction and room for professional growth. Although she was not, at the time of termination, involved in a serious love relationship, her social life was active and rich, and she was capable of maintaining serious, long-term commitments. She had recovered vivid and explicit memories of her early abusive experiences and had grown, with extraordinary effort, to accept the reality of these experiences and the enormously disruptive consequences that had been imposed on her life. In spite of this progress, however, she was still subject to periods of intense self-doubt and would wonder out loud if there were any chance that she could have "made up" a substantial part of what she remembered.

A year after terminating treatment, the patient contacted her therapist, ostensibly to obtain a referral for her sister, who now appeared ready for therapy. At the time the patient reported that the post-termination time had been difficult, but, all things considered, she believed that she was doing well. The therapist heard nothing more from the patient for approximately 4 years, after which time she received the following letter:

> The most extraordinary thing has happened. It is not so much the event itself, which could have been anticipated . . . but the remarkable effect it has had upon me, even after all the years of analysis. My sister has remembered her abuse! She flew in last weekend just to talk to me. She said she could not bear to talk of it on the phone. We both sat up all night long . . . I guess it had to be at night. We talked and cried all night long. Some things we remembered exactly the same . . . some things slightly differently . . . but all the essentials were close enough!
>
> But back to the effects I mentioned. Literally within seconds of realizing what it was she was about to say I experienced the most extraordinary and overwhelming sense of relief. It is truly difficult to put the sensation, the experience of mental and physical release, of tension actually flowing from my body into adequate words. My immediate impulse was to scream my sanity from the rooftops. So many of the tears were for my dead crazy self. She died so fast after all these years of vitality. My sister said it was all real; one other human voice in my midnight prison, and the uncertainty was gone. I was irrevocably sane!
>
> I've thought a lot, lately, of the others. Those who were alone in their dream. There is inside of me now a place I can reach. It is palpable . . . a place of ineffable sadness, for the girl I once was, and for all the others who can never entirely escape the endless, maddening, doubts. What is real? What was a dream? How can you possibly know who you are, if you can't first determine where you have been?

Chronic Doubting and Therapeutic Validation

We report Melissa's experience in some detail, because it is perhaps only as her endless doubting comes to an end that we along with the patient herself can comprehend the maddening entrapment that such an unfamiliarity with one's own basic experiences can engender. Adult survivors of childhood sexual abuse begin treatment with dramatically different degrees of confidence in their own childhood memories. Many patients begin with vivid memories of the abuse they suffered as children, along with a high degree of confidence in the reliability of such memories. Others, however, begin with no memories at all, or only the vaguest sense that all was not right along with a history and symptom picture that brings to mind the possibility of childhood sexual abuse. Where such memories begin as nonexistent or vague—and only emerge in clear form for the first time during therapy—the patient's confidence in the reliability of such memories is subject to the most intense doubting. This could be expected. Of enormous interest, however, is the fact that, even when patients begin treatment with vivid incest memories, a sense of chronic doubting and questions about the accuracy of these recollections almost inevitably plague the therapeutic process. Chronic doubts about what did and did not happen, along with a persistent inability to trust one's perceptions of reality, are perhaps the most permanent and ultimately damaging long-term effects of childhood sexual abuse. Such doubts make it extremely difficult for the patient to arrive at a point where she can come to believe in her own life history. It would be hard to exaggerate the pain an incest survivor feels as she struggles to regain confidence in the working integrity of her own mind or the intense pressure that such doubting induces in the analyst to either confirm or disconfirm the patient's questions about the reality of her own abuse.

It is ironic that the whole issue of childhood sexual abuse comes to the fore at a time within the theoretical evolution of psychoanalytic thinking in which there is serious question about the possibility of establishing historical truth within such a treatment setting. Certainly, the current momentum within psychoanalysis is toward the recognition of narrative truth within a social constructivist model (Hoffman, 1991). Such truth grows out of the ongoing interaction and mutual interpretive dialog between patient and therapist, with a sense of history and reality growing *not* out of some special access to the past but out of interpersonal experience as it emerges within the therapeutic encounter. Such a theoretical preference presents unique problems for the clinician working with incest survivors, where the balance between memory and fantasy in the establishment of personal history becomes all important (Slavin, 1992). Is such a theoretical and clinical dichotomy reconcilable within the actual clinical work?

Most clinicians who work regularly with survivors of childhood sexual abuse are all too familiar with their patients' needs for validation and confirmation of early abuse-related memories. Particularly in the case of incest, where the unconscious participation of the nonabusing parent is so often a part of the clinical picture, the therapist's open and frank readiness to believe in the patient's reports are often critical to the working-through of the traumatic material. Indeed, most of the literature on the subject is unequivocal on the therapist's need to substantiate the patient's beliefs, or else risk a reenactment of the parental neglect or denial that accompanied the original abuse. When the patient offers up her early memories with certainty, the therapist must stand ready to believe in their essential truth.

Our own experience, however, indicates that the working-through of chronic problems with reality testing in general, and the patient's relentless doubts about incestuous memories in particular, is rarely as simple as this formulation would indicate. The mere expression of therapeutic support, in fact, does little to effect permanent change in these areas of ego dysfunction, and, although it is often necessary, it is rarely sufficient to end relentless doubting. The patient who is convinced of the reality of her abuse and the dubious or denying therapist are only one form of reenactment that may occur around this issue. Indeed, there are at least as many times when it is the therapist who becomes adamant about the conviction that the patient was sexually abused as a child and the patient who remains doubtful or staunchly denying. Here, the therapist walks the ever-controversial line between therapeutic zeal and transferentially reinforced suggestion. The reenactment in the transference-countertransference can go one of two ways: either the patient prematurely "accepts" the therapist's experience of reality as her own and begins to construct incest "memories" in a transferential need to please the therapist; or, as is more often the case, the patient becomes uncomfortable exploring her own trauma-related images and memories, because the therapist's certainty about their meaning forecloses on her own psychic elaboration of these thoughts. Here the therapist treads dangerously close to the parent who superimposed his view of reality onto that of the child during the original abuse. In either of these two scenarios, something is being forcefully inserted into the experience of the child. In the first scenario, the patient submits to the therapist's construction of "truth"; in the second, she fights back by keeping the therapist's formulations, although true, from penetrating her defenses. Either alternative seriously distorts the patient's capacity to apprehend her own reality.

Most often, the roles of "believer" and "denyer" shift back and forth between patient and therapist in all forms of transference-countertransference reenactment. As the therapist becomes more convinced of the realities of the patient's early traumatic abuse, it is not uncommon for the patient to begin expressing more questions and doubts: "Could it all be made up, a creative invention of fantasy?" Selma Kramer (1983) was one of the first clinicians to describe this process of shifting belief and disbelief. Kramer called this process "object-coercive doubting", but believed it to be present only in cases of maternal incest occurring before the completion of the separation-individuation process. Here the shifting of doubtful experience between patient and therapist was viewed as a failure in boundary functions between mother and child, reenacted in the transference. Such an enactment of this process could happen around the question of whether or not the incest occurred but could also be argued about any two mutually incompatible views of a reality-based situation. Kramer reports on a patient who argued vehemently with the therapist about whether or not she was wearing a pin on the lapel of her blazer.

Although we agree with Kramer's clinical depiction, our experience has shown this process to occur in most cases of parental incest, regardless of whether the perpetrator was the mother or father. We view it as a reenactment via projective identification in the transference-countertransference of the dissociation, intrusion, and boundary distortion suffered by the adult survivor. It would seem that the therapist firmly convinced of the patient's abusive history, becomes an object of envy to the survivor ripped apart by endless misgivings, leading to an activation in the transference of the patient's sadistic introject. Here, in a game of turnabout, the patient, in identification with the abusing parent, begins an insidious attack on the therapist's reality-testing functions. One can also view this sense of confusion and unreality to be further enhanced by the presence of verbally unencoded traumatic residues that are both felt to be there but are as yet unnamed and unrecognized.

How, then, should therapists deal with the patient's doubting and uncertainty, both as a resistance to understanding her own experience and as a countertransference experience that tends to confuse and derail the therapist's hold on what is occurring in the clinical situation? If we hold to a belief that history will essentially repeat itself within the transference-countertransference drama, we can direct ourselves toward the emerging relational reenactments within the treatment situation in order to illuminate this often circuitous route. Indeed, within such a model, the patient's and therapist's very real doubts about the historical accuracy of incestuous images, especially those doubts that volley back and forth between the two participants in the analytic process, will serve to reinforce rather than undermine the truth of such suspicions. For such a volleying of belief and disbelief in the accuracy of one's perceptual capacities does reflect a reenactment of the invasion of body and mind associated with childhood sexual abuse.

Therefore, all issues related to the patient's and therapist's opposing views of reality, particularly those that emerge during therapy, should be carefully attended to. As they are addressed directly between patient and therapist, certain changes will occur. First, as patient and therapist together explore their versions of the therapeutic interaction, differences in perception will be unavoidable. As these are explored, negotiated, and compromised, the patient's reality-testing skills will be indirectly called into service. There will be points of agreement, points of continued disagreement, and compromises that feel wholly satisfactory to neither. It is not the specific content of what is in dispute that is essential but the way in which patient and therapist, together, create an environment where disagreement, compromise, and ambiguity can intermingle. If agreement, disagreement, and compromise are reached without a loss of integrity on either side, the process of negotiation itself will precipitate a repair in seriously affected reality and boundary functions. To give in on a point without losing oneself; to hold on to one's own view without shutting out the other person's experience entirely; to hold rigorously to what one believes, beyond doubt without undo aggression and devaluation, are the interpersonal avenues of such ego repair.

Second, the therapeutic process should highlight ways in which early, traumatic abuse permanently affects a child's sense of reality even in areas not directly related to the incest itself. The unsymbolized nature of traumatic memory, the dissociation that keeps such memories unintegrated with any others, the fact that incestuous abuse is rarely, if ever, spoken of between perpetrators and their victims, the fact that most sexual abuse occurs at night when the child is already in a semisomnolent state all contribute to the mental disorganization that accompanies the reemergence of such memories. As the historical meaning of such confusion is interwoven with the day-to-day negotiation of reality issues in the immediate treatment setting, the therapist should begin to see serious shifts in the patient's willingness to evaluate the accuracy and primacy of reenactments as they occur in therapy and to experience a significant diminution in his or her own sense of confusion and disorientation with regard to traumatic memory.

One cannot emphasize enough that, ultimately, it is the patient who must come to know and believe in the reality of her own incestuous experience. It is, concretely, the patient who chooses the words with which to give voice to her own internal states—and thus labels the connection between these states and historically significant events in her life. When the therapist's constructions and words lead the therapeutic journey, the patient's difficulties with reality and boundary issues are never addressed, and the treatment itself becomes a reenactment of yet one more form of invasive control by a powerful and needed other. In most cases, the specific difficulties with reality testing that are manifested by adult survivors of childhood sexual abuse are not related to the accuracy of sexual abuse memories per se, but they are secondary to the ongoing mental invasion implicit in such abuse.

Compromises in Reality Testing

In examining the complex compromises in reality testing that result from chronic childhood sexual abuse, one can look specifically at the dual nature of ego organization emphasized in the preceding section. For the adult patient who presents for treatment, the effects of chronic abuse on reality-testing skills are subtly interwoven into characterological patterns and particular nuances in interpersonal relatedness, such as (1) the capacity to tolerate dramatically different experiences and interpretations of specific events simultaneously; (2) the tendency to organize one's understanding of reality around the perceived needs of important objects; and (3) the tendency toward obfuscating truth and meaning as expendable, unreliable, and, ultimately, unknowable.

There are three specific areas of developmentally mediated ego impairment that serve to impede the consolidation of reality orientation in adult survivors of childhood sexual abuse. The first involves the individual's ability to relinquish the world of infantile fantasy and magical omnipotence and deal with the realistic frustrations and anxieties that inevitably arise without recourse to a regressive reactivation of this infantile state. The second impedes the ego's capacity to contain contradictory experiences of self and other, to move beyond projection and projective introjective mechanisms, to ultimately move beyond a rigidification of object relationships at a part-object level. The third involves the complete disruption of ego functioning brought on by recurrent flashbacks of traumatic events in the individual's life. Such flashbacks are a reactivation of earlier memories that bring on a loss of orientation to time, place, and person.

Magical Thinking and Omnipotent Control

Developmentally, the capacity to adequately apprehend reality and enter into experiences of mutual intersubjective relatedness (Benjamin, 1990) presupposes the necessary renunciation of magical thinking and omnipotent control (Ogden, 1986; Winnicott, 1951). Without reviewing the entire developmental literature, it can surely be said that, for such steps to be taken, the child must come to believe in the essential benevolence of the world outside herself. Such a notion includes the order and predictability of Erikson's (1963) "basic trust," the exquisite, fine tuning of Winnicott's (1960) "good enough mothering," the presymbolic internalization of Bollas's (1987) "transformational objects," Kohut's (1971) notions of "transmuting internalizations," Bion's (1962) ideas about "containment," and a plethora of others that might have been singled out. Despite their theoretically divergent points of view, these works, when taken as a whole, weave an intricate background pattern of developmental prerequisites for adequate ego structuralization. The "good enough parent," to borrow Winnicott's notion, must nurture, organize, respond empathically, withstand assault, and, ultimately, not retaliate.

How different is the experience of the sexually abused child. Here the world is dangerous and invasive; there is no order and predictability; people are either betrayers or abusers. The child's emerging sense of efficacy and mastery is demolished by repeated experiences of traumatic helplessness. At a time when magical thinking, defensive idealization, and omnipotent control of others should be giving way to more realistic experiences of success and failure, this extreme helplessness strikes a devastating blow. The world is shown to be unsafe, significant others betray or fail to protect, and the self is experienced as hopelessly inept and worthless.

It is only in a world of fantasy that such bad self and object representations can be omnipotently disposed of and make-believe saviors magically empowered. It is a world created as the temporary hiding place of an abused and helpless child, whose reality-based adaptational alternatives have failed to offer protection. It is to this world of rescue, retribution, and control that she learns to retreat during abusive episodes, although it is, unfortunately, also this world that eventually comes to hold her captive. Vulnerable in the extreme to experiences of personal inadequacy (because they are the rationalized excuse for abusive parental behavior), the world of magical wish-fulfillment becomes too compelling an alternative at any point of personal frustration and struggle. Thus, the childhood development of realistic self-soothing skills is severely constricted; narcissistic resilience based on successful experiences of struggle and mastery are prematurely aborted in fearful avoidance of an infusion of poisonous self-representations. Fantasy remains an easily accessible and overused alternative, and the boundary between fantasy and reality becomes potentially problematic. It is this world that the therapist enters when she begins to work with a survivor of traumatic abuse. It is a world of profoundly depleted and magically empowered others who begin to inhabit the transference-countertransference field of the analytic work. The world so constructed between patient and therapist ultimately introduces the therapist to the internal world in which the adult survivor has stayed hidden.

Certainly, the very circumstances of abuse would appear to mitigate against realistic adaptation and, by extension, integration. Though many theorists have struggled with the question of illusive thinking, of exactly what gratification of developmental need maximizes the transition from one more primitive mode of relating to another higher order, all apparently agree that, at least in part, the slow accretion of positive, nurturing, empathic, relational experiences prepares the self to withstand the potentially disruptive containment of negative self and object representations (Kernberg, 1976; Klein, 1952; Ogden, 1986.) Where abuse prevails—and adaptational skills are so dramatically constricted—where omnipotent fantasy and magical thinking represent the most compelling alternative to frustration and struggle, this safe, protective, context for aggressive fantasy is never internalized. There is no safe holding environment, to contain and contradict the angry projections of a rageful child. It would appear, in fact, that the natural developmental progression toward integration is reversed. Rather than fostering a movement out into the world of healthier, more gratifying object-related experiences, integration threatens to flood the entire structure with poisonous and malev-

choose a treatment method that in itself is technically orchestrated to facilitate fantasy and regression, particularly for a population so vulnerable in this regard?

The answer, fortunately, is clear. No other treatment method will permit so thorough an investigation of the actualities of the abusive experience, the long-term intrapsychic adaptation, and the powerful interpersonal corollaries as will psychoanalysis. However, work with any survivors of real chronic trauma forces us to reconsider several of the key assumptions that structure and organize our analytic approach. Here we will focus specifically on those which appear to impinge most powerfully on the ongoing dialectic tension between reality and fantasy. We will explore ways in which the treatment setting must be accommodated to the specific needs of our patient population.

We have gone to some length to demonstrate how the adult survivor of childhood sexual abuse approaches treatment with a flawed hold on reality and a consequently diminished capacity to trust her own interpretations of experience. Her own reluctance to interpret events is often greater than what should ensue from the particular ego deficiencies we have mentioned. Nevertheless, when taken in concert, these two difficulties place the entering analytic patient in a very vulnerable position and present the therapist with several striking and paradoxical dilemmas.

Above and beyond all else, victims of childhood abuse need to begin to understand the kinds of interpersonal difficulties that recur with regularity in their lives, so they can begin again to trust their own perceptions and interpretations of emotional interactions with others. Until patients can believe in and, therefore, come to defend their own view of the world, they are subject to constant manipulation and insidious abuse by others, even those with the most well-meaning intentions. Submission to another person's interpretation of events, regardless of whether that view is more or less accurate, is experienced by an adult survivor as a symbolic reenactment of the mind rape that exists at the heart of all child abuse. Clearly, patients need to have their experiences validated. But the therapeutic dilemma is clear. How do we validate the experience of those patients whose reality testing we have just called into question? How do we encourage them to believe in their own experience if we ourselves, in another voice, continue to reframe and reinterpret these same events according to our own emotional urgency or theoretical preconceptions—if, in other words, we presume our own reality to be of a higher order?

Adult survivors must, by slowly confirming interactions with significant others, rebuild a sense of confidence in their own interpretive skills. Here, the therapeutic interaction becomes particularly important, an arena in which to repair such capabilities. Such a task, however, requires a closer look at some of the subtle nuances of analytic practice, with particular emphasis on the processes of transference and resistance interpretation.

The Process of Interpretation

Some of the long-held psychoanalytic cornerstones deserve to be reevaluated. First, we look at the notion of the analyst as a blank screen upon which the patient plays out via projection and displacement early, pathological object relationships. The very notion of such unresponsiveness in work with our patients is dangerous. It was, after all, the denial and indifference, the, if you will, blank stare of the nonabusive parent that allowed the trauma to continue. Often, adult survivors flee treatment or regress unnecessarily, because this "opaque parent" becomes symbolically reactivated in the transference. Here, the patient's rage is so intense, with such a disorganizing effect on ego functioning, that even the most active interpretation will fail to reverse what essentially becomes an iatrogenic retraumatization. It is a psychotic transference unlikely to generalize to the rest of the patient's functioning but that nonetheless makes interpretation less useful and certainly less intense than the symbolic damage that can be done.

During the initial phases of treatment, many adult survivors of childhood sexual abuse appear highly resistant to interpretations on the part of the analyst that suggest a new or different way of looking at old behavior. Clearly, such interpretations threaten the tenuousness of the patient's own point of view and challenge long-held patterns of relating to internalized self and object representations. Such interventions are therefore capable of causing considerable disorganization. To the extent that the analytic environment is one of omniscient commentary by the analyst, not of collaborative inquiry by both parties involved, such resistance is intensified. Patients report feeling overwhelmed, penetrated, or out of control. The analytic situation is, again, dangerously close to the original trauma. In addition, the omniscient stance of the analyst is subtly infantalizing and consequently undermines and undervalues the patient's own contributions toward understanding his internal life.

It has been our experience in treating adult survivors that the *process* of mutuality and collaboration in the analytic work becomes at least as important as the content of the therapist's communications. This includes the analyst's attempts at collaborative inquiry and, of course, the patient's resistances to it. We believe that, particularly at the outset of treatment, interpreting such resistances to a more mutual investigation will further the analytic process, whereas prematurely penetrating interpretations of content threaten to incur the patient's frightened, self-defensive foreclosure on any further uncovering. Work with those who have been sexually abused must proceed at the patient's pace. Those clearly sensitive to experiences of forcible penetration and humiliating exposure must, initially and to some degree throughout, feel control over the process of self-disclosure. Of course, the time will come when the patient reports feeling forced, penetrated, or humiliated by the analyst despite all these adjustments in technique, and to some extent this is necessary. Patients must begin to explore their particular sensitivities in this area. It is only when a strong foundation of equality, mutuality, and respect has been laid, as a context for exploring more abusive, potentially disorganizing negative transference reactions, that this crucial aspect of the work can be carried through without a complete loss of reality testing.

Similarly, when transference is viewed as an asymmetrical, one-sided affair, where the patient's observations of the analyst are repeatedly denied and viewed as pathological distortions that come solely from the patient's own early life, the enhancement of the patient's reality testing is dealt another serious blow. Though the tradition of eliminating the therapist's own behavior from analytic scrutiny has recently been questioned for all patients (Aron, 1991; Gill & Hoffman, 1982; Greenberg, 1991; Hoffman, 1983, 1991) it is particularly deleterious in the case of abuse survivors. So often it is viewed, transferentially, as the analyst's attempt to abrogate responsibility for his or her own behavior, to indirectly blame the patient. Here, too, the transference becomes inextricably confused with the patient's traumatic past, where parental behavior was obfuscated and responsibility externalized onto the patient. Past and present, fantasy and reality blur, and verbal interpretation is often inadequate to redress the resulting confusion.

Quite different is the dialog that ensues when transference is regarded as the patient's more or less unique response to more or less selective aspects of the analyst's real behavior (Hoffman, 1983). Distortion is a mutual process, with the past of each participant casting an intense shadow on the perception of the other. Certainly, the therapist's personal analysis proves indispensable in disentangling the views and observations of each; however, no one's analysis is infallible, and distortions and misperceptions occur on both sides. Where the analyst listens to the patient's observations with respectful consideration, not strained forbearance, such respect is internalized, and the patient proceeds with an enhanced capacity for self-reflective activity.

Transference interpretations are most difficult. Although an extra-transference interpretation can be offered to further a patient's understanding in a particular area, to enhance her experience of an event by offering parallel meanings, a transference interpretation, as used by some therapists, implies distortion or exaggerated response on the part of the patient. The analyst is, in effect, saying, "No, I have not done what you say . . . you experience me in this way, because. . . ." Here we tell the patient, "What you think is happening is not happening . . . you only misperceive it that way . . . do not trust your own perceptions." How confusing to tell the patient to trust in what she suspects happened in the past but not to trust what she knows to be happening in the present. And yet, what of the analyst who truly believes that a major distortion is occurring in the transference?

The most contemporary literature on countertransference and projective identification (Gill & Hoffman, 1982; Grotstein, 1981; Joseph, 1989; Sandler, 1987; Tansey & Burke, 1989), considers the possibility that the patient has accurately perceived some aspect of the therapist's behavior of which the therapist is unaware. We believe the patient's behavior and her unconscious fantasy invite certain activity by the analyst, particularly the kind of penetrating, overstimulating activity the patient is most hypervigilant to. Likewise, we believe that the analyst's behavior invites similar responses on the part of the patient. By seriously considering his own behavior as a powerful precipitant to certain transference reactions, the analyst accomplishes two important clinical tasks. First, he opens up for analytic scrutiny certain unconscious processes within himself and the patient that, via projective and introjective identification, might otherwise remain elusive. And, second, he acknowledges that the patient's transferences are often rooted in very accurate perceptions of the analyst's behavior, therefore supporting the patient's capacity to accurately perceive and interpret her world.

Therefore, we listen with great interest to the patient's perceptions of the therapist's behavior and to her interpretations of and fantasies about the possible meanings of such behavior. We ask specifically what aspects of the therapist's behavior led the patient to the conclusions she has drawn. We ask her to explore all the possible reasons she can come up with for why she believes the analyst may have reacted in such a way. Particularly when the patient accuses us of being abusive, intrusive, controlling, sadistic, seductive, overstimulating and so on—words that speak to significant reenactments in the transference-countertransference process—do we focus our attention not on what this tells us about the patient's past, but what it can illuminate about the therapist's experience in the present. If, for example, the patient experiences the therapist as unnecessarily seductive, the therapist could interpret this perception as a simple displacement from a past significant relationship; or he can integrate an awareness of his own seductive behaviors into his attempts to clarify the unconscious or as yet unformulated (Stern, 1985) aspects of transference-countertransference paradigms being reenacted in the present therapeutic situation.

Again, we are placing therapeutic communication via an attention to process over therapeutic communication via interpretation of content; intent in our belief that a process of mutuality and respect ensures that content will follow. Though we can suggest that in certain cases the patient *may* have misinterpreted the meaning and intent of certain aspects of the therapist's behavior, one should not *assume* that this is the case. It is equally likely that the patient has simply perceived or experienced some aspect of the therapist's behavior or attitude that has remained defensively dissociated and needs to be integrated into the current therapeutic dialog.

The Nature of Resistance

Similar issues emerge when considering the particular resistances that often impede the progress of treatment for adult survivors. From the inception of psychoanalysis, therapists have tried to remove the negative connotations from the word *resistance*. Although all therapists struggle with this, particularly in formal teaching situations or written material, the informal dialog about "resistant patients," belies the unconscious negativity inherent in the term. After all, resistance is, by definition, an opposing force. Those of us who think developmentally, however, regard the capacity to resist, to say no, to disagree as a developmental milestone. It is necessary for survival; it is endemic to separation and individuation. Without this capacity, the patient lives in constant fear of impingement, invasion, and ultimately mental annihilation. However, adults who have survived significant childhood sexual abuse are severely limited in their ability to say no. As children, physical resistance was a threat to survival; mental resistance could occur only via dissociation and outward compliance.

Because our patients have so little faith in their capacity to discern what is true from what is false, what is helpful from what is destructive, what is pleasurable from what hurts, the invitation to consider an interpretation, particularly one that challenges the patient's perspective on an issue, can set in motion an experience of intense anxiety, even panic. The patient finds it enormously difficult to reject an interpretation. Such a rejection would, in essence, stimulate abandonment terror commensurate with that of the abused child who could not question his parent's denial or distortion of reality. The child could not depend on the parent whose reality testing, that is, sanity, was at question. Therefore, transferentially, the analyst's intellect, judgment, and ultimate superiority must be absolute. Critical appraisal and evaluation, because of the partial rejection implied, is out of the question. Grateful for the thoughtful attention and concern, patients can, on occasion, accept any and all interpretations in a dramatic show of outward compliance. The interpretations are, therefore, perceived as "brilliant" and can stimulate an exciting outpouring of eager associations. The power of the therapist, at the outset of such treatments, is unrivaled, an example of the dangerously compliant misalliances described earlier. What then, becomes of interpretations that are incorrect? At such times, splitting is reinforced. Disagreement and objection, along with the anger and anxiety they generate, are relegated to the domain of the dissociated child persona and of her abusive counterpart. Conscious idealization dominates the analytic space.

As always, the most dangerously seductive resistance lies in countertransference. Being loved by a patient who has searched so long and hard for a savior is intensely moving for the analyst. What more could be asked by anyone than to be brilliant and virtuous, simultaneously. Nonetheless, within this magical province of unmitigated mutual regard, an insidiously invisible malignant growth proliferates. For the patient is swallowing up, whole, the analyst's view of her own internal reality. There is no loyalty to self, and where there is no conflict, there can be no integration. Having been prostituted for mere survival, the patient is more than willing, even eager, to repeat this pattern in order to secure a long-sought-after, idealized love. The dissociated underside of conscious, mutual idealization is abusive control and forced submission. Under the cloak of the powerful countertransferential experience, it becomes one of the most easily missed resistances to the analysis.

Ultimately, the therapeutic task in such a situation involves questioning the patient's unremitting and outward compliance. Does she ever disagree with an interpretation? How is it that the analyst is always so smart? Does she ever say what she thinks the analyst wishes to hear rather than what she believes to be? If the analysis succeeds in helping the patient to see how she supplants her own reality with that offered by the analyst or any idealized other, the therapist and patient together can explore the most crucial question of where the patient's own experience of reality has been hidden. We can rest assured, in our work with child abuse survivors, that such a reality has been held safely intact, in a clearly dissociated system of self and object representations.

A supervisee complains during a recent supervisory session that his patient has become "argumentative, nitpicking, and highly resistant." He complains that she rewords whatever he says and in each and every instance feels compelled to take exception to some component of the interpretation, no matter how inconsequential. She questions his competence, demands to know what training he has had, whether he is a certified analyst.

The therapist insists that he has "interpreted the resistance time and time again, but the patient will not hear it!" "My pointing out her resistance seems to make her angrier." The patient threatens to leave the treatment. Perhaps the therapist is too inexperienced. The supervisor feels that the therapist is whining and somewhat petulant. What has the supervisor done or not done that this once-perfect treatment has now gone seemingly sour?

The patient is a 36-year-old female attorney with a history of sexual abuse between the ages of 4 and 9. She is regarded by her colleagues as a successful litigator, and her thinking, as revealed in sessions, is incisive and logical. The early phase of her treatment has been a "honeymoon period." She has worked eagerly, and although she has been angry on occasion, there have been no periods of protracted negative transference. She has responded to interpretations with willingness and, in general, has taken care to fuel her analyst with steady doses of gratitude and appreciation. She has asked relatively few "tough questions," and appears to have assiduously avoided any areas of potential vulnerability in the therapist.

Now she has begun to quibble over interpretations; to demand certain information about her analyst. The therapist is annoyed; he calls her resistant; he wants the supervisor to tell him how to deal with her resistance. He wants his good little, obedient—perhaps seductive—girl back.

Here is an example where the most dangerous resistance is not the most obvious one. The patient is not *becoming* resistant, she is simply changing from a form of resistance that the therapist found highly enjoyable to one he experiences as more distasteful. She is probably doing this because the therapist and supervisor have not been quick enough in calling her attention to the more subtle process. They have been distracted by the powerful content. The patient is doing everyone a favor. Was it not odd that this incisive thinker, this highly successful litigator, had never made an objection, never asked her therapist to state his credentials, up front, for the record? Did she not have a right to do this?

Of course, the patient is confused and angered by being called resistant. In her mind, she is simply being self-protective, critically evaluating ideas before she accepts them, and asking for the training credentials of the therapist to whom she has entrusted her emotional future. It is this confusion that is making her so frightened and angry; the impingement of a reality so different from her own, by a therapist whose protection and good wishes she so values. Does she succumb to his view of the matter as she has all along, or assert her own mind, and risk losing all?

The most appropriate question to ask clinically is not why she is resisting, but why it has taken so long for the patient to exercise her most fundamental rights in this interpersonal situation. Far from going sour, the treatment has progressed to a point where the patient trusts her therapist's integrity and good will enough to permit the emergence of more negative transference constellations. Hopefully, the *therapist's* resistance will not impede the progress of this treatment.

We do not mean to suggest here that masochistic compliance is the only manifestation of transference resistance in adult survivors. Certainly, it is equally possible for the patient to express her fear of abuse or abandonment via an unremitting counterdependent stance, in which she *rejects* any and all interpretations offered. Our point is only to emphasize this less obvious expression of negative transference that is often missed.

Assaults on the Therapist's Reality-Testing

There is one further interface between reality-testing ego functions and the process of psychoanalytic treatment for adult survivors. It is a phenomenon well-known to those who work in this area, and it has to do with the patient's attempts to destroy the analyst's reality-testing capabilities. This can occur at particular crisis points in the treatment, or it can weave its way, like a leitmotif, throughout the course of therapy. Clinically, it almost always bears some connection to the emergence of the sadistic introject, that is, of that part of the patient who is closely identified with the abusive parent and is now remobilized within the transference. As these aspects of the patient's personality emerge, often in dissociated form, the therapist can become, via projective identification, the subject of several different forms of confusion.

When the sadistic introject emerges in a purely dissociated form, there can be direct assaults on the analyst's reality testing. One patient, a 26-year-old incest survivor, would repeatedly rearrange the cupboards and take food from a refrigerator in the kitchen off her therapist's waiting room. The therapist began to feel that she was going crazy. Only when it became clear that these experiences always followed this particular patient's sessions did the therapist feel calmer. The patient, however, strenuously denied any involvement in these activities and was so offended by the analyst's suggestion that the treatment was seriously jeopardized. It appears that this behavior occurred while the patient was in a dissociated state. Only when she began to recover memories of how her mother had constantly rearranged her things when she was a child so that she never knew where anything was at the same time that she had denied being in the patient's room did a look of recognition came over her face, and the dissociative gap was bridged. Here, the patient was reenacting in a dissociated form the kind of "mind attack" that she was subjected to as a child. The analyst becomes the victimized child and is allowed to experience some of the confusion, fear, loss of control, and disorientation that filled her patient's early years.

Because victims of sexual abuse can slip in and out of dissociative states so quickly and imperceptibly, patients can say and not say things simultaneously. This can go on between sessions, or from moment to moment within the same session. Patients can recount vivid memories of their abusive experiences on one day and then claim no recall of what was discussed at their very next session. Similarly, patients can say something during the course of a session, yet look mystified and confused when the therapist responds to the statement, claiming no memory of having said the remark referred to. The latter usually takes the form of, "You must have heard me wrong . . . I never said that." When this becomes a pattern, a therapist unfamiliar with the vicissitudes of dissociation can become either deeply enraged or deeply confused and troubled about his own sanity.

Another very common way in which survivors attack their therapists' hold on reality, one that often threatens to destroy the treatment entirely, is the "I'm sorry, I made the whole thing up" phenomenon. Rarely is a therapist as shaken as she is the first few times this happens. However, it is almost to be expected, because it represents a reenactment of the abusive experience on so many different levels. On the simplest level, the patient strives to re-dissociate material she has begun to recover, so that it truly feels for a while like something she may be making up. One patient used to say, "These words come out of my mouth, as if a stranger lives inside of me. I don't remember these events, but the stranger is trembling and hysterical. Why would she be so scared if this wasn't real?" This process of recovery and redissociation of traumatic experience can be expected to continue for some time.

Although such a sudden reversal represents a redissociation of traumatic memory on one level, at a deeper level, it represents a further reenactment of the traumatogenic object relationship. Here the patient as abuser turns to the unsuspecting therapist, and with a direct frontal assault on her reality says, "This terrible thing we've been going through together . . . forget it . . . it never happened." Here again, through a form of projective identification, the patient has communicated to her therapist the deep confusion and terrible despair of being told by her attacker, "This never happened . . . we will never speak of it again."

The most vicious form of this attack on the therapist usually comes from patients whose abuse has been particularly sadistic and humiliating in nature. Here, the patient's reversals are infused with powerful contempt, invoking in the analyst not only a sense of confusion and disorientation but also a humiliating experience of extraordinary stupidity and gullibility. One can almost see the evil core of this introject rearing its head to further torment and torture the victim by mocking her capacity to love and trust. Here the self-loathing of the child-victim/analyst is palpable. "How stupid to have believed in and trusted someone else." Our experience reveals, however, that, rather than creating untenable doubt for the therapist, such a dramatic reversal should serve as a confirmation by the patient that the abusive reality-distorting experiences recounted in the therapy experiences did, in fact, take place.

There is one final place where the therapist's loss of reality testing appears to signal a reenactment in the transference. The critical experience here is one in which language appears to lose all meaning for the patient, the therapist, or both. The patient stares blankly at the therapist, seemingly mystified by the most basic of interpretations. The meaning of words seems to fail. It is difficult, if not impossible, for the therapist to reach the patient. We understand this experience as a reactivation in the treatment of a childhood experience where the grownups spoke and the child could not comprehend the meaning of their words, when, because of multiple deceptions, the child had no faith in the content of what was being said, therefore abandoning any interest in, or commitment to the spoken word. When the communicative value of words fail, the therapist must be aware that he or she is dealing with the split-off child persona, and all of the ego deficits detailed come into play.

The opposite transference-countertransference paradigm can also become activated in the treatment setting. Here, through a form of complementary projective identification, the therapist fails to make any sense of the patient's words. The experience is one of incredible stupidity. The therapist feels that the patient is speaking a foreign language. The particulars may take many forms, but the overriding experience is one in which the therapist listens in disbelief, unable for protracted periods of time to make any sense out of the patient's words.

In all of the situations described, the therapist can easily be moved to experiences of intense rage. Sadistic retaliation or angry withdrawal are both common responses. It is imperative that the analyst remember that these are *induced* countertransference responses, designed to communicate verbally inexpressible phenomena. When they are used by the therapist to facilitate the patient's recovery of further memory or of a vivid first-hand experience of her own internalized sadistic wishes, they can be among the most critical and ultimately curative moments in the treatment.

In attempting to integrate a conceptual frame with a clinical-experiential substrate, it is critical to remember that the abused child's life represents an ongoing compromise with reality. Such distortions as we have described should not be surprising. Nor should they necessarily be viewed as representing an underlying psychopathy. Rather, they are an accommodation, a mode of relating to experience that allows unspeakable events to occur and not occur simultaneously. Although survivors can dissociate and repress the particulars of their past abuse, the specific modifications in ego structuralization described continue to permeate the individual's psychic adaptation and interpersonal relations on all levels.

CHAPTER 7

Exposure to Danger, the Erotization of Fear, and Compulsive Self-abuse

C HALLENGING SUCCESSFUL TREATMENT of many survivors of childhood sexual abuse is the dazzling array of violent, often self-destructive behaviors in which these patients frequently engage. From suicidality to self-mutilation, substance abuse, promiscuity, reckless driving, eating disorders, self-battering, stealing, and repeatedly placing themselves in potentially dangerous situations, such as walking on deserted streets alone at night or hitchhiking, survivors often put into action rather than consciously experience and process memories, affects, self-representations, identifications, and fantasies that threaten to seriously endanger them. The relentlessness and drama of a survivor's self-destructive enactments can overwhelm the therapist as well, endangering the therapeutic alliance and, ultimately, the treatment.

It is thus crucial that a therapist working with a sexual abuse survivor be familiar with the purposes and meanings of violent enactments within this patient population. We will in this chapter look at (1) an exploration of the multilayered psychic meanings of violent, acting-out behavior within a psychoanalytic framework; (2) an integrated model for the psychologically and physiologically mediated eroticization of fear and for the compulsive self-mutilating behavior that often accompanies it; and finally (3) an attempt to integrate this multidimensional model into specific treatment recommendations that will, it is hoped, bring about a cessation of compulsively self-abusive behaviors. We attempt to describe here the cyclical and synergistic pattern we have come to expect with patients as they volley endlessly between intensely sexualized hyperarousal states and the kinds of satiated, exhaustive aftermath of periods of intensely dangerous and life-threatening exposure to self-abuse.

The Significance of Self-abuse to Psychic Equilibrium

In recent years, violent, self-abusive behaviors have been associated most often with diagnoses of borderline personality disorder. Through such work, clinicians have become familiarized with the view that violent acting-out behavior represents the intensification of sadomasochistic identifications and interpersonal relations with which borderline patients struggle. This, exacerbated by poor impulse control, diffuse boundaries, and an envious need to defeat the therapeutic efforts of the therapist by controlling via imperious demands on the therapist the therapeutic endeavor have all come to serve as the therapeutic bedrock of understanding of this type of behavior.

However, newer research on the subject shows that between 75% and 87% of patients diagnosed with borderline personality disorder also have histories of violent childhood abuse (Herman et al., 1989). Furthermore, clinical reports also show the consistent relationship between self-mutilation and histories of childhood physical and sexual abuse (children with histories of repeated surgery can also show such a symptomatic picture). In fact, Simpson and Porter (1981) summarized the clinical findings in this way: "Self-destructive activities were not primarily related to conflict, guilt and superego pressure, but to more primitive behavior patterns originating in painful encounters with hostile caretakers during the first years of life " (pp. 428–438).

One can consider the way in which self-inflicted abuse turns a passive trauma into an active one for the sexual abuse survivor who is attempting to gain mastery over early trauma and its aftermaths. Through self-destructive behaviors, the survivor regulates the timing, pace, and severity of her victimizations, paradoxically experiencing a sense of empowerment. Ostensibly no longer at the mercy of an external perpetrator, the patient assumes control of her abuse. We say "ostensibly," because the self-destructiveness, in fact, assumes both continued bondage to the abuser and identification with the abuser's ruthlessness. In addition to providing an illusion of control, such enactments help the patient to manage potential disruptions of her internal and external worlds by keeping at bay traumatic memories with their associated mental contents and affect states. This aspect of coping may be particularly important for the patient who has no conscious memories of her abuse, or maintains an apparently loving relationship with her abuser.

For example, Katie was tied to a bed and sodomized by her uncle, who lived with her family, over many years of her childhood. When she presented for treatment, she had no memories of her sexual abuse; she knew only that she felt vaguely frightened and constricted in her uncle's presence. Shortly after beginning therapy, Katie began a relationship with a man who liked to engage in "rough" sex, including binding her to the bed during anal intercourse. This was not her first involvement with a man who bound and sodomized her. During these sexual encounters, Katie reported feeling both terrified and intensely aroused.

In this case, the reenactment of sexual activities reminiscent of her abuse protected Katie from contacting the memories of her actual victimizations by channeling emerging traumatogenic material into real adult relationships. Furthermore, voluntarily engaging in bondage and anal intercourse allowed Katie to relive her abuse at least apparently on her own terms. This enactment also preserved the homeostasis of her internal world, preserving attachments to her uncle and to her parents who had failed to protect her from exploitation. Finally, the almost exact duplication of her childhood trauma embodied in the enactment, combined with her intense, ambivalent affective state, communicated the nature of her early sexual victimizations long before Katie consciously remembered them.

Most survivors who engage in violent enactments are aware of wanting to punish themselves. These patients, at their core, are convinced that they are unfit human beings. Filled with shame, they experience themselves as profoundly defective and horribly toxic. Often, they have internalized the scourges hurled at them in childhood: whore, bitch, manipulative devil, worthless shit, lying little dummy. Frequently told by their abuser(s) that they provoked and wanted the sexual attacks, survivors see themselves as malevolently powerful. Moreover, they often reach adulthood with introjected, lying, malevolent, worthless, toxic self representations long ago split off and projected by the perpetrator (Fairbairn, 1943). As adults, when some internal or external event evokes a sense of having been "bad," survivors may physically attack themselves or take life-threatening risks to punish themselves.

Pauline was told by her father that, if she ever told anyone about the incest, he would cut her tongue out. Long before she consciously remembered this threat, Pauline stuck her tongue with a safety pin whenever she was furious with herself and watched in detached satisfaction as droplets of blood fell from her mouth. In this case, the method of self-punishment was also an enactment of the punishment threatened by Pauline's father and can be viewed as an attack by her abusive introject. Literally possessed by a bad object, the patient put into action the threat she had yet to recall to conscious memory. Not surprisingly, Pauline pricked her tongue frequently when she began to talk about her abuse in therapy.

Although being victimized is painful for the survivor of childhood abuse, it is also familiar. Often, being a victim is the most secure identity the survivor has. To initiate self-protective behavior as an adult means to loosen the survivor's attachment to her internalized objects and to her most familiar organization of self. In addition, at an often deeply unconscious level, continued victimization in adulthood validates for the survivor the reality of the violations of the past; to relinquish victimization today is experienced by some survivors as undermining their own and others' belief in the veracity of the earlier sexual abuse. In a confusion of past and present, these patients similarly feel that, if they protect themselves from danger now, it proves that they are capable of preventing abuse, and it suggests to them that they could have and should have protected themselves from childhood exploitations. They deny the differences in physical prowess, autonomy, cognition, and resources that separate children from adults. All these factors contribute to the difficulty some survivors have in ending enactments that position them as actual or potential victims.

Always juxtaposed alongside the survivor's identification as victim, running parallel to it—though less consciously available—is her equally strong identification with the perpetrator of her abuse. The ruthlessness and icy sadism survivors can display toward their own bodies, minds, and emotions are shocking to witness. In part, this often represents an identification with the abuser's blatant lack of regard for his or her child victim. The enacting survivor takes up where the perpetrator left off, turning fury and frustration against herself in appallingly vicious ways.

The patient's identification with her abuser preserves relational bonds to the internalized and often external victimizer, as well as to other nonabusing but unavailable early figures. Many survivors enter treatment with current ongoing relationships with their abusers. Often, neither the adult survivor nor the perpetrator has spoken of the abuse. Even if the survivor is no longer in contact with her victimizer, a strong attachment to the internalized object is tenaciously protected and preserved. This may be particularly potent if the survivor has not yet remembered her abuse. Identification with victimizing aspects of the abuser pays tribute to the survivor's real and internalized relationships, protecting the patient from experiencing painful object loss.

In addition to preservation of relational bonds, the survivor's identification with the perpetrator protects her from contacting the helplessness and vulnerability of her victimized self. Survivors report a paradoxical sense of power and control when they cut themselves, drive recklessly, or engage in sex with men they hardly know. Identifying with her perpetrator, the survivor experiences this illusory empowerment, denying that her self-abuse is hurtful. In fact, survivors report, especially early on in treatment, that they do not feel physical pain when they cut, burn, or batter themselves. Like their victimizers, they successfully split off a sense of themselves as vulnerable, scared, and out of control.

To help a survivor to recognize that she has incorporated and identified with aspects of her abuser is difficult work. The more she has remembered, affectively relived, and integrated her sexually abusive experiences, the more the idea that she is in any way like her perpetrator is anathema to her. Interpretation of this element of enactments must be handled sensitively, lest the survivor's already potent sense of toxicity and malevolence be intensified unbearably. If that occurs, the survivor may become disorganized and enact even more intense self-abuse, this time in an attempt to concretely destroy the internalized object.

If survivors are loathe to acknowledge that their enactments betray an identification with their abusers, they are equally reluctant to recognize that their behaviors convey thoughts, feelings, or fantasies about current figures in their lives, including the therapist. Quite often, however, survivors self-destructively enact powerful reactions to others in their lives. Terrified of the imagined power of envious, rageful, hateful feelings, survivors may deny the interpersonal implications of these affect states, instead turning them against themselves. As children, they introjected their abuser's badness and projected their own goodness onto others to preserve the hope of eventually receiving love and care. Now, adult survivors continue this process; they deny the relational failings of others, assuming the mantle of responsibility for making relationships work. When someone the survivor loves or needs disappoints or angers her, these feelings are often turned back on the self. At the core of this process may be a dreadful fear of abandonment.

For example, Winnie was sexually abused by her father, who told her she would be sent to an orphanage if she told anyone about the incest or failed to perfectly comply with his instructions during sexual activities. As an adult, whenever Winnie's fiancé criticized her or let her down, Winnie outwardly placidly accepted his behavior. Later, however, she inevitably dug tweezers into her thighs. She was conscious only of blaming herself for provoking the relational disappointments, a position consistent with her perception that she had "made" her otherwise wonderful father molest her. It was a long time before Winnie was able to accept and integrate the idea that her self-abuse stemmed in part from the hurt and anger she felt toward her fiancé but was afraid to express directly, lest he refuse to marry her.

Most difficult for survivors to acknowledge is that, once they are in treatment, their violent enactments almost always contain a transferential component, the acting-out element of enactment. Like their parents once were, the therapist becomes a needed figure depended on by survivors to see them through the terrifying and painful working-through of their abuse and its consequences. As survivors loosen their grip on real and internalized objects and are confronted with those losses, the therapist assumes an even greater importance in their lives. As they once protected their parents from their mistrust, terror, and rage, they also deny negative reactions to the therapist and, instead, act them out, often self-destructively. Sometimes, the enactment represents a vicious attack on the therapist's ability to contain and to heal, a ruthless attempt to disrupt the interpretive and integrative work of treatment. At other times, the enactment speaks for the survivor's bitter hurt, voiceless rage, and desperate envy.

Compulsive Self-abuse and the Erotization of Fear

For some adult survivors of childhood sexual abuse, self-injurious behaviors truly reach frenetic intensity. Many become life-threatening, and even when this is not the case, the ongoing moment-to-moment struggle between enactment and self-control becomes relentless, consuming an ever-increasing percentage of the patient's conscious sensorium. Like the perpetrator who once kept his victim in a state of fearful anticipation of the next abusive episode, the survivor, session after session, holds the therapist hostage to the possibility of the patient's impending self-mutilation or death. As the situation goes on, the therapist may move from feeling deep concern and empathy to experiencing terror, impotent rage, and eventually, numbness and seeming indifference to the outcome, countertransferentially enacting the abused child's earlier responses to abuse. The therapist may even begin to think, "Okay, okay. Just do it, and get it over with," a countertransferential response similar to the victimized child's impatience for the abuse to occur again just so the unbearable anticipation is relieved.

Such behavior becomes clearly compulsive, and the pressure to perform this painful, self-abusive activity is essentially addictive in nature, a quality that is underscored by its therapeutic intractability and resistance to all forms of interpretation. Indeed, there are patients for whom active interpretation appears only to intensify the cycle of overstimulation and abuse. Such abuse includes nonlethal forms of cutting, burning, bingeing, vomiting, and compulsive, often painful forms of masturbatory activity. In this area, psychodynamic formulations alone prove inadequate and must be integrated with knowledge gained about the specific psychology of adult survivors, and about the psychophysiology of abuse and its aftermath.

Hyperarousal, Erotization, and Guilt

One thing we have come to know about adult survivors of childhood sexual abuse is that they have an enormously difficult time modulating even mild-to-moderate degrees of arousal (Kardiner, 1941; Kolb, 1987; Pittman, Orr, Laforgue, & De Jong, 1987; van der Kolk, 1988). It is often irrelevant whether such arousal presents in the form of anxiety, fear, pain, pleasure, or anticipatory excitement. The slightest trigger can catapult the patient into a maelstrom of breathless, physiologically mediated hyperarousal that proves to be disorganizing and unmodifiable in the short run. Such hyperreactivity is one of the unquestioned long-term effects of traumatic childhood abuse (van der Kolk, 1988). This process appears to be controlled by a complex system of emotional, maturational, and physiological factors.

Certainly, an individual's sense of safety and control is strongly influenced by the supportive presence of those to whom he or she is positively at-

tached. When a person can no longer cope with traumatic situations by relying on his or her own internal resources, the presence of auxilliary support
in the form of loving others helping from the outside becomes even more
significant. We know that the presence of loving and supportive others plays
an important role in helping children to contend with the extreme states of
hyperarousal specific to traumatic situations. Likewise, traumatized children, alone or in the presence of strangers, are likely to experience extremes
of under- and overarousal that are physiologically mediated and cognitively
disorganizing (Finkelhor & Brown, 1985). Such decreased capacity to modulate physiological arousal by relying on the presence of loving and trustworthy others would also explain the patient's inability to call upon reliable internal representations of loving and supportive others at times of acute
distress. Indeed, there is a decreased ability to use symbolic mental operations at all, and under the sway of such arousal and disorganization, where
mental processes fail, the trauma survivor becomes used to responding to
threats or perceived threats via action rather than thought.

In adult survivors of childhood sexual abuse, these states of emotional
and physiological hyperarousal have by dint of constant pairing and fundamental learning paradigms become intensely sexualized as well. Those arbitrary triggers that have become conditioned stimuli for traumatic levels of
responsiveness, particularly those that elicit fear or anxiety reactions, will
also generate states of intensely eroticized hyperarousal. In response to images that evoke frightening possibilities or the anticipation of pain, such reactions set the groundwork for a reciprocal and synergistic intensification of
fear, hyperarousal, and sexualization of the entire situation, that often spirals
desperately out of control, creating havoc in the patient's life and within the
therapeutic relationship. Yet, such a connection between the fear and anticipatory anxiety that accompanies chronic abuse and later eroticization of similar "trigger" situations is virtually unavoidable.

For example, Tracey was an adult survivor of particularly sadistic and
harrowing abuse at the hands of her psychotic and dramatically sadistic
mother. Beginning when Tracey was four, at which time the patient must
have begun to masturbate, her mother would insist on "checking" her to
make sure that she had not been "touching herself in her evil parts or thinking any evil thoughts that would make her be wet down there." Tracey's
mother would send her to her room, ordering her to strip and lie down on
her bed with her legs apart "as wide apart as you can get them." Tracey
would lie there, stripped naked, completely vulnerable and exposed for in-
determinate lengths of time ranging from what she remembers as minutes to
hours. Occasionally, her mother would look in to make sure she was lying in
the right way. Terrified and shivering from the cold and from the physical
and psychological exposure, Tracey would anticipate the many things her
mother had done in the past: inserting objects into her; cold and hot water

douches; examining her with knives that she sharpened as the child lay waiting, her panic and hysteria escalating out of control. Tracey would begin to
contract her vaginal muscles in the only form of protection she could use to
bar her mother's entry. Of course, the contraction and release of these muscles, accompanied by the hyperarousal state, was intensely stimulating. Her
mother would finally enter the room. "It's time to check you now," she
would say. Inserting her finger deep into the child's contracted vagina, and
massaging it along the way, she would coo, "You love it, you love it you
know; wet like a little whore you are!" Too young to know that it was her
mother's growing sexual arousal and sadistic behavior that was in fact creating the sexual stimulation, Tracey could do nothing but accept the horrible
truth of her mother's hideous proclamations.

Although this example may seem extreme, it is, unfortunately, only one
of hundreds of such stories we have heard in our work with survivors of
childhood abuse. To most of us, such sadistic and mind-bending torture is
inconceivable in actuality, and, yet, we assume that to the reader of this
book, the story as told is at least mildly arousing. One cannot help but respond to such raw and eroticized sadism. If we monitor our own responses,
our own guilt at being sexually moved by such a hideous story, we can only
begin to comprehend the confusing panoply of bodily somatic states and
conflicting psychological reactions that become embedded and recorded
around this mental representation of Tracey and her mother. An organization of experience that clearly defies any coherent verbal representation, yet
continues to exist in the naked cold body, the contracting vagina, the
mother's sadistic laughter, the sense of self as evil, unlovable, and twisted
beyond comprehension.

The realization that frightening and painful situations or fantasies are
likely to stimulate intensely sexual responses is one aspect of the intrapsychic organization of adult survivors that most confirms and maintains the
survivor's sense of inner badness and blame. Such stimulation becomes for
the survivor a perverse confirmation that she in fact "enjoyed" her abuse,
that she was, as her abuser may have tormented her, secretly turned on and
excited by the incestuous activity. Indeed, therapists themselves have on occasion used the fact that a patient masturbated to the image of incestuous
memories to try and demonstrate the "pleasureable part of the incest" or the
"patient's complicity and participation in the incest." We believe such an interpretation to be not only wrong, failing to take into account the intense
eroticization of fear that we have been discussing, but also destructive in its
reification of the patient's guilt and self-blame as well as a serious risk factor
in potentiating new rounds of self-punishing and self-abusive behavior.

Of course, we realize that some incestuous behavior can at the outset
seem pleasureable to the young child. It is often the case that when one parent is absent or emotionally unavailable such activity is the most intimate

contact available. Before it becomes too physiologically intense or too physically painful; before familial complications secret the patient in a hidden and isolated world cut off from those she has previously turned to; before threats are made to ensure that she will maintain her silence; before she begins to wonder why no one protects her from this frightening and overstimulating process; before all of this begins to crystallize, there may be moments of pleasurable physical sensation—moments that may even interface with specific preabuse fantasies. It is these very fleeting moments of pleasure that the adult survivor of childhood sexual abuse holds to tenaciously as the living testament to her eternal sense of shame, rottenness, humiliation, and damnation. It is her proof positive of complicity and unconscious participation in the dreaded events. When such vague and far-away memories are buttressed by the current awareness of a sadomasochistically oriented sexual or fantasy life, when painful self-abuse or dangerous situations leave the patient highly aroused, these horrific fears of complicity and guilt are reinforced. This is when the vicious and rapidly burgeoning cycle occurs of anxiety, leading to fear, escalating to hyperarousal, ultimately eroticized, leading to guilt and mortification, creating yet greater levels of terror and hyperarousal also eroticized, and so on—all in a context devoid of others who can help to soothe or contain or devoid of the mental representations of others who have in the past helped to soothe and contain. It is ultimately possible, although this would be a subject for future research, that it is the very capacity to evoke such soothing representations of self with other in an atmosphere of safety and containment that protects those who have not suffered such object-related trauma from the states of escalating hyperarousal we have described. Certainly, analysts have, for many years, recognized an informal connection between the infants' early experiences of their parents and certain self-regulatory ego functions. Although analysts have understood this connection in terms of identifications and transmuting internalizations, might not the capacity to evoke soothing images of self and object together, in itself, prove to have a powerful impact on the physiological mechanisms that control arousal and reactivity?

Hyperarousal and Transference-Countertransference

For the adult survivor of traumatic childhood sexual abuse, the establishment of repetitive patterns of self-mutilation becomes the internalized and ever-present representation of the abused self in perpetual, never-ending relation to the abusing other(s). By engaging in endless struggles to protect herself from what is experienced as the overwhelming drive to hurt and punish herself, the adult survivor, in essence, lives the original abusive experiences, on a continuing basis every day of her life, remaining at least in part absorbed with the cast of characters around whom the abused child's internalized system of self and object representation was organized and split off in dissociated form. The victim, the abuser, the idealized savior, as well as a host of unseeing others who failed in their protective duties toward the child, come into the immediate foreground of the patient's life with the arousal of each self-destructive, particularly self-mutilating thought. As this system of self and others becomes crystalized in the foreground, as the patient struggles against her self-abusive behaviors, trying to control the cutting, burning, bingeing, purging behavior that wreaks havoc in her day-to-day existence, the same state of physiological hyperarousal and dramatic anticipatory erotization described is symbolically triggered. Most patients are not only bewildered by the connection between self-mutilation and sexual responsiveness but also take it as further proof of their ultimate guilt, responsibility, and perversity. They are usually unable even to articulate it and terrified beyond all else to mention it to the therapist.

Further reinforcement of this synergistic and escalating process flows from the fact that, as transference-countertransference paradigms become triggers for the somatic sensations embedded within the patient's relationship to her abuser(s), the patient will also experience these episodes of eroticized hyperarousal vis à vis the therapist. For many survivors, this is the most unbearable aspect of reenactment in the treatment, and it can lead to abrupt terminations, escalating self-abuse, or suicidal behaviors if not interpreted and worked through during sessions. Because of the abuse victim's inability to modulate any state of arousal, and because most of these states become sexualized, any experience of intensification in the treatment setting can result in such erotic responses to the therapist, even an intensification of the positive and loving feelings within the dyad. However, arousal that accompanies the reemergence in the transference of the sadistic introject is what is most intensely shameful and simultaneously incomprehensible and disorganizing. To be enraged at one's therapist and sexually aroused at the same time, merely confirms for the patient her own worst fears of horrible perversity. Likewise, the position of being sexually aroused at a time when the therapist has been moved to a frighteningly angry position. Let us return to Tracey, with a vignette that will hopefully highlight some of these issues.

Tracey arrived for her session one day enraged, because the therapist, who usually returned her "emergency" phone calls, had failed to do so the night before. The therapist was expecting an either angry or depressive response but did not anticipate what followed. The patient's words conveyed her feeling at being uncared for and unloved by the therapist and of being convinced now that the therapist's proclamations of concern were a sham, just like everyone else's. She claimed to feel suicidal, not worthy of living, too alone and unloved to tolerate life any longer. She had, she stated, decided it was time to die, and, although she did not state so explicitly, she made it clear that it was the therapist's failure to respond that had "made her mind up for her." It was as if this one failure, this one event, erased all other positive experiences that had gone before, a clear example of splitting in the transference. Although Tracey was clearly upset by what had happened, and although her words were sad and depressed, her mood did not seem depressed. In fact, she appeared palpably energized by her anger. Her energy was almost frenetic, uncontainable, and yet oddly pleasurable for the patient, who clearly felt that in her game of "I gotcha," she had the therapist in a vulnerable position. She seemed eager, beyond words, to extract her guilty pound of flesh, and she made it clear from the beginning that she was going to enjoy the process.

At first, the therapist fell right in with the therapeutic agenda, attempting to bring into focus both the times when she had failed the patient and the many times she had in fact "come through for her"; the coexistence of loving and hating feelings; and her faith that the patient could experience both without destroying or being destroyed. Although the interpretation sounded right, the patient became more excited, more abusive, and seemed more out of control. The therapist was clearly trying to defend herself, and this only enhanced the patient's experience of sadistic glee in her identification with her own abuser. She flounced down in a chair, the otherwise nondescript black dress she had been wearing slipped seductively off one shoulder, a large satchel-type bag she was carrying placed across her lap. She smiled with startling triumph and began to breathe noticeably harder:

PATIENT: I want you to know that I have a gun in my bag (she placed both hands inside the pocketbook), and I intend to shoot myself with it sometime before I leave your office today. I'm sorry to do this, but really you leave me no choice. You've lied to me and deceived me for the last time.

THERAPIST: I see . . . [The therapist is aware that her heart has begun to race and that she is compellingly drawn into the horror of the moment. She has known the patient for a long time and doubts that she truly has a gun, yet this is a patient with a long history of self-abusive behavior, and it is certainly not outside the realm of possibility that she is in fact telling the truth. In the absence of anything brilliant to say, the therapist chooses to work toward the obvious need to contain the patient's now out-of-control behavior.] You know that I can't let you do anything to hurt yourself in my office. And you know, too, that you can't bring a gun in here. We need to talk seriously about how you're challenging the strength of our relationship right now. Clearly, you want to see how far I will go, and let me be clear that I won't go this far!

PATIENT: I don't care what you want anymore, bitch! Go ahead and try to stop me. [The patient begins to almost writhe in her chair, she is inviting the therapist to pull her pocketbook away, to try and restrain her physically. She is hyperventilating and moving her hips in a particularly erotic way.] I'm loading the gun now. [She moves her hands inside the pocketbook.] Let's see how many bullets I will be needing.

[The therapist's breathing is also escalating. She feels frightened and rather helpless. She hopes that if she finds just the right words, the right interpretation, she can contain the patient's behavior and reverse what is happening in the session. But she feels stupid and unfit to the task. Perhaps this patient is too much for her. However, she is certainly energized, alert, at her peak, and even, to her momentary horror and mortification, slightly sexually aroused. With this recognition comes a glimmer of the emerging transference-countertransference paradigm being reenacted in the moment, and of an obvious shift in tactics with the patient.]

THERAPIST: If only I can say the right thing to you . . . if only I can be good enough and smart enough and clever enough, then maybe I can say something . . . maybe I can say or do exactly the right thing, and you won't do these terrible deeds.

PATIENT: [Looks momentarily confused and disoriented] What are you talking about, bitch, don't try and confuse me . . . you're a tricky little thing aren't you . . . very slippery . . .

THERAPIST: Can you hear that you even sound like your mother now. "You little bitch." That's what she always called you, wasn't it? I think you're showing me in the most powerful way you can what it was like to be you when your mother teased and tormented you in the same way you're teasing and tormenting me.

In an obviously unconscious move, the patient pulls her dress back around her shoulders. This signals to the therapist that she is on the right track and that the patient is feeling more contained, less anxious, and therefore less aroused. Perhaps, there is also a beginning shift in the dissociated self and object relationships available to the patient and therapist.

THERAPIST: I don't know what's real and what's not real. I don't know if you'll do this terrible thing or not. I don't know if you're awful for making these abusive threats, or if I'm awful for forcing you to do it.

PATIENT: I'm not being abusive. You are. You're the one who didn't call me back. Don't turn this whole thing around on me like she did . . . that's abusive.

THERAPIST: I agree with you on that, and I'm not trying to blame you . . . I don't think either of us is to blame. You're angry at me . . . very angry . . . maybe rightfully . . . maybe not . . . all that seems less important right now than what you're doing with that anger. You sound like

Mommy. I think this is the Mommy that lives inside of you. She comes out when you're angry. . . . She threatens me, but she also threatens you . . . like when she wants you to hurt yourself . . . I think you want me to help you to control her, so that you can learn to do that when I'm not around. She's very scary, and very confusing, and very hateful, and I have to say more than a little exciting."

PATIENT: Exciting, what do you mean exciting?

THERAPIST: When you were so enraged and you started to provoke and tease, for a minute I thought the whole thing was a little sexual in a way.

PATIENT: That's disgusting . . . what kind of a pervert are you . . . you're supposed to be helping me . . . first you say I'm letting the mommy in me come out . . . then you say she turns you on. My god! You're no better than she was! [The patient has begun to breathe heavily again, shifting around in her chair and frantically scratching at her wrists.]

THERAPIST: But that's the point, I think. . . . I'm reacting just as she did . . . and so are you . . . between the two of us, we're re-creating exactly what used to happen between you and Mommy. . . . She would terrorize you, and the more scared you got, the more excited she would get . . . You saw that, maybe you couldn't put it into words back then, but you could see it . . . you've called it the funny look in her eyes . . . you said she'd be breathing funny . . . she was sexually excited by your fear . . . as you got more and more scared, she'd get more and more aroused. Your body couldn't help but get overstimulated too . . . in all ways . . . by that kind of sexual provocation . . . just as mine couldn't. I think you call me disgusting because you've always lived with the fear that being sexually aroused meant that you liked what happened.

PATIENT: So now you know . . . of course, I must have wanted it . . . or I wouldn't have reacted that way . . . my body wouldn't have done what it did.

THERAPIST: And I think you feel that way even more strongly in here sometimes when we're fighting and you start to feel too aroused . . . or when you're at home hurting yourself also . . .

PATIENT: [Crying now] Okay, so it's not you, it's me, you stop it . . . I'm the disgusting one. I know that. I'm not stupid. I've known that all along.

THERAPIST: But it's not disgusting . . . and it doesn't mean that you wanted your mother to do the things she did . . .

PATIENT: [The patient looks up, stops crying, stops scratching at wrists, seems to really be listening for the first time in this session.]

THERAPIST: Sure you may have been stimulated. The vagina is a bunch of nerve endings; you rub a child's vagina, and it responds; but that doesn't mean you were aroused for all those years and continue to be now, because you liked the things that your Mommy did. It happens to all kids who've been so badly abused . . . she stimulated your vagina at the same time that she scared the daylights out of you and enraged you beyond words, so many times and with such relentlessness that the terror and the sexual feelings and the rage got all mushed together. Now, they come as a package . . . it's almost impossible to sort them out. Now when something scares you it also arouses you; when you get aroused, you also get scared and feel like something bad is going to happen. It all makes you furious, and by the time you're finished, you're left with exactly the confusion of feelings we've both been through in this session.

This very dramatic vignette helps not only to elucidate how such a transference-countertransference reaction can trigger the described states but also to convey an understanding of how active interpretation of the relational paradigms being reenacted can help to undercut these terribly complicated moments in the treatment. It should be noted that this example comes from a point quite late in Tracey's treatment, when she was able to tolerate this level of interpretive work. It is an example of the kind of analytic work that can and must occur with adult survivors. However, it should be emphasized that the therapist needs to assess the patient's capacity to sustain such intensity at earlier points in the treatment.

Stress-Induced Analgesia

As if the cycle of terror, hyperarousal, and self-abuse was not confusing enough, there is one more bewildering complication. From animal research, we learn that organisms exposed to inescapable shock, the experimental paradigm believed to most resemble chronic childhood abuse, develop stress-induced analgesia when they are reexposed to stress shortly afterward (Amir et al., 1980; Miczek, Thompson, & Shuster, 1982; van der Kolk, 1989). In humans, Vietnam veterans with diagnosed PTSD demonstrate an analgesic effect (equivalent to an injection of 8 mg of morphine) after watching 15 minutes of a combat movie. Thus, it would appear likely that self-abusive behavior may produce the same effect as the administration of exogenous opioids (van der Kolk, 1989). Van Der Kolk (1989) concludes:

> If recent animal research is any guide, people, particularly children, who have been exposed to severe, prolonged environmental stress will experience extraordinary increases in both catecholamine and endogenous opioid responses to subsequent stress. The endogenous opioid response may produce both dependence and withdrawal phenomena resembling those of exogenous opioids. This could explain, in part, why childhood trauma is associated with subsequent self-destructive behavior. Depending on which stimuli have come to condition an opioid response, self-destructive behavior may include chronic in-

volvement with abusive partners, sexual masochism, self-starvation and violence against self or others (pp. 401–402).

Therefore, although we have shown how the *anticipation* of self-mutilation triggers a state of hyperarousal, disorganization, and erotic overstimulation, the abusive act *itself* can come to serve as a conditioned stimulus for the release of endogenous opioids, which will in effect tranquilize and relax the out-of-control patient. Most patients tell us that they feel better after they have cut or burned themselves. They describe a pattern in which the trauma reaction is triggered by some internal or interpersonal event, the hyperarousal response builds to an uncontrollable and intolerable level, some act of self-mutilation is performed; and with the pain comes the sought-after release of uncontainable arousal. A sense of calm follows the self-abuse. The physiologically addictive nature of most self-mutilating behavior and the connection between such symptomatology and histories of childhood abuse and violence are now an accepted part of the literature on post-traumatic stress, but they have not been incorporated into our understanding of the psychoanalytic process with compulsively self-abusive patients (Graff, Mallin, 1967; Pattison & Kahan, 1983; Rosenthal, Rinzler, and Wallsh, 1972; van der Kolk, Herman, & Perry, 1987).

It is imperative that the therapist explain to the patient this process of addiction to self-abusive behavior and its connection to histories of childhood trauma, along with the kinds of intrapsychic interpretations of self-abuse described. Such an understanding on the patient's part serves a twofold purpose. First, it alleviates, via a kind of biological normalization, the intense shame and humiliation that accompany most compulsive self-abuse, and it encourages the patient to incorporate her self-destructive symptoms into the therapeutic dialog without reexperienceing this shame and mortification within the transference. Given that such an experience in the transference could in itself trigger a cycle of self-abusive acting-out behavior, such a short-circuiting of this enactment will go a long way toward facilitating a safer holding environment for the patient. Second, by encouraging the patient to talk of her self-mutilating activity in sessions, such an understanding of these acts will allow patient and therapist together to explore other forms of self-soothing behavior that the patient can turn to at times of extreme stress. These therapeutic options will be discussed in the next section.

Ultimately it is only in the context of a thorough working-through of the relational paradigms implicit in the triggering and escalation of the hyperarousal states and in an elucidation of the physiological and psychological addiction to the maintenance of such behaviors that the intractible and dangerous violence one sees in the acting-out behaviors of adult survivors will begin to give way to healthier adaptations.

Therapeutic Implications

It goes without saying that episodes of violent or self-abusive behavior will call forth powerful countertransferential reactions, involving the therapist in oftentimes dramatic therapeutic reenactments of the relational paradigms with which the adult survivor organizes her internal object world and her external interpersonal relationships. Inherent in such enactments are the seeds of a power struggle for control of the patient's body and mind. This struggle, once lost by the abused child, may be fought to the death or near death by the adult survivor, who is convinced that control of her own person is more important than any other single motive in her life. Against the force of such violent assault, the therapist working within a psychoanalytic frame will find it impossible to maintain a neutral position. Here the therapist will be ultimately forced to act—and in so doing will become an active participant in the patient's enactment.

To the extent that the therapist remains neutral, committed to a purely interpretive role in the process, it is almost inevitable that she will be seen as reenacting the role of the uninvolved parent who either implicitly or explicitly allowed the child to be abused by standing by and doing nothing. In such a case, the patient will up the ante, escalating the violence and dangerousness of her behavior until the therapist does something to try and control the situation. Even very experienced analysts have been moved to what can only be considered "counterabusive" behavior in an attempt to control the patient's escalation of violence within the session. Having maintained a purely interpretive position up to a point—and having stood by helplessly as the patient's violence became more and more uncontainable—they clearly found themselves in the role of the victim who faces her abuser with a sense of increasing desperation and rage. One senior analyst, in describing his work with an adult survivor, recalled guiltily how he had "virtually wrestled her to the floor" in an attempt to get hold of a bottle of lethal pills she was threatening to consume in his office. "I was convinced," he said, "that she was going to take the damned things and this was the only way to save her life. As I grabbed them from her, she smiled at me in triumph, 'Go ahead and hit me,' she claimed, 'You know it was only a matter of time.'" Here the therapist's attempt at maintaining a position of neutrality called forth a full-scale attack by the internalized sadistic introject to involve him in a completely dissociated reenactment of her violent physical abuse by an out-of-control mother.

To the extent that the therapist remains disengaged from the survivor's violence, he or she may repeat the neglectful parent's unavailability or stimulate an episode of dissociation and projective identification within which she reenacts the patient's terror and helplessness in the face of an out-of-control abuser.

On the other hand, the therapist who moves too quickly to try and stop the patient's self-inflicted violence challenges the adult's right to autonomous control of her own person. Here the therapist is likely to be experienced in the transference-countertransference paradigm as an abusively controlling and intrusive object, unempathically blind to the fact that self-inflicted injury is both empowering and addictively sedating. It feels good. Oftentimes, the therapist who is eager to contract with the patient for complete cessation of self-abusive behavior is viewed as the intrusive parent who prohibited masturbation or other forms of self-soothing behavior.

Arlene's mother would sexually molest her whenever she caught the child masturbating in bed. She would "put something in there to keep me from doing it and then tie my hands behind my back. I had to try and fall asleep that way. I couldn't stop the throbbing in my vagina . . . I knew I was a bad girl for feeling that way . . . for wanting to touch myself . . . but I knew that only touching myself would make the feeling stop." Here is the quintissential example of the sexually abusive parent's assault: to overstimulate; project blame and responsibility; and ultimately to prohibit self-soothing behavior. Arlene became a compulsive wrist cutter, beginning in adolesence. As she and her therapist struggled to recover memories and piece together the fragments of her story, this behavior escalated to alarming proportion. Arlene's frantic attempt to maintain her right to engage in such actions clearly became the symbolic equivalent of her need to masturbate despite her mother's prohibitions, and to do it, transferentially, in full view of the therapist seen as her intrusively controlling mother. Interpretation of this reenactment did little to stop or lessen the self-abuse. In fact the interpretation itself became the "thing in the vagina" artificially inserted and overstimulating. It was only when this interpretation of the reenactment was coupled with the therapist's acknowledgement that the self-abusive behavior was in fact soothing to Arlene and that she used it often to control her feelings of escalating panic and helplessness that the patient could attain any distance from the dangerous situation. At that point, patient and therapist could work together to find other ways of self-soothing that were less potentially lethal. In Arlene's case, temporary medication, followed by learning specific behavioral, self-relaxation techniques slowly broke the cycle that had become so addictively entrenched. Only when the wrist cutting behavior no longer served as an addictively self-soothing behavior could its symbolic power and its embeddedness within the transference-countertransference reenactment be interpretively incorporated by the patient.

So here, as therapists, we dance on the head of a pin, caught maddeningly between the dangers of under- and overreaction to the patient's violent behavior. We assume, as we have all along, that we will fall prey to both extremes of the countertransferential valence. It is only as we fail the patient that we enable her to rework the dissociated matrices of relational paradigms that have become her unique legacy. However, we are well aware that in this particular aspect of reenactment, we move from the symbolic to the dangerously concrete. It is important to remember that sexual abuse survivors are two to three times more likely than nonabused women to make a serious suicide attempt (Bagley & Ramsay, 1986; Briere & Runtz, 1986). Their suicidal proclivities must, therefore, be taken seriously.

We have found it most effective to combine active interpretation of the therapist's dilemma, i.e., whether to underreact or overreact and the resulting transference-countertransference paradigms, with acknowledgment of the physiologically and psychologically addictive qualities of the behavior itself. We have had our best successes in helping patients control their self-abusive behavior when interpretation of the emerging relational patterns has been accompanied by acknowledgment of the patient's addiction and active efforts to search together for gradual substitutes for this self-soothing activity. In such situations we go to great lengths to educate our patients with the latest research on the physiological processes underlying addiction to self-abuse. We acknowledge its soothing potential and try to find other ways in which the patient can achieve the same or similar effects. Such methods vary from patient to patient but have in our experience included meditation, self-hypnosis, yoga, writing in a journal, playing or listening to soothing music, drawing, painting, and so on. The sadomasochistic struggle for control between patient and therapist becomes replaced by a joint effort to control the dangerous acting-out behavior of the dissociated abusive introject. We do wish to emphasize, however, that such substitution of more appropriate forms of self-soothing for the self-abusive behaviors described is by no means a simple process. Such a change may take years of active interpretation, containment, and struggle—with many many failures along the way. It may be helpful to remember that when the therapist is most angered and enraged by the abusively out-of-control patient, feels most challenged and teased, and verges on all forms of counterabuse, she is indeed struggling with a dissociated aspect of the patient's identification with her own aggressor. Behind this challenging and out-of-control patient is a terrified and abused child waiting to be shown a way out of her endlessly violent and life-threatening nightmare.

Unfortunately there will be times, particularly with patients who have been very sadistically abused, where all attempts at interpretation will fail, and the patient's behavior will reach life-threatening proportions. Here the therapist must err in the direction of taking whatever measures become necessary to safeguard the patient's life. It is ultimately the therapist's responsibility to show the patient that whatever measures are necessary to stop her abuse will be taken. By containing the lethal intentions of the sadistic introject, therapists symbolically communicate to the patient that they will not let her life be threatened, that they will stand by her and do whatever is necessary to protect her from her abuser—now, of course, dissociated and internalized.

If the patient cannot or will not contain life-threatening enactments, hospitalization may be necessary. Optimally, the therapist will maintain some therapeutic contact with the patient during this hospital stay. When the patient is released, it is crucial that the therapist pursue transferential reactions to the hospitalization. Was the clinician experienced as a cruel abuser, taking away the patient's freedom by placing her in captivity? Or did the therapist appear to be a strong, resourceful parent capable of protecting the patient when the latter could not protect herself? Inevitably, some mixture of positive and negative reactions will be discussed.

Whenever Diana felt abandoned by the therapist or by some other figure in her life, she soothed herself by walking, alone and at night, from the east side of New York's Central Park to the west side and back again, along winding pathways off the main roads. When Diana disclosed this habit to the therapist, the latter pointed out the suicidality inherent in the behavior. She commented that it was only a matter of time until Diana was mugged, beaten, raped, or killed on one of her nocturnal strolls. Furthermore, the therapist suggested to the patient that if she could not contain this behavior, hospitalization would have to be considered in order for treatment to continue. The patient was enraged, recalling how she had always been labeled the "crazy one" in her family. On a deeper level, she feared being sent away by the therapist because she had spoken to her of the abuse. However, Diana was also relieved at the therapist's clear and forceful stance, and her nighttime walks were not repeated.

A similarly active position is required when the survivor is engaged in enactments that present an acute threat to her health and availability as a patient. The survivor who chronically abuses alcohol or drugs must be willing to participate in rehabilitation or a 12-step program designed to maintain sobriety. A survivor who is actively anorexic or bulimic must agree to work with a physician who monitors her physical symptoms and viability. Again, it is important to pursue the transference reactions to the therapist's insistence on these ancillary treatments.

Finally, the therapist is committed to an active, forceful stance whenever a patient discloses that a child is being abused. The abuse must be reported to the appropriate state or local agency. In fact, it can be a reparative and therapeutic experience for the survivor to make the report herself if she is willing. At all times, the message from the clinician is that continued work with the survivor depends on cessation of the abuse and protection of the child. Here, it is important to keep in mind at all times the patient's ultimate identification with her own victim. This therapeutic stance clearly differentiates the therapist from others in the patient's life who may have passively allowed physical or sexual violations to go on for years. It communicates to the patient the therapist's commitment to protecting the helpless child, whether dissociated and internalized, or dissociated and projected onto another innocent victim, and it emphasizes the imperative that cycles of abusive violence can and must be stopped.

Therapists repeatedly confronted by the violently enacting survivor must have a substantial tolerance for chaos and for dissociatively, split-off, and behaviorally expressed sadism. They must be able to bear, sometimes for protracted periods of time, powerful feelings of shock, fear, impotent rage, and potential impending disaster, much like those the survivor experienced as a child in relationship with her abuser. Furthermore, they must be willing to forcefully and actively meet potentially lethal enactments, a level of activity that may be unusual for some clinicians. The strain of this work should not be underestimated; it can be exhausting, disorganizing, and emotionally draining. It is most helpful for therapists working with violently enacting patients to consult regularly with colleagues familiar with this population, as isolation only increases the stress under which the clinician labors—as well as the overwhelming responsibility and potential guilt.

CHAPTER 8

The Impact of Trauma on Transference and Countertransference

T HERE ARE FOUR major traumatogenic complications to analysis of the transference and countertransference in work with adult survivors of incest and childhood sexual abuse. The first is the extent to which these patients present with unorganized, unsymbolized experiences that begin to emerge during treatment, frightening and confusing the survivor and often threatening the continuation of therapeutic work. The second complication is related to the survivor's use of dissociation as a coping skill, defense, and vehicle of communication. Third, there is the more general defensive structure common to sexual abuse survivors—splitting, denial, acting out, omnipotence, projective identification. Finally, there are countertransference reactions related to the clinician's personal attitudes or experiences with trauma and to her transference to psychoanalytic thinkers and mentors.

The Effect of Unsymbolized Experiences

Many adult survivors of childhood sexual abuse arrive in treatment with no conscious memories of their abuse or with only vague, hazy impressions. Often, the traumatic experiences remain unorganized and unsymbolized within the patient's psyche. Once treatment is under way and transference-countertransference paradigms reach a critical level of intensity, these unsymbolized memories begin to emerge, frequently in the form of unexpected reactions to external stimuli. At this point, the patient often feels besieged, literally, as if she were possessed by terrifying, formless affects and body sensations for which she has no words and over which she is able to exert little control. In Fairbairn's (1943) terms, the patient *is* possessed by the emerging return of bad objects who once physically and emotionally overstimulated her and over whom she had no control. During this period of treatment, patients who were functioning very well in many areas of their lives may suddenly experience a dismantling of ego functions that disorganizes and scares them. In addition, the patient's anticipation of the disorganization accompanying the emergence of unsymbolized memories is itself experienced as traumatic and recapitulates the child's fearful anticipation of sexual abuse.

One highly successful attorney unexpectedly found herself feeling physically little—about the size of a 5-year-old girl—whenever the demanding senior partner of her firm asked to see her. Entering his office, her vaginal muscles began to contract; she felt pale, dizzy, shaky, and terrified of some unnamed danger; she was unable to muster her characteristic assertiveness and spunk. This continued for months until she began to recover memories of her uncle's sexual abuse. It was this uncle who had helped her secure her current position; the senior partner who suddenly terrified her had been her uncle's law school classmate.

To fully appreciate the power of these unsymbolized memories, it is important to differentiate them from the return of the repressed. The traumatic aspects of abusive experiences represented in these memories were never symbolized and then repressed. So overwhelming were the traumas to body and psyche that they were experienced as huge, formless, nameless, and dreadful and were stored unorganized and unrepresented. In treatment, they emerge the same way, and it becomes the task of therapy to help the patient to name, form, and symbolize them. For this to happen, the patient must remain in treatment.

Not surprisingly, the patient struggling with these unsymbolized experiences is often tempted to precipitously bolt from therapy. She quite accurately attributes the emergence of these dreadful feelings and sensations to the deepening of the therapeutic relationship. To her, the solution appears simple—end the therapy, and the assaults on mind, body, functioning will also stop. It is sometimes helpful to interpret the role and meaning of emerging unsymbolized memories. Interpretation, at this point, begins to establish some understanding of and control over these phenomena; it starts to drive a wedge between past and present. Some patients will, nonetheless, end treatment at this time. Those who stay challenge the holding capacity of the therapist and of the psychotherapeutic space.

First, it is crucial that the clinician assure the patient that the unorganized affects and somatic reactions being experienced have meaning, meaning that patient and therapist together can discover and name. It is helpful when the unsymbolized experiences occur more and more in the consultation room and less and less in the patient's extratherapeutic life. This localization within treatment can be assisted by the therapist's requesting the patient to imagine and relive each incident in the room associating to the disturbing stimuli and resultant reactions. Understandably, patients often resist entering or staying with these experiences, and it is up to the clinician to encourage without demanding that the patient do just that.

During this stage of treatment, the explicit and implicit messages from the therapist are that (1) the clinician can bear the intensity and confusion of the patient's unsymbolized experiences; (2) unlike the original trauma, the patient is not alone now; (3) therapist and patient together can eventually symbolize the currently formless; and (4) the patient can control the timing and pace of this segment of the work. The therapist, in other words, remains consistent, available, able to think when the patient's capacity to think is overwhelmed; able to reason, judge, and function when the survivor's ego functioning is flooded and faulty. Maintaining thoughtfulness, integration, confidence, and clarity is not a simple task for the therapist working with a patient beset by unformed memories. Like the patient, the clinician frequently is besieged by frightening, formless countertransferential experiences and projective identifications that challenge the integrity of her functioning. We have felt inexplicably nauseous, terrified, bigger, or smaller, have had tingly skin, numbness in an extremity, headaches, dizziness, vaginal pain, or contractions, or have experienced states of sexual arousal, all of which were disorienting and alien to a normally functioning ego. Like the patient, the therapist may be tempted to "bolt" therapy by withdrawing in self-protectiveness from this overstimulation and chaos. It is, of course, imperative that the clinician marshal observing and processing capabilities to manage and contain these transference-countertransference reactions. Consultation with colleagues experienced in this work often provides a much-needed container for the therapist struggling to hold and contain the survivor.

The dreadfulness for the patient of this period of treatment should not be underestimated. She feels crazy, regressed, disorganized, out of control. Frightened, her transference shifts between increased need for the clinician and increased mistrust, with a concomitant desire to get away from the therapeutic situation. Extra sessions or between session phone contacts are often vital in maintaining the holding and containing function of the therapy. Sometimes, just hearing the therapist's voice is enough to hold the patient until the next session. Although the increased availability of the clinician is often vital at this point, there is also a danger that the patient will be frightened by her increased dependency on the clinician. The delicate balancing act for the therapist is to offer herself as dependably available without moving in too quickly or overwhelmingly. Offering too much too soon can be viewed by the patient as an interpretation that the survivor is unable to contain her experiences while continuing to function. Here, the clinician is challenged to be just good enough (Winnicott, 1960b).

Although the importance of the holding capacity of the therapist and the corresponding transference to the clinician as a container during this phase of treatment should be emphasized, this transference-countertransference paradigm is not the only one in play. The therapist urging a patient to stay with an overwhelming, disorienting experience is not uncommonly viewed as a sadistic abuser, perhaps "getting off" on the victim's agony and help-lessness. At other times, the therapist is perceived as a stupid, unseeing, un-available adult who fails to rescue the survivor from her victimizations. The very availability of the therapist can be seen as a seductive promise to com-pensate the patient for all that she has missed and suffered. The clinician, of course, experiences corresponding feelings of abusiveness, ineffectiveness, and a wish to rescue. What is challenging about the emergence of transfer-ence-countertransference paradigms during this phase of treatment is that the patient frequently is as unable to symbolize and articulate these reactions to the therapist as she is to symbolize and name the traumatic memories with which she is struggling. Her symbolic capabilities are temporarily sub-merged in formlessness, and transferential reactions to the clinician become another thread in an unsymbolized mass. Much of the interpersonal action occurring between therapist and patient at this point is communicated non-verbally, and it is thus particularly important that the clinician be available and attend to his countertransferential responses. They are the map guiding the clinician through the hidden shoals of the transference during this period of treatment.

The Impact of Dissociation

An equally challenging complication to analysis of the transference and countertransference with adult survivors of childhood sexual abuse is the patient's use of dissociation. We have discussed the phenomenology of dis-sociation and have stated that successful treatment depends on the analyst's willingness to fully enter into the dissociative world of the patient. If the clinician is willing to be guided in this way, the abused child ego state will lead the therapeutic triad (adult patient, abused child self, therapist) to the memory/affect bank of trauma.

Clara is a 36-year-old survivor of particularly horrific incest and physical abuse that included bondage, burning, sodomy, and rape. When Clara's dis-sociated self emerges, therapist and patient engage in a ritual that signifies entry to the store of traumatic memories, fantasies, and affects. This little-girl part of the patient asks the clinician a series of questions, "Do you have the flashlight? Do you have a sword? Do you have a map in case we get lost? Did you eat your breakfast?" The therapist answers affirmatively, saying, for instance, "Yes, I ate and am fortified for this journey with you."

Thus assured, the child "takes" the clinician down a long hallway, lined on both sides with closed doors, and eventually opens the one just beyond the last one entered. Inevitably, the patient then relives an aspect of the trauma, often poignantly reexperiencing physical and emotional pain. Although many interpretations of the whole process and of the ritualized questions come to mind (e.g., "Did you bring the flashlight?" means, "Can you help me shed light on the experiences I had as a child?," and, "Do you have the sword?" means, "Can you protect us both from all those who would do us harm [and from our murderous impulses toward each other]?,") the therapist frames responses that primarily represent participation in the child patient's drama and only secondarily, if at all, bring into awareness the anxieties encapsulated in the inquiries. We advise uninterpreted enactment here, because the patient's traumitized child self is engaged in something new; she is trusting a grown-up person with the abuse she endured, risking to relive it within the clinical space.

Once the therapist has made the decision to proceed in this way, the transference-countertransference complications become apparent. One is the pluralization and rapid shifts in transference and countertransference paradigms associated with dissociative phenomena. These, in turn, are linked to two sources—temporal shifts in the dominance of each ego state, and intraego state changes in reactions to the therapist and to the other ego state.

A patient presenting with two autonomously functioning ego states will shift from one state to another during session. At times, these shifts are rapid, resulting in kaleidoscopic parallel changes in the transference and countertransference. Shifts may be triggered by the emergence of traumatic material or by the attempt to defend against emergence of that material. A case example clarifies the way in which this occurs. The following material is taken from a session of a patient whose dissociated abused child self held the memories and affects associated with father-daughter rape. The dissociated child had relived much of the abuse with the therapist, and the adult patient was aware of the content of the trauma, although she looked with contempt on the child part of herself.

PATIENT: I went to my parents' house to do laundry yesterday—my mother had called complaining that I hadn't been over in a long time. While my clothes were washing, I had tea with my mother and father.

THERAPIST: How was it for you being there?

PATIENT: It was fine. Why wouldn't it be? Actually, I was aware of how stiff I am around them. But I don't know if I've always been stiff around them, or if I feel stiff now because of this stuff I've been telling you. Frankly, I'm not sure it's true at all. Maybe you're getting off on all this. And even if it isn't a lie, who wants to know this stuff? If it did happen, it's over and done. It happened to another part of me anyway—that disgusting kid part we've been talking about. She probably asked for it anyway—and you think she's so fucking innocent! If you like her so much, why don't you fucking adopt her or something and leave me alone, the both of you. [At this point, the patient begins to cry, turns over on the couch, curls up, and continues in a very little-girl voice.] I was so scared going there yesterday. My Daddy still is really mean to me—he said it was a waste to send me to college—I should just get married and raise more dummies like me. My mommy just laughed and said, "Oh, Dad, you know you don't really mean that. Drink your tea." I didn't say anything, because I didn't want Daddy to yell at Mommy. But I wish I could've been here where it's safe. I wish she/I didn't have to go there all the time.

THERAPIST: You sound very scared talking about being with your mommy and daddy. I'm glad you can talk about that here.

[Now, the patient sighs, straightens out on the couch, and looks at her nails.]

PATIENT: What is going on here? I get so confused. One part of me thinks you're right—another part thinks my father's right. My whole life is unraveling thanks to my alleged therapist and this stupid kid part of me—monster part of me, I'd say. And I'm supposed to feel safe? She thinks it's safe here? The only place that's really safe is home alone in my apartment with absolutely no one around me.

THERAPIST: The different parts of you have different ideas about who and what is safe right now. To the kid inside you, at this moment, I'm safe— I guess because I listen to her. To you, I'm at best well-intentioned but misguided; at worst, stupid, abusive, blind to what's really going on in front of my eyes. The solution you suggest—being alone, taking care of yourself—is one you've relied on for many years. It's worked well in some ways and not so well in others.

This vignette illustrates the kaleidoscopic changes in transferential material accompanying interego shifts in dominance. The abused child self's transference, at this point, is most clearly trusting and dependent, although one might wonder at the child's less available transference to the clinician as someone who "lets" the adult ego state take her back to her parents. The adult patient, on the other hand, is furious at the therapist, experiencing her as an abusive object, sadistically "getting off" on violent sexual abuse or as a naive object, duped into accepting the lies told by the abused child self, much as the patient's mother once accepted her husband's facade, failing and continuing to fail to see and address her spouse's abusiveness. In the interpretation, the clinician addresses all the manifest transferences, accepting the current disagreements between ego states. At this point, uninterpreted is the adult patient's identification with the abuser in her contemptuousness toward the abused child self and the therapist.

Working with transference and countertransference in the patient who dissociates is something akin to doing couples or family therapy. Each ego state has a plethora of transferences to the therapist and to the other ego state. In this vignette, for instance, the adult patient holds the abused child in contempt, thus defending against experiencing the child's—and, therefore, her own—vulnerability. At this point in treatment, the predominant transference of the abused child self to the adult patient is one of mistrust, with expectations of betrayal and invalidation. The task of the clinician is to enable all participants in the therapy to observe and work through the various transferences and countertransferences. Because the adult patient and the dissociated abused child usually begin their work with each other with mutual hostility, mistrust, resentment, and envy, the clinical task is difficult. Gradually, the abused child part of the patient must learn to trust the adult part, empathizing with her strivings to function in adult domains of her life. Through the therapist's acceptance and interpretation of the adult's successes and ways of relating, the abused child ego state can come to respect the ambition, decisiveness, thinking capacities of her adult counterpart. Similarly, the adult must learn to trust, respect, and parent the traumatized child part of her. As the adult patient incorporates the traumatic memories, affects, and fantasies long borne alone by the child, she recognizes the strength and resiliency of her child self. As the mutual hatred and mistrust abate, adult and child grieve together the loss of fanstasied good parents and of a fantasied, unmarred childhood. Concurrently, the adult patient frequently rediscovers the playfulness, creativity, and spontaneity long split off and held by the dissociated child self. One survivor, for instance, joyfully told of putting up a Christmas tree for the first time in years, explaining how she "let" the child part of her choose the tree and a number of new ornaments.

Eventually, the third stage of the emergence of the transference and countertransference gives way to the fourth stage, in which the rigid boundaries between the ego states relax. This stage extends for a protracted period of time, as adult and child get to know and gradually come to terms with one another. It is through the therapist's patient, consistent acceptance, and interpretation of each ego state's existence, memories, feelings, fantasies, transferences, and countertransferences—to the clinician and to each other—that the two grow toward mutual understanding, respect, and affection. For a long time, the subjective experience of each ego state is that she is a separate entity, having an autonomous cognitive, affective, and relational existence. Neither wants to relinquish her independence; both want to preserve the hard-won closeness they now enjoy. Psychically isolated for so long, each ego state cherishes having a trustworthy other around all the time. The therapist must respect the subjective experience of the patient(s), continuing to analyze both the transferences and countertransferences of each ego state to the clinician and to each other. In our experience, this clinical stance facilitates a gradual integration that occurs in barely perceptible, yet definite, steps until there is one patient sharing the therapeutic space with the therapist. Often, the adult survivor will signal that integration is occurring by mourning the loss of the reified little girl, reminiscing with the therapist about their journey from the "bad, old days" of mutual fear and disdain to the current situation in which the child cannot quite be found anymore. As one patient said, "I know her qualities and memories are still with me, but now they are me. I don't see her standing outside me or even curled up under my ribs anymore. It's so bittersweet—I'm much more whole, but I miss her. She was a neat kid." The therapist will often find himself countertransferentially also grieving the departure of the abused child ego state.

Saying this brings to light a potential countertransferential pitfall. In working with the patient presenting with dissociated ego states, the clinician must beware of "playing favorites" between the ego states, just as the couples or family therapist avoids overaligning with any one member of the system. Some therapists might be much more comfortable with the abused child self, and their maternalism, protectiveness, or rescue fantasies elicited by her fragility and brokenness. Other therapists might be more at home with the adult patient's verbal acuity and intellectualism. Because the ultimate therapeutic aim is integration of the disparate ego states, the clinician's position must be equidistant from each ego state, with an overriding connectedness to the whole, integrated person, who, for a long time, exists only as a potential. Although a dissociated ego state cannot be iatrogenically created, it can be iatrogenically perpetuated by a clinician who becomes invested in a continuing relationship with a fragmented part of the whole rather than with the whole person. In other words, it is critical to the therapeutic process that the clinician accept and validate both patients/participants—both ego states—without being particularly curious about or invested in either more than in the other. This can be especially difficult when it comes to the abused child self. Dissociation itself is fascinating; the emergence and treatment of the child ego state are fascinating. The tricky job for the therapist is to do the work without being too fascinated. Once again, we exhort the benefits of collegial consultation to work through potential countertransferential acting out in this area.

Although with most patients the process of integration proceeds naturally, it can happen that a survivor becomes invested in continued dissociation to defend against examining present-day dynamic conflicts. One patient, for instance, who initially had rejected vehemently the existence of the child ego state, eventually integrated all the abusive memories of the traumatized child. As far as could be told, the adaptive and communicative functions of dissociation had been worked through. The patient faced, however, a number of thorny present-day relational conflicts, for example, whether to end or continue a long-standing affair with a married man. Whenever the therapy turned to these issues, the "little girl" suddenly appeared on the scene. In this case, the clinician chose to interpret the resistance. Interpretation was chosen to address the patient's use of what had become by now an old, growth-inhibiting relational pattern.

We want to stress again that the level of dissociation we discuss represents that found in the prototypical survivor that we treat. We certainly see patients who come to treatment with full memories of their abuse and who dissociate not at all or only to a minimum degree; their treatment will not include the emergence of a dissociated ego state. On the other hand, we also treat patients whose abuse was so early or so horrific that dissociative phenomena include three or more autonomously organized ego states. These patients often warrant the diagnosis of multiple personality disorder, and the analysis of transference and countertransference is correspondingly more complex and chaotic.

The Effect of the Patient's Typical Defensive Constellation

Adult survivors of childhood sexual abuse typically employ a constellation of defenses that include splitting, projection/introjection, denial, acting out, omnipotence, projective identification, and dissociation. We have discussed dissociation at length. Now, we focus on the impact of the other defenses on the development and analysis of transference and countertransference in sexual abuse survivors.

Splitting

Denial, acting out, projection/introjection, omnipotence, and projective identification all are, to some extent, variants of splitting. In denial, the patient splits off and disavows knowledge or affect; the person acts "as if," what is true is not. For the survivor of childhood sexual abuse, this parallels her childhood experience in which the abuse was denied. In acting out, behavior is split off from thought and verbal processing. Rather than knowing about and understanding a conflict or set of feelings, the survivor enacts them, much as the abuser once enacted, rather than contained and processed, sexually aggressive impulses. In projection, disavowed self representations or affects are split off and placed in fantasy onto someone else. For the sexual abuse survivor, this often replicates the nonabusive parent's projection of self-loathing onto the patient and the subsequent attribution of the victim's experience as self-induced. In omnipotence, the survivor splits off an inadequate, vulnerable self representation, defending against its emergence into consciousness through presentation of an invulnerable, all-powerful facade. For the survivor who was once so helpless and vulnerable, omnipotence often also represents an identification with the abuser who seemed himself totally dominant and powerful. Finally, in projective identification, one set of self representations is split off from others and transferred onto the therapist, with the clinician identifying with the projected aspect of the patient's self. Splitting thus becomes both a defense and a manner of processing internal and external stimuli. Transference and countertransference phenomena will therefore reflect the patient's use of splitting in its various derivatives.

Grotstein (1985) offers a good definition of splitting. He positions splitting as both a defense and a cognitive organization of the self, object, self-object, and object-object interactions. He stipulates first that aspects of the self can be split from one another, as when an incest sexual abuse survivor perceives herself as wholly bad and "whorish," splitting off any self representations of herself as good, worthy, respectable. Next, Grotstein suggests that aspects of objects can be split from one another, as when the father-daughter incest survivor consciously clings to a perception of her father as totally warm and caring, splitting off his exploitative, abusive aspects. Finally, Grotstein states that the internalized relationships of objects to one another can be split. This can occur, for instance, when a grandfather-granddaughter incest survivor holds fast to a perception of her mother's relationship with the perpetrator as wholly unsatisfactory to her mother, splitting off the aspects of the relationship the mother obviously enjoyed. This is done to protect her internalized mother from rage and disappointment.

For the sexually abused child, especially the incestuously abused child, splitting is a mechanism vital for psychic survival. The persistent sexual and emotional betrayal of a child by a loved and trusted other represents an assault against the ego that is too overwhelming to be handled by repression (Scharff, 1982). Instead, the child must split off the bad aspects of both the abusing and nonabusing family members. The child, after all, needs her family. Because of her need, helplessness, and dependency, the sexually abused child splits the object into good and bad and then further splits her own ego, identifying with the bad object and projecting her own goodness onto the family. In this way, as poignantly captured by Fairbairn (1943), she preserves internal representations of good parents and assumes the mantle of badness herself, thus preserving the hope that she can obtain love and care by learning to be be good enough. Further, splitting is imposed by the perpetrator and by the family system that refuses to acknowledge or name the abuse or frequently blames the child for bringing the trauma on herself. Splitting thus becomes the fundamental basis for the organization of self and object representations and it is carried into adulthood where it becomes the relational template upon which interpersonal relationships are forged and understood. Because the failure of splitting releases extremely potent memories, affects, self and other representations, the patient unconsciously, yet tenaciously, clings to this defense and relational processing mechanism. As Gill (1982) stipulates, the defense—in this case splitting—is an intrapsychic process that becomes evident through the transferential relationship with the analyst. The primary early mainfestation of splitting in the transference is resistance to awareness (Gill, 1982) of the full range of transference reactions to the therapist. We see this most particularly in resistance to awareness of negative feelings about the clinician that are acted out or conveyed through projective identification rather than being consciously observed and expressed.

As the child once protected her internal relationship with her parents by projecting her goodness onto them and introjecting their badness into her self representations, the adult survivor of childhood sexual abuse ostensibly protects the therapist from rageful, hateful reactions by denying them, consciously maintaining a positive image of the clinician and turning the rage and hatred toward herself. Such acting out also involves unconscious fantasies of victimizing the therapist by shocking and by rendering the clinician powerless. Because the split-off rage and hate are so potent, their acting out can be quite impressive, including suicidal gestures or attempts, self-mutilation, substance abuse, reckless driving, potentially dangerous sexual promiscuity, and anorexia or bulimia. Transference expressed in this way not surprisingly evokes powerful countertransferential reactions that are important to process and understand.

Acting Out

It is important to understand that acting out by the adult survivor once she is in treatment *always* has some transferential component. This is not to negate genetic or current extratherapeutic factors; a given piece of acting out is usually multidetermined. Once the patient has arrived in treatment, however, reactions to the therapeutic relationship are always involved in acting out.

Vivian is a father-daughter incest survivor who presented to treatment with a history of nonlethal cutting of her forearms. When she began treatment, she was engaged in an affair with a married man about the same age as her father. During one session, Vivian and the therapist were once again exploring the meaning of this relationship. By now, Vivian had become aware of some of the dynamics enacted through the affair—it allowed her to gain mastery of the abuse by having some control over the sexual relationship with her lover/father; it provided the opportunity to express hostility toward the lover's wife/the patient's mother by sleeping with this man; it enacted the self-representation of a whore—the name her father called her during the abuse; and it revived a sense of triumph in winning the oedipal battle. The evening after the session in question, Vivian's lover canceled a date at the last minute. On the phone, she responded with placid understanding. About an hour later, she dug into her forearm with a scissor. She reported the entire episode at the next session. Despite the clinician's attempts to explore what the cutting meant in terms of the analytic relationship, Vivian attributed the self-mutilation entirely to her rage at being stood up by her lover. Even this rage was not consciously experienced but was accepted intellectually as "making sense."

It was only much later in the treatment, after a number of similar episodes, that some transference reaction involved in the cutting was made explicit. Like Vivian's lover, the therapist set the terms of her availability to the patient. The clinician was not necessarily on hand when Vivian most needed her but was available only at certain times, times over which the therapist had more control than Vivian did. To Vivian, both the therapist and her lover seduced her, then set the parameters of their relationship with her, much as her father once totally controlled his relationship with her. In addition, both lover and clinician, albeit in different ways, insisted on the confidentiality of their relationships with her, to some extent replicating the secrecy of the incest. When Vivian's lover canceled dates, it evoked unconscious rage toward him in the current situation, unconscious rage toward her father's control and secrecy, and unconscious rage toward the therapist, who was also—to some degree accurately—perceived as unilaterally dictating the boundaries of the "secret" analytic relationship. The cutting in this case represented an attempt to self-regulate and contain powerful split-off affective reactions to past and present figures.

It is imperative that the therapist address the transferential meanings embodied in acting out. Not to do so invokes the image of the abuser who disclaimed responsibility for the victimizations or of the nonabusing parent who looked but did not see. A very tempting countertransferential position to assume when confronted by a patient who cut her thighs to ribbons after the last session, or who got drunk, picked up a man, and engaged in unprotected sex the night before the current session, however, is to deny the transference meaning of the behavior, focusing instead on genetic or current extratherapeutic factors. This countertransference stance protects the clinician from experiencing the patient's vicious assaults on his goodness and caring by erecting a fantasy within the therapy that the abusiveness is "out there" rather than "in here." However, this stance will also ensure continuation of the acting out, often in ever-escalating intensity or frequency.

Projective Identification

The other major way in which the adult survivor resists awareness of negative transference reactions while indirectly communicating them is through the use of projective identification. Projective identification is a slippery concept for which many definitions have been proposed (Grotstein, 1985; Kernberg, 1976; Klein, 1952; Ogden, 1979; Porder, 1987). Most definitions, however, include at least two steps. First, the patient projects a split-off internalized self representation onto the therapist to control good or bad aspects of the internal world. Second, the clinician identifies with the projected aspects of the patient's self, subjectively experiencing himself in a way that is usually ego-alien but perfectly congruent with the projected contents.

When projective identification is occurring, there are often three levels of relational interaction simultaneously in play. One involves the patient's conscious experience of the therapist and whatever countertransferential reactions that evokes. The second level encompasses transference reactions that are currently out of the patient's awareness that can be brought to consciousness gradually through questioning and interpretation. These transferences are accompanied by an expected range of countertransference responses. Finally, at the level of projective identification, are profoundly split-off transference reactions that are projected onto the therapist, with which the therapist identifies, and against awareness of which the patient tenaciously defends. Because the transference communicated through projective identification is so intense and so alien to the therapist, the clinician's reactions frequently include disorganization of her thinking capacities. A clinical example helps elucidate this elusive concept.

Helen, a 40-year-old survivor of father-daughter rape, sodomy, fellatio, and regular beatings, had been in treatment for 6 months. She frequently cut her thighs with a razor some hours after a session and spoke weekly of struggling not to drive her car off a river embankment. In session, she steadfastly denied any transferential meaning to these self-destructive thoughts and behaviors. In fact, Helen denied that the cutting and suicidality were relationally associated with anyone, stipulating that they encompassed only her contempt for her "stupid, worthless self." Helen's conscious experience of the therapist was of a warm, caring professional, who, for some unfathomable reason, was interested in helping her. At another level—unconscious but tolerable for Helen to explore in session—was a perception of the clinician as well-meaning but naive, duped into believing there to be something worthwhile about Helen, and blind to her "obvious" lack of substance and intelligence. This transference was to the therapist as the patient's mother who failed to see the obvious within her own family. Helen was unaware of the contempt encapsulated in this transference, consciously expressing liking and respect for the therapist. The clinician's countertransference to this level of transference were maternal feelings of caring, mild annoyance at the contempt for her power of discernment, and dismay at the patient's lack of self-worth. Coexisting with these two transference-countertransference constellations was another paradigm secured within a projective identification that conveyed more primitive experiences of self and object.

Although consciously and somewhat intellectually defined as worthless, Helen, at a deeply unconscious level, identified with the vicious sadism of her abusive father. Through the apparently self-victimizing cutting and suicidality, she launched a powerfully sadistic attack on the therapist's containing and healing functions. Each time she left a session, acted out, then reported it in the next session, Helen was unconsciously saying to the clinician what her father once said to her, "Take this, you bitch. You're a worthless nothing who will never amount to anything. You're a nothing piece of shit." Identifying in this way with her father, Helen projected her victimized self representation onto the therapist. Furthermore, the clinician identified with the projection, experiencing herself as paralyzed, frozen with terror and impotent, unexpressible rage, much as Helen had experienced herself as a child.

The clinician in this case dreaded Helen's appointment time and felt a sinking, hopeless feeling in her stomach when the waiting room door opened, signaling Helen's arrival. This very much paralleled the patient's childhood dread when she heard her father's footsteps outside her room at night. In session, the clinician felt beaten up by the relentlessness of Helen's self-mutilation and suicidal ideation. She felt terrified that Helen would in fact die and was impotently enraged at the ongoing attacks on her therapeutic effectiveness. The therapist, identified with Helen's projected victimized self, was afraid to confront the patient's sadism, fearing an escalation of acting out. Again, this was congruent with Helen's induced speechlessness as a child. As the therapist began to sort through and process the projective identification, she gradually loosened herself from the countertransferential stranglehold and began to openly address with Helen what was happening between them.

Although projective identification is a disorienting, deeply disturbing experience for the clinician, it is also, like dissociation, an invaluable venue for communicating information about the self that is intolerable for the patient to consciously know about and express. Through projective identification, the therapist comes to know about aspects of the patient's self-experience at a visceral level that can result in heightened empathy and understanding. It is helpful for the therapist working with an adult survivor of childhood sexual abuse to anticipate that projective identification will be an important component of work in the transference and countertransference. If it is expected, the clinician is less likely to self-protectively withdraw from the powerfully ego-alien disruptions inherent in projective identification, a countertransference pitfall that unconsciously communicates to the patient that the self aspects being transferred onto the therapist are unacceptable. As such projections are already unacceptable to the patient, the therapist's withdrawal from the projective identification renders the projected self representations of the patient unanalyzable and, ultimately, threatens continued treatment.

The turbulence of development, emergence, and analysis of transference-countertransference work with adult survivors of incest and childhood sexual abuse is clear. The violence, intrusiveness, seduction, and betrayal inherent in this therapeutic endeavor evoke countertransference reactions derived not only from the work itself but also from analysts' transferences to psychoanalytic tradition and from personal experiences with abuse, if any.

The Impact of Therapist Attitudes

On a personal level, it is crucial that therapists examine their attitudes and beliefs about childhood sexual abuse before embarking on a therapeutic journey with a survivor. Analytically oriented clinicians are all products of a theoretical and clinical tradition that underestimated the frequency and pathogenic impact of childhood sexual abuse; they are also members of a society that only recently began to open its eyes to the victimizations of children. The therapist's willingness to acknowledge the reality of a patient's abusive history, to engage in the demanding transference-countertransference constellations inherent in the work, to be guided by the patient's need for the clinician's full participation in the relational matrix emerging from the work, to stretch the parameters of analytic therapy to include work with a dissociated child self may be complicated by countertransference reactions that are, in fact, embedded in perhaps long-standing transferences to supervisors, training programs, theoreticians, and, generally, traditional and even more contemporary understandings about development, pathology, and acceptable ways of conducting analytic work.

For example, a therapist who works with a number of incest survivors participates in a supervision group led by a senior clinician. One day, a colleague presents his work with a patient with whom powerfully disruptive, sadomasochistic transference and countertransference paradigms have been set in play. In discussing the patient's history, symptoms, character structure, and relationship with her therapist, the clinician who works with sexual abuse survivors begins to wonder if the patient may have been sexually traumatized earlier in life. She suggests this to her colleague who is presenting the case. He acknowledges that he has not asked his patient about a history of sexual abuse and, further, is concerned that such questions could be suggestive to this patient whom he has conceptualized as "severely borderline."

At this point, the senior clinician somewhat teasingly remarks, "Well, maybe this woman was abused, but you people who work with sexual abuse also seem to start seeing it everywhere." The senior analyst then offers the presenting therapist a perfectly plausible formulation of the transference-countertransference bind with this patient. It is based on contemporary psychoanalytic thinking about borderline pathology and treatment, and it does not include the possibility of a reenactment of abuse. The therapist who *does* work with sexual abuse suddenly feels ashamed and somehow "slimy." She experiences herself now as outside this peer group, different from them, because she is "bad" in some way.

Driving back to her office, the therapist begins to wonder if indeed she is making too much of the prevalence and impact of childhood sexual trauma. Maybe she even is being suggestive with her own patients. And she hated that feeling of shame and not belonging she had experienced within the supervision group. Even if she *is* right when she thinks she detects the possibility of sexual abuse in a colleague's patient, maybe she just should keep quiet about it. Her peers do not want to hear about it anyway, and now the senior clinician, whom she likes and respects and from whom she desires admiration and respect, is making fun of her. It just is not worth it. She can keep her ideas about sexual abuse to herself and still learn from and contribute to the peer-supervision group. And they will like her better.

That afternoon, the therapist works with one of her patients who was abused sexually and quite sadistically by her father for many years of childhood. The patient has been struggling for months to accept the reality of what happened to her. To acknowledge that the abuse occurred requires her to loosen her grip on and experience the loss of the compensatory internalized good father to whom she has been attached tenaciously. The patient's relationship with the clinician as a figure who believes in the actuality of the sexual trauma has been crucial to the patient in this phase of the work. During that afternoon's session, the patient tearfully states that she thinks she finally may be able to bear knowing the unbearable truth that her father abused her and, sobbing now, asks the clinician once again if she thinks it really happened. Uncharacteristically, the therapist hesitates just a bit before affirming her belief in the reality of the abuse. Always acutely attuned to the clinician's internal states, the patient hears the hesitation and panics. She accuses the therapist of tricking her, of leading her on to accept something that is not even true, of needlessly robbing her of her good father. It is some time before the rupture in the therapeutic relationship is healed. Well, what has happened here?

First, in this vignette, we see an enactment of relational patterns inherent in sexual abuse at play in the therapist's peer-supervision group. The therapist hears that her colleague's patient may have been abused sexually and attempts to disclose that possible trauma within the supervision group. To this extent, she enacts the role of the sexually abused child who tries to speak of her victimizations within the family. Consistent with what might happen in an incestuous family, the abused child, now located within the therapist, essentially is told that she is crazy; her suggestion that her colleague's patient may have been traumatized sexually is dismissed. Congruent with her enactment of a sexually abused child, the therapist assumes responsibility for what has occurred—she is ashamed and experiences herself as slimy and bad. She also feels that her acceptance within the supervision group will be endangered if she continues to bring up the subject of sexual abuse; this is consistent with the sexually abused child's fear that she will lose her family if she speaks of the trauma.

As the therapist muses over the peer-supervision session in the car, she continues an identification with a victim of sexual abuse. She begins to doubt her own knowledge and reality; she speculates that perhaps she really does not know what she knows. Furthermore, to preserve her real and internalized relationship with the idealized senior clinician, she decides to stop talking about sexual abuse in the supervision group. Like the abused child, she protects important relational ties by splitting off sexual abuse from the rest of family life. At this point, also dissociated is the rage the therapist might otherwise feel toward the senior analyst and her peers for the invalidation she experienced that morning. Again, we see congruence with the abused child's splitting off of rage she might feel toward abusive and/or neglectful others.

Back in her own consultation room, the therapist enacts her internalization of and transference to the morning's events in a disruptive countertransference response to her patient. Now identified with the senior clinician and her peers, and, in turn, with their more traditional psychoanalytic conceptualizations about pathology and treatment, the therapist subtly invalidates her patient's growing acceptance of her abusive history. Within the supervision group, the therapist, at least in fantasy, becomes the silent, compliant, invalidated child. Within the therapeutic dyad, the therapist enacts the betrayal of the patient's early objects. Although one can speculate that there were dynamics within the treatment that also drew the therapist into this enactment, her transference to psychoanalytic tradition as expressed through the relational matrix of the supervision group seems to have been the primary source of the countertransferential empathic failure.

As this vignette indicates, to successfully enter into analytic work with a survivor requires the therapist to rethink her understanding of psychoanalysis and psychoanalytic psychotherapy. It often necessitates that the clinician brook the disapproval of actual and internalized supervisors, mentors, colleagues, and personal analysts who may strenuously disagree that what the therapist is engaged in is at all congruent with analytic tenets and techniques. The analytically oriented therapist engaging with the patient in the way described may struggle with strong internal dissonance created by discrepancies in what she perceives as necessary and effective treatment strategies and the real or fantasied skepticism or criticism of important transferential figures in her own life. This struggle may manifest in the treatment as inconsistencies in therapeutic stance that confuse and even frighten the patient who is especially hyperattuned to inconsistency. We again recommend consultation with colleagues working with survivors as a way to identify and work through countertransference emanating from transferences to psychoanalytic writers, supervisors, and colleagues.

Therapists who are also survivors may be especially susceptible to particular countertransference complications. First, they may not remember their own abuse and may begin to recall traumatic memories through work with a survivor. This may require them to reenter treatment, evoking a myriad of transference reactions to former and new analysts, as well as strong countertransference feelings about the patient(s) who "caused" the memories to emerge. Therapists who know they are survivors may assume a persistently masochistic position with patients, provoking ever-escalating sadistic attacks through their patients' self-destructive or abusive acting out. This position is often multidetermined. Through it, clinicians maintain an unconscious attachment to their own abusers by remaining victims in the therapeutic relationship. By ignoring patients' victimizing transference reactions, clinicians also preserve an identification with their own nonabusive parents who were blind to the abuse going on before their eyes. At the same time, the therapists avoid experiencing their own often disowned abusiveness by unconsciously agreeing that patients will enact those feelings for them. Another countertransference stumbling block for survivor/therapists may be a reluctance to allow themselves to be fully experienced by patients as bad objects. Uncomfortable with their own aggression and even more uncomfortable with any identification with their own abusers, clinicians may subtly, or not so subtly, defuse patients' aggressive transference reactions. This countertransference position preserves the therapist as a good object, a self representation she may have worked hard in analytic treatment to achieve and believe in. Keeping the relationship with patients primarily loving and "nice" may also represent survivor/therapist attempts to compensate patients and themselves for the wonderful childhood neither ever had.

It is also true that survivor/therapists bring their traumatic backgrounds to their work in ways that enhance their effectiveness with patients. Certainly, they can empathize with the terror, rage, and loss encapsulated in childhood sexual abuse at levels nonabused clinicians may never reach. Ultimately, it is the extent to which they have worked through traumatogenic issues within the transference and countertransference of their own analyses and within their supervisory relationships that allows them to use their experiences to further rather than restrict analytic work with patients.

CHAPTER 9

Eight Transference-Countertransference Positions

W E HAVE FOUND that there are eight relational positions, expressed within four relational matrices, alternately enacted by therapist and survivor in the transference and countertransference, that repeatedly recur in psychoanalytic work with adult survivors of childhood sexual abuse. These include the uninvolved nonabusing parent and the neglected child; the sadistic abuser and the helpless, impotently enraged victim; the idealized, omnipotent rescuer and the entitled child who demands to be rescued; and the seducer and the seduced. Although these, of course, do not account for every aspect of the transference and countertransference with every patient, our experience is that these eight positions and four matrices are enacted with sufficient regularity that a thorough familiarity with their clinical manifestations is invaluable to the analytic work.

Because they encompass self and object representations that are frequently split off from the consciousness of the patient, these eight relational positions are often identifiable only through the therapist's careful attention to his own countertransference. It is in the countertransferential reactions that the clinician experiences powerful projective identifications with aspects of the patient's self and object worlds. It is the intensity of the countertransference experience, along with rapid shifts in transference-countertransference states, that complicates analysis of the transference and countertransference with survivors. Further challenging the therapist is the extent to which, for a protracted period of time, these relational positions and constellations are enacted rather than verbally identified and processed. The relational matrices emerging from the clinician's and patient's enactments come alive in the consulting room with an affective loading and sense of action unlike that which takes place with many other, nonabused patients. Sexually traumatized children are abused motorically—in action. Healing for the adult patient demands an engagement with transference-countertransference roles that is similarly active, even when motoric discharge is contained. It is the therapist's willingness to embrace and enact, through the creation of an illusion in the analytic space (Khan, 1971b), the relevant transference-countertransference positions that eventually allows the patient to identify, tame, and integrate long split-off elements of her self and object worlds. In fact, unless all combinations and permutations of relational roles are experienced and worked through in the transference and countertransference, the treatment will not be complete. At the same time, we stress that enactment alone is not enough. It is the enactment and interpretation of transference-countertransference phenomena combined that facilitate integration and healing.

In presenting our understanding of these four essential relational matrices, we hold fast to a conviction about the vast ambiguity of human experience. Truly creative work in the transference-countertransference cannot be understood as a search for preconceived structures or mental configurations. Rather, we think of our schematization of these powerful relational paradigms as offering the reader what might be considered points of orientation; beacons of directional light when the storm of transference-countertransference enactments becomes otherwise blinding and cognitively disorienting.

The Unseeing, Uninvolved Parent and the Unseen, Neglected Child

Whenever a child is sexually abused, someone's eyes are closed. Certainly, when the abuse is incestuous, one or both parents deny the violations of the child's body and mind and present themselves as emotionally detached from the victim. Some contemporary trauma researchers (Steele, 1986; van der Kolk, 1987) cite the loss of secure attachment that is emblematic of parental neglect as a profoundly damaging trauma preceding the more vividly identifiable sexual trauma. One can speculate, in fact, whether child sexual abuse could extend over time if parents were awake, attached, and attuned to their children's behaviors and emotional life.

One aspect of the internalized world of the adult survivor, then, is a relationship between a neglectful, unavailable parent and an unseen, neglected child. Because this parent was also loved and needed by the child, this relational constellation is split off from consciousness. The patient preserves a conscious image of a loving, available parent while setting into motion within the treatment the long-held-at-bay relational configuration just described. Within the transference-countertransference, the patient enacts either side or both sides of the relational matrix sequentially, while the therapist projectively identifies with and enacts the complementary role. Manifestations of this transference-countertransference paradigm are varied.

At times, the patient identifies with her parent and enacts the latter's coldness, unavailability, and rejection in the therapy sessions. The patient may be profoundly withholding, remaining silent for long periods, or she may respond minimally to queries or overtures from the clinician. When identified with the uninvolved parent, the patient may accuse the therapist, verbally or nonverbally, of "bothering" her; of demanding more attention from her than she is willing to give. The patient may appear bored, disdainful, narcissistically preoccupied, hostile to the interpersonal engagement sought by the clinician. During these periods of identification with the neglectful parent, the patient treats her own vulnerability, emotional needs, and affect states with the same cold neglect that she heaps on the therapist. The patient may even verbally berate herself for any detectable emotional "weakness," much as her parent(s) once overtly or covertly dismissed her feelings and yearnings to be cared for.

When the patient is identified with her uninvolved parent, the clinician frequently countertransferentially takes on the role of the patient's disowned self representation of a neglected, unseen child. The therapist experiences herself as unwanted, unimportant, utterly bereft of vital connection with the patient. The clinician may begin working very hard to reach the patient, and, when these efforts fail, as they once did for the child struggling to make contact with her parent, the therapist sequentially may feel frustrated, inadequate, enraged, and, ultimately, depressed. The therapist also may cringe at the coldness with which the patient addresses her own vulnerability and affect, finding the patient's hostility toward her own needs almost unbearable. Eventually, the clinician may be tempted to give up, withdraw interest from and empathy for the patient or may even wish the patient would just go away.

It is crucial for the treatment that the therapist resist the temptation to abandon the patient emotionally, thus replicating the original parental disavowal of the child. Remembering that the nonabusing parent(s)'s often hostile neglect was in many ways as damaging to the patient as the overt sexual abuse, the clinician must continue to strive to stay alive and in relationship with the patient. She must be particularly vigilant to signs of emotional withdrawal like sleepiness, daydreaming, and inattention. The therapeutic message to the patient is that the clinician can bear the unbearable; that she can tolerate, contain, process, and, ultimately, make explicit the profound negelct the patient suffered as a child.

In another enactment of the uninvolved parent/neglected child paradigm, the patient identifies with herself as a child and responds to the clinician as she once did, at least initially, to her parent. Here, the patient denies her own needs and feelings in order to care for the therapist. Certain that the only way to obtain emotional supplies from the clinician is to tend to the latter's perceived needs, the patient is solicitous of and, at least superficially, compliant with the therapist and the demands of the therapeutic situation. Associations may appear to flow freely, but, in fact, the patient "protects" the clinician from her deepest pain, rage, and bereavement. She also is quite likely to "protect" the therapist from the memories of her abuse, much as she once shielded her parent from the reality of the sexual victimizations.

During this period of treatment, the therapist may collude with the relational matrix being enacted by not seeing the "false self" (Winnicott, 1960) aspects of the patient's presentation. If this transference-countertransference configuration extends for some time, the patient is likely to become enraged at once again not being truly seen or heard. As she did when she was a child, the patient may split off rageful responses in order to maintain a tenuous attachment to the therapist/parent. Instead of expressing them in session, the patient may act out her rage in extratherapeutic relationships or by engaging in self-destructive behaviors such as cutting, substance abuse, or promiscuous sex, or she may become increasingly depressed. With this relational matrix in play, the therapist may feel bored, annoyed, increasingly angry as she senses that the treatment is mired in apparent superficiality. Once again, it is vital that the therapist use the countertransference eventually to make explicit the relational constellation enacted in the consulting room rather than self-protectively withdrawing from, or in some way castigating, the patient as the parent did earlier in the survivor's life.

Finally, an overt transference to the therapist as an unseeing, uninvolved parent may develop, in which the patient experiences the clinician as neglectful. Sometimes, the patient angrily and repetitively berates the therapist for somehow "missing" her; for not noticing, hearing, correctly interpreting, remembering feelings, behaviors, facts, dreams, memories the patient considers crucial. Here, it seems that nothing the therapist does or does not do is "right."

In this case, the patient is once again identified with a hostile parent who expected to be cared for by the child and who berated the patient for her ineptness in meeting the adult's needs perfectly. Overtly or covertly, this parent threatened abandonment if the child failed to attune to and gratify her parent's emotional needs. Beneath the sometimes amazingly intellectualized criticism and carping is a wildly terrified patient, who, literally beside herself, strives to hang on to the therapist by a relational thread in the only way she knows how without directly exposing her vulnerability and need. Countertransferentially, the therapist, much to her or his chagrin, may enact stupidity, forgetfulness, inadequacy. It is with such a patient that therapists uncharacteristically double-book a session, miss an "obvious" connection among associations, or forget dream material. The clinician, again identified with split-off aspects of the child, feels panicky, stupid, frozen, and inadequate. She may begin to dread sessions with the patient. Once again, it is important for the clinician to use the countertransference experience to gradually help make explicit the split-off terror of the patient and to refrain from self-protectively emotionally abandoning the survivor.

The relational matrix of the uninvolved parent/neglected child is frequently the first transference-countertransference paradigm to emerge in the treatment. We agree with other writers (Bernstein, 1990; Burland & Raskin, 1990; Gabbard, 1992) that until this transference-countertransference configuration is enacted, identified, and at least partially worked through, it is unlikely that the patient can tolerate fully the recovery, working-through, and integration of traumatic memories. Even the patient who presents to treatment in crisis due to unsymbolized body memories, nightmares, or flashbacks usually shifts into the uninvolved parent/neglected child aspect of the therapeutic work once the crisis has abated. She only returns to work through more thoroughly traumatic material once this transference-countertransference paradigm is at least partially resolved. Reemergence of this relational constellation occurs, however, at various points in treatment, sometimes as resistance to proceeding further with the recovery of painful memories. Similarly, the next relational matrix to be discussed, the sadistic abuser/helpless, impotently enraged victim, may be in evidence sporadically, long before it becomes central to the treatment.

The Sadistic Abuser and the Helpless, Impotently Enraged Victim

One focal aspect of a sexual abuse survivor's internalized self and object worlds is a relationship between a greedy, sadistic, impulsive abuser and a terrified, helpless, impotently enraged victim. Like the patient's internalized relationship with the uninvolved parent, this relational paradigm frequently is split off from consciousness in order to preserve a positive image of the perpetrator. This is particularly true when the victimizer was also a loved and needed parent. Split off from awareness, the relational constellation is detectable in powerful transference-countertransference phenomena that emerge in the treatment. Working within this relational configuration is particularly upsetting for both therapist and patient, both of whom experience themselves and each other as victim and victimizer. Because this relational paradigm is so pervasive within the patient's internal and external relational worlds, the transference and countertransference manifestations are intense and varied.

We know that any child who is sexually traumatized over time, especially by a parent, will internalize and identify with those aspects of the perpetrator, who is also a loved and trusted figure in the child's life. Through this identification, the child attempts to preserve her bond to the perpetrator by becoming like him. As an adult, the patient's unconscious identification with her victimizer allows her to keep at bay experiences of herself as helpless, terrifed, violated. Instead, she projects her "weakness" on to another, thus feeling to some extent empowered. Then, she constructs a relational view, in which the other deserves the devaluation she visits upon him. The whole process, of course, replicates the defensive maneuverings of the original abuser. Finally, the patient's identification with her abuser also facilitates the expression of contempt and rage that she usually carefully keeps out of awareness because of its power.

In the transference, one manifestation of a patient's abusiveness is her tendency to penetrate and invade the therapist's personal and psychic boundaries. Some patients, for instance, literally burst on the treatment scene, entering the room in an intrusive, forceful manner. Occasionally, patients have knocked on the door of the consulting room or even opened the door, knowing very well that the clinician was in session. In addition, some patients have a way of staring intently and penetratingly at the therapist as if they are trying to get inside and control him. Other patients persistently notice and comment on many aspects of the clinician's personal appearance or office. These comments are often disparaging or seductive, and, even when they are complimentary, their relentlessness can be unsettling. Adult survivors also often are attuned to the therapist's moods; their accurate and insistent interpretations of these to the clinician have an invasive and unbounded quality. Finally, these patients are often creatively determined to learn about the therapist's personal life. One patient, for example, met and slept with her therapist's son, creating a therapeutic and personal quagmire for the clinician.

Through her invasion of the therapist's boundaries, the patient betrays her identification with her abuser(s). In all the transferential manifestations of this identification, the patient communicates an unconscious fantasied intention to intrude on and control various elements of the clinician's personal and professional life. In so doing, she is replicating in the treatment her perpetrator's ruthless lack of respect for and greedy smashing of physical and psychological boundaries. For the abuser, nothing was sacred. For the patient attempting to master her early trauma while keeping at a distance her vulnerability and fear, unconscious identification with and enactment of her abuser's lack of boundaries offers some sense of power and inviolability.

Countertransferentially, the therapist being intruded on by the patient may experience great discomfort at and anticipatory anxiety about being exposed and penetrated. Identified with split-off victimized aspects of the patient, the clinician may find himself dressing differently, straightening up the office, trying to be in the "right" mood, and avoiding eye contact with the patient in order to stave off episodes of intrusion. The clinician may think about upcoming sessions well in advance with anxiety and dread. At this point, of course, the therapist is reenacting many of the behaviors and emotional states the patient experienced in relationship with her abuser(s) and tries to protect himself from the inevitable intrusions by guessing what might "set off" the patient and fixing it ahead of time or by avoiding real engagement with the patient. All this, of course, replicates the kind of strategies the patient employed to try to protect herself from her victimizer(s).

Another way in which a patient can abuse her therapist is through entitled demands for attention, such as extra sessions, between-session phone contact, lengthened sessions, and so on. Often, the clinician has set the stage for this by responding to crises with increased availability. For example, when a patient is struggling with disorganizing body memories or flashbacks, the clinician may offer more frequent contact, responding to a real need in the patient. Suddenly, however, the therapist is besieged by demands for more and more until he feels overwhelmed. Initially, he may submit to the patient's escalating demands, even blaming himself for initiating this pattern. Gradually, however, the therapist begins to feel used, furious, but helpless to extricate himself from what has become a regular way of relating with this patient.

Here, is we have another dramatic recreation of an early relational matrix within the transference-countertransference of the treatment. The patient, in this case, exploits the willingness of the clinician to be available and, as her perpetrator did before, develops an insatiable demand for more. In turn, the clinician experiences aspects of the patient's victimized self; the therapist assumes the blame for the abuse, feels violated and enraged but helpless to do anything else but accede to the patient's demands.

Yet another manifestation of the patient's identification with her perpetrator(s) is the self-destructive or violent enactments in which the patient often engages. Here is the transference-countertransference meaning of acting out that bespeaks the patient's role as abuser within the treatment. When the patient acts self-destructively and presents the therapist with a fait accompli, often accompanied by disturbing, visible physical evidence such as cuts or burns, it is, at one level, a vicious attack on the therapist's holding and containing effectiveness. There is often a sense of the patient saying, "Take this. Don't think for one minute that you can really have an impact on me because, in the end, I'll do exactly what I want."

The clinician confronted with a patient's self-destructive acting out often is shocked and paralyzed by the intense rage and violence inherent in the acts. Frequently, the clinician feels unable to interpret or to intervene in any way, fearing that to do so will provoke an escalation of action. The therapist feels attacked, helpless, and fearful about where the acting out might ultimately lead. The therapist also feels trapped by the patient's acting out; he may search for exactly the right intervention in order to prevent his patient from spinning completely out of control.

In this paradigm, we see still another enactment of the patient's relationship with the abuser, in which she assumes a victimizing role. Like her abuser, the patient translates impulses into direct action, action that terrifies and impotently enrages the therapist, who, in turn, assumes the role of victim. Identified with the victimized aspects of the patient, the therapist feels trapped, paralyzed, and intent on somehow preventing escalation of action. This, of course, is congruent with what the patient experienced as a child as she struggled to prevent escalation of sexually abusive activities.

There is at least one more way in which these patients enact identifications with their abusers, and that is to destroy hope. In most cases, adult survivors are terrified that good things cannot last, that promises will always ultimately be broken. Rather than waiting for the inevitable disappointment to occur, patients with sexual abuse histories often intervene in the buildup of anxiety that accompanies hope by assuming control of the situation and shattering what they are convinced is only an illusion anyway. They do this by threatening premature termination, resuming self-destructive acting out after long periods of abstinence, developing new symptoms such as psychosomatic disorders, or sabotaging extratherapeutic successes in relationships or jobs.

Countertransferentially, the therapist feels deflated by these attacks on hope that often occur when things seem to be going particularly well in the treatment. The clinician may become depressed and is sometimes tempted to passively accede to hopelessness through relational withdrawal, loss of energy, muted affect.

In this paradigm, we see another reenactment of the patient's past. Often, the sexually abused child experiences periods of hope, during which the perpetrator stops abusing for one reason or another, presenting himself more consistently as the good object for whom the child yearns. Inevitably, however, the abuse resumes, or a younger sibling begins to be victimized by the same abuser with our patient's knowledge. In treatment, when things are hopeful, the patient may identify with the perpetrator and seemingly smash to bits progress and hope. Identifying with the victim, the therapist experiences the despair and deflation once held by the victimized child.

Therapists working with a patient who is enacting an identification with an internalized abuser find themselves executing a delicate therapeutic balancing act. To the extent that they ignore or minimize the patient's abusiveness, they recreate the unseeing, uninvolved parent and, ultimately, lessen the perceived safety of the analytic space. To the extent that they remain locked into a countertransference experience of victimization, they are likely to evoke intense feelings of toxicity and guilt in the patient. These patients perceive themselves to be powerfully toxic anyway and struggle with chronic, free-floating guilt. When they sense unconsciously that they have victimized the therapist, unbearable states of shame and guilt are engendered. Protecting themselves from conscious awareness of these intolerable affects and self-representations, they project them onto the therapist, who then is perceived as toxic and deserving of attack, and the cycle begins again.

Eventually, the transference-countertransference paradigms in play have to be made explicit, so that the patient can begin to tame and integrate currently disowned self representations and identifications. This is delicate work when the self representation or identification that is activated is that of abuser. More than any other relational position, the adult survivor of childhood sexual abuse eschews acknowledging and making explicit her identification with her abuser(s). The thought that she might actually sadistically mistreat another after having been so badly used herself nauseates and enrages her. Premature interpretation, which can be precipitated by the clinician's desire to extricate himself from the role of victim, can engender defensive denial and rage, along with further splitting off and enactment of the identification. Too early interpretation also can evoke intensified guilt and self-punishment, with concomitant submerging rather than integration of the abusive self-representation.

Some classical writers (Greenacre, 1949, 1950, 1967; Shengold, 1989, 1992) explain the adult sexual abuse survivor's abusiveness in terms of the reactivation of early sadomasochistic impulses and fantasies. There is no doubt that the relational paradigms encapsulated in psychoanalytic work with these patients contain and express both sadism and masochism. We feel, however, that the classical viewpoint overlooks both the loving attachment to an abuser that is preserved through identification, as well as the mindless, wordless terror encompassed in the self representation of victim against which the patient defends through enactment of an identification with the perpetrator. To keep these factors in mind can help therapists to tolerate and process their countertransference responses to the patient-as-abuser. Then, they can focus their interventions on the love, pain, and terror around which the patient is organized when she is abusive.

It is crucial for the treatment for the therapist to experience and enact the role of victim to the patient/abuser. Only in this way can the clinician begin to truly appreciate at a visceral level the terror, paralysis, hopelessness, and impotent rage lived by the patient when she was a child. At the same time, we advocate gradually making explicit, and when necessary setting limits on, the patient's attacks and intrusive demands. We find this works best when the underlying terror and love of the abuser are also discussed with the patient. Her abusiveness can be framed as an attempt at relational preservation and mastery rather than being presented as a pejorative criticism of sadomasochistic impulses.

During psychoanalytic work with a survivor, a transference-countertransference configuration of patient-as-victim and therapist-as-abuser will alternate with the constellation just described and will become evident in a variety of ways.

First, there are elements inherent in the treatment situation that can evoke feelings of victimization in the patient. The relationship is not equal, no matter how egalitarian we perceive ourselves to be. We engage the patient in "treatment," during which, if we are successful, we "penetrate" defensive barriers to "get inside" the patient. The patient "submits" to a fee and a frame of our making and agrees to "open" herself by freely associating and sharing her psychic contents. All of these aspects of psychoanalytic work are often particularly conflictual for the adult survivor of sexual abuse; they can evoke a transference to the therapist as abuser, while the patient assumes a familiar victim role. The patient may readily and passively accede to the demands of the therapeutic situation, failing to make explicit doubts and resentments about the frame. Or she may rail in rage against every element of the clinical parameters. In either case, the therapist may begin to feel abusive about usually minimally conflictual frame issues. To rid himself of this disturbing self-experience, the clinician may bend the frame, not in response to real patient needs but simply to avoid feeling abusive. Suddenly, the roles switch—the therapist feels victimized, and the patient is viewed by the clinician as manipulative. In fact, the therapist acted out in order not to feel abusive!

Sometimes, the therapist unconsciously enacts an intrusive, controlling role with the patient, because she consciously is intent on not duplicating the patient's uninvolved parent. When this occurs, the clinician often intrudes on the patient to limit some form of self-destructive acting out. Here, the therapist assumes control of the patient's mind and body by unnecessarily hospitalizing her or by engaging her in complicated, essentially unenforceable contracts about her behavior. Often, the patient plays a complementary role. For a protracted period of time, she may have provocatively and abusively taunted the therapist with her behavior, unconsciously wanting the clinician to take control of her functioning. Finally, the therapist reacts and, again, there is an immediate exchange of roles. The abusive patient becomes a victim of the victimized therapist's countertransferential abusiveness. The patient rails at the clinician for the latter's betrayal, and the therapist is left confused and guilty.

A very similar enactment occurs when a therapist who has been berated contemptuously by a patient, perhaps for months, "suddenly" explodes into a verbal assault on the patient. The formerly abusive patient is now the wounded victim; the previously abused clinician is, correspondingly, a verbally sadistic victimizer.

Other, more subtle ways in which the therapist enacts abusiveness are through premature interpretations, intrusive questioning, or encouraging a patient to stay with a traumatic memory beyond what is therapeutically indicated in order to satisfy voyeuristic fascination with the abusive experience. In each case, the therapist, in an enactment of victimization, exploits the patient's vulnerability and dependency as once the patient was exploited by her abuser. The patient, in turn, may respond with woundedness, or she may passively submit to the victimizing aspects of the therapist while storing up uncommunicated, impotent rage.

Sexual Encounters between Patient and Therapist

The most serious enactment of analyst abusiveness/patient victimization occurs when the parties engage in an explicit sexual relationship. Here, as during the original trauma, identifications, in the form of transference-countertransference reactions are expressed in actuality, rather than symbolically. The result, of course, is the tragic reabuse of the patient. It is tempting to account for all such experiences by assuming serious therapist psychopathology. Some form of unresolved pathological identification is, in fact, a factor in all explicit sexual encounters between a therapist and his patient. In addition, the clinician is ultimately responsible for maintenance of necessary therapeutic boundaries. At the same time, the fact that sexual encounters with therapists are most often reported by adult survivors of childhood sexual abuse (Kluft, 1990c) also bespeaks the power of transference-countertransference pressures to enact rather than symbolize; these pressures must be acknowledged in work with this population.

In her identification with her abuser, the adult survivor of childhood sexual abuse plays out a truly dazzling array of seductive, cajoling, pleading behaviors that, via projective identification, are capable of evoking within the clinician confusion and disorientation comparable to that of the child whose experience of reality was so seriously impinged upon. Here, the abuser within the patient maintains an intense investment in reenacting—with the roles reversed this time—the childhood trauma. This compulsion to repeat the sexual abuse within the therapeutic relationship represents the ultimate triumph of the sadistic introject. Although the patient may experience consciously an illusion of mastery—she will initiate and control the sexual activities this time within a truly loving relationship—the enactment also offers, tragically, equally illusory "proof" that she is a powerfully seductive and dangerously toxic figure who can drive any man to lose his mind.

In one common manifestation of the drive to repeat, the patient, in her most appealing wounded child persona, appeals to the therapist as protector and savior. She has been so sexually traumatized by her original perpetrator that she "needs" a different loving experience of sexuality that "only her therapist can give." It will be therapeutic, she claims, in her most seductive and persuasive incarnation. Here, she enacts an identification with a needy, infantile, cajoling abuser. In the countertransference, the therapist may feel empowered toward acts of sexual "reparenting and redoing" that attempt to salvage the sexual future of the patient hidden within a grandiosity that is the analog of the abused daughter's attempt to salvage and nourish a perpetrator who is believed by the child to be bereft.

In a very different scenario, the patient becomes intrusive and assaultive in her sexual demands. The therapist receives erotic phone calls, is stalked or followed by the patient, or is confronted with the patient undressing before him. Here, the patient enacts an obvious identification with the abusive parent. The clinician, in what becomes a "she asked for it" countertransferential response, identifies with that part of the patient who blames herself for the abuse she suffered.

These two scenarios are only two of many possible ones. What is clear is that whenever an actual sexual relationship comes about between clinician and patient, any hope for future therapeutic work is destroyed. Sexual contact has replaced much-needed interpretation and explication of relational paradigms. Reality falls on the therapeutic space, as it once did much too early on the patient's childhood, with a cruel and deadening thud. What is left is an abusive therapist who mislabeled aggression, need, retaliation, and projective identification as allowable attraction, even love, and a badly, perhaps dangerously, retraumatized patient.

As disturbing as it is for both therapist and patient to relate as abuser and victim, it is only through the enactment, observation, and eventual interpretation of these transference and countertransference constellations that the sexual abuse survivor can integrate into her internal world these split-off self and object representations. This process is protracted and constitutes a central aspect of psychoanalytically oriented treatment with survivors. As the patient works through and resolves experiences of herself and the therapist as victim and victimizer, she begins to more fully affectively process the loss of her childhood innocence and of her fantasied good parents. At this point, another relational matrix, present in the therapy from the beginning, moves into sharper focus and assumes a focal role in the treatment.

The Idealized, Omnipotent Rescuer and the Entitled Child

Throughout treatment with an adult survivor of childhood sexual abuse, there are times when the therapist is powerfully drawn into enacting the role of omnipotent, all-giving rescuer. It is a countertransference enactment that may be easily evoked for many clinicians anyway; we have chosen, after all, to live our lives as professional helpers. The abuse and neglect reported by sexual abuse survivors and the evidence of psychic damage with which they present, however, often elicit strong caretaking responses. These can mushroom into more driven enactments of rescue when, for example, patients are besieged by body memories or flashbacks or are reliving traumatic events in the consultation room. Suddenly, we find ourselves wanting to save the broken child before us from the torment she continues to suffer as abusive internalized relationships are revitalized through the therapy. Perhaps guilty for "making" the patient remember and relive awful childhood events, we now unconsciously resolve to make it all better.

In part, the countertransferential position of omnipotent rescuer can be viewed as an identification with an enactment of the patient's childhood attempts to rescue her abuser by sacrificing her own needs and growth. Abused children, as do all children, unconsciously attune to the relational yearnings and the psychological damage within their victimizers. At great personal cost, they strive to repair the brokenness of adults they love. One root of a survivor's pervasive shame, in fact, is her perceived failure to rescue the victimizer whom she desperately loved despite his abusiveness.

Although clinicians working with adult survivors may experience and enact a wish to rescue throughout the treatment, we have found this countertransferential stance to be particularly potent when the patient begins to integrate and more fully affectively mourn the loss of her childhood and of the fantasied good parents. The pain associated with this phase of treatment is acute, perhaps even surpassing that connected with accepting the reality of the sexual traumas. The patient, stripped now of her compensatory fantasies, is bereft and lost. One patient said: "This is too much. I can deal with the abuse . . . I think . . . maybe I can. But the idea that this is all there will ever be, that when I think of being little, all I feel is pain and terror and aloneness . . . that's too much . . . I can't live with that. I can't stand knowing I never was and never will be a child."

There is tremendous poignancy to this phase of treatment. It challenges the therapist's capacity to withstand the patient's despair and the limitations of the clinician's own ability to alleviate suffering. During this phase, the pull to rescue is often great. However, because the patient must be allowed to experience and express her grief in full measure, it is important that the therapist refrain from presenting herself as an omnipotent rescuer, thus truncating the patient's complete working-through of horrendous losses. Monitoring fantasies of omnipotent rescue is one way for the clinician to do this.

It also frequently happens, particularly during the mourning periods of therapy, that the patient enacts a long split-off self representation of a wounded child who expects to be compensated for all that she has suffered and lost. A universal fantasy among sexual abuse survivors seems to be that, once she relinquishes the fantasied childhood that came complete with good-enough, loving parents, someone will provide a new, wonderful childhood. That someone often turns out to be the therapist. In this case, the patient reasons that, because the clinician "made" her know what happened to her and somehow got her to give up her fantasied good objects, it is now up to the therapist to make up for all the pain and loss. At times, the patient's demands for compensation become strident and entitled. Often, the clinician who has been deeply moved by the patient's courageous therapeutic journey

finds the patient's demands to be perfectly reasonable and sets about to provide the asked-for compensation. We have had fantasies of including patients in holiday or vacation plans, of sharing afternoons in the park, of
going on exciting shopping sprees in special toy stores.

Here, the clinician once again is challenged to proceed with delicate balance. In part, the emergence of entitled demands for compensation for a lost
childhood represents the reawakening of long-buried relational strivings
and yearnings to play, an activity often alien to sexual abuse survivors. For
those healthy strivings to continue to unfold, it is crucial that the therapist
allow the creation of an illusion within the therapeutic space (Khan, 1971b)
in which clinician and patient can play, and fight, and love, and hate with
the shameless passion and vitality known only to children. At the same time,
the patient must be allowed to rail against and grieve the original losses as
well as the limitations to reparation available within the therapeutic relationship (e.g., sessions do end, clinicians take vacations, therapist and patient
will not spend Christmas together in a a concrete way). If the work of this
phase goes well, however, the internalized presence of the therapist will accompany the patient on vacations and at holidays in a way that encourages
passion, play, and continued relational unfolding.

As in other transference-countertransference constellations discussed in
this chapter, patient and therapist each will enact relational positions of rescuer and entitled child.

We have already described the extent to which abused children try to rescue the psychologically damaged abusers with whom they are in relationship. As adults, this striving is combined with the need all patients experience to cure their therapists (Searles, 1975) and is manifested in treatment
through the patient's attempts to rescue the therapist. Patients who were
sexually abused often are remarkably sensitive to and accurate about their
therapist's moods and dynamics. Frequently, if a patient senses that her
therapist is distraught or in pain, she will move quite lovingly to repair the
clinician. We are aware, of course, that these loving efforts coexist with the
patient's anxious fear that she must tend to the therapist, lest the attachment
be threatened. At this point, we selectively focus on the love and gratitude
encapsulated in the wish to repair.

One evening, for example, a patient accurately perceived that the clinician
was preoccupied with something worrisome, and she cared for her by talking about interesting and funny job-related issues. The therapist, in fact, felt
better by the end of the session. When the session was later discussed, with
the relational aspects of it made explicit, the patient expressed great joy that
she could have a curative impact on the clinician. Over the course of treatment, she referred to this incident many times with gratitude that the therapist had allowed the patient to attend to her in this way. We certainly are not
advocating mutual analysis (Ferenczi, 1932), in which the analyst regularly

shares personal problems with the patient and uses the latter as a therapist. We are suggesting, however, that one transference-countertransference enactment that will arise in work with a survivor is the patient as rescuer of the clinician and that, when this spontaneously occurs as in the vignette above, it can be therapeutic for the patient to succeed in curing the therapist. Among other things, it relieves the patient's intense sense of herself as toxic.

In addition to specific attempts by the patient to rescue the therapist, psychoanalytic work with sexual abuse survivors pushes clinicians to the limits of their creativity, mindfulness, and availability. We have heard over and over again from therapists working with this population that these treatments stretch them beyond the parameters of their training, their more traditional ways of thinking, the processes and outcomes of their personal analyses; these observations are certainly congruent with our own experiences. Work with adult survivors of childhood sexual abuse demands an aliveness, a presence, a relational combination of strength, availability, and vulnerability that are both terrifying and transforming. Clinicians who allow it will be changed by this work, "rescued" if you will, from personal and professional limitations.

Finally, we look at the therapist as entitled child. This countertransferential response often is elicited when the clinician feels that she has given and given and given to the needy patient only to be asked for more, with no expression of gratitude from her. At these junctures in the treatment, the therapist may identify with a split-off self representation of the abused child who gave and gave to the abuser only to be required to do and to give more. The therapist may feel used and entitled to some recognition of her therapeutic efforts. It may be tempting for the clinician to retaliate by withdrawing from the patient who then feels abandoned and bereft.

The Seducer and the Seduced

Pervading the psychoanalytically oriented treatment of adult survivors of childhood sexual abuse is an ambience of seduction. Throughout the work, therapist and patient seduce and are seduced by each other. If therapy is successful, however, there will be, over time, a shift in the nature and experience of mutual seductions.

Early in treatment, and for a protracted period, the patient is likely to experience split-off self representations that include flirtatiousness or more overt seductiveness as horribly dangerous. These are qualities, after all, that, in the patient's mind, got her into trouble in the first place. Yet, from a young age, this patient was trained to seduce and to be seduced to maintain a primary relationship. It is what she knows how to do best. Early on in treatment, then, the patient's seductiveness is split off and enacted or projected while she consciously preserves a sexually conservative, even rigid, attitudinal facade through which she disdains sexiness in others.

First, the patient may present provocatively dressed and openly flirtatious while evidencing a total lack of awareness of her impact on others. The totality of the split between her physical appearance and mannerisms and her consciously held beliefs about herself can be startling to the clinician. One patient, for example, regularly appeared for sessions dressed in skin-tight mini-skirts and halter tops. As she sat provocatively draped in the chair and gazed invitingly at the therapist, she frequently decried the sexual objectification of women in modern society and railed against men who made passes at her.

The therapist confronted with this split-off, yet intense, seductiveness may feel both attacked and sexually aroused. There is an aggressiveness to the patient's seductions at this point that are often experienced by the clinician as coercive. At the same time, the therapist may respond erotically to the raw sexuality of the patient before him and then feel guilty about having sexual feelings toward a patient who once was abused badly by an authority figure. Whether experiencing himself as victimized or aroused, the therapist feels overstimulated, much as the patient once did, and may be tempted to self-protectively withdraw from emotional engagement with the patient. It is important, however, for the clinician to remain engaged while processing the countertransference reactions. To withdraw is likely to evoke shame and feelings of toxicity in the patient.

Not all survivors present with their seductiveness split off from a provocative facade. Some patients dress and make up appropriately, or even asexually. Still, in the early phases of treatment, there is likely to be a strong sense of split-off seductiveness that will come into play within the treatment space.

Another way in which the patient initially seduces the therapist is to tease the clinician with partial disclosures about her intrapsychic and interpersonal life by presenting tantalizing fragments of traumatic memories. This is not the patient's painfully difficult struggle to retrieve memories or to finally speak the unspeakability of her abusive history nor her fear of being seen and exposed through her verbalizations. It is a split-off seduction that is unconsciously designed to overstimulate and frustrate the therapist. Once again, we see a reenactment of the sexual abuser's sexual and relational overstimulation and frustration of the patient when she was a child. Here, as before, it is the clinician's attention to his countertransference that allows him to differentiate seductive teasings from the patient's shame and fear-based difficulties in speaking openly. When seductiveness is in play, the therapist can set limits, as the abused child never could, on unending tantalizations by wondering with the patient about the relational paradigm enacted in the consultation room, eventually making explicit the transference-countertransference issues in force.

The therapist, too, seductively engages with the patient in the early days of treatment. He or she may hear an uncharacteristically flirtatious tone in his voice when addressing the patient or he may tease the patient to reveal more about herself in a way that is erotically tinged. On the other hand, the clinician may be so concerned and guilty about sexualized reactions to the patient that, in a process parallel to the patient's own, the therapist splits them off and, instead, presents a rigid, overcontrolled facade that deadens the treatment and evokes terror in the patient about the power of her own sexual impulses.

During this extended phase of treatment, the therapist is challenged to convey to the survivor that sexual feelings and seductiveness are acceptable aspects of human experience, while maintaining the integrity of the thera-peutic boundaries. It is this combination of acceptance, availability, and boundaries that eventually allows the patient to differentiate between be-nign and malignant seductions, opening a pathway to integration of her own sexuality. Newirth (1992) outlines this well when he says: "The successful treatment of sexually abused patients involves the development of a positive identity as a woman who can experience herself as sexual and desireable without experiencing guilt, shame, or sadomasochistic relatedness. . . . Sexual feelings in the countertransference can involve recognition of the pa-tient's capacity to be a sexual person without the threat of action. . . . The ability to recognize patients as sexual subjects, as women who have desire and are desireable is an important part in the personality intergration of the sexually abused patient's self" (pp. 15, 17).

As patient and therapist grow to accept and even enjoy sexual feelings about each other, the nature of mutual seductions between therapist and pa-tient begins to change.

A very touching period of treatment with an adult survivor encompasses a phase during which the patient and clinician engage in a form of oedipal romance that facilitates a reparative reworking of the former victim's long-held-at-bay sexual impulses. At first tentatively and shyly, the patient, now more consciously, flirts with the therapist about whom she experiences childlike, romantic feelings. She may compliment the clinician on his appear-ance, present him with flowers, food, poetry, or other small gifts, and pro-duce overt associations or derivatives suggesting jealousy about real or fan-tasied partners and other patients in the therapist's life. There is a possessive longing for the therapist at whom the patient gazes with childlike adoration. The clinician, in turn, feels flattered, moved, and wryly amused at the oedi-pal forces at play.

We suggest that the therapist acknowledge and play within the patient's oedipal romance. Adhering to our position that new relational strivings be enacted rather than made explicit, we delight with the patient about her ro-mantic feelings. Like a good-enough parent (Winnicott, 1960), we make ourselves available to the patient's oedipal fantasies while maintaining therapeutic boundaries. The patient, at this stage of treatment, will be alert to any sign of disapproval or rejection of her rebudding sexuality. At the same time, she will be hypervigilant to signs of impending abuse. Still not wholly convinced that her sexuality did not provoke the abuse as well as the accompanying parental neglect, thus rendering her forever dangerous and toxic, the patient will watch carefully for signals that the therapist is uncontrollably aroused or stiffly intimidated by these new relational overtures.

If this treatment period proceeds well, the patient will, at some point, seemingly leap into a more adolescent burgeoning of sexual strivings directed toward the clinician. The shy, tentative child is suddenly a postpubescent teenager experimenting with new hairstyles, makeup, and fashion statements. Like a real adolescent who struggles to integrate and make sense of her sexuality, the patient appears one day as a little girl in bib overalls, then as a businesslike professional, then as an amazingly sexy young person shooting off electric sexual sparks. At the same time, the patient tests the therapist's capacity to allow her to engage in intimate extratherapeutic relationships. Often, the sexually abused adolescent, especially the father-daughter incest survivor, is clung to possessively by the abuser or is completely rejected by him when she seeks the companionship of peers. In treatment, therefore, the patient will be hyperalert for evidence that the clinician intends to prohibit appopriate extratherapeutic relational strivings or that he will abandon the patient entirely for seeking intimacy outside the therapeutic dyad.

The clinician working with the adult sexual abuse survivor during this treatment phase may be quite startled at the patient's newly shown off sexuality. The therapist, in fact, may feel jealous, possessive, abandoned as the patient pursues new or more imtimate extratherapeutic relationships, may envy the patient's enhanced attractiveness and sexual vitality. Finally, of course, the therapist may find himself sexually aroused by and drawn to the patient in a way that is disconcerting and evocative of guilt or shame. The clinician's ability to acknowledge and process his countertransferential responses to the patient's emergence as a more integrated sexual being, neither abandoning the patient nor possessively clinging to her, will ultimately facilitate the patient's increased comfort with and ownership of her sexual impulses.

An impressive piece of work has been accomplished when an adult survivor of childhood sexual abuse and her therapist relatively nonconflictually accept and appreciate each other as sexual beings who share a range of feelings and fantasies about each other—some erotic—but who also respect the boundaries between them.

For the sake of simplicity and clarity, the eight transference-countertransference stances are presented here in terms of four relational matrices that comprise complementary interactive configurations. Life in the consulting room, of course, is not so neatly schematic, simple, and clear. As we suggested earlier, the transference and countertransference shifts in this work are rapid and confusing for protracted periods of time. At one moment, the therapist experiences himself as abusing the patient with a premature, penetrating interpretation, only moments later to be cast into the experiential role of victim by the patient who is berating the clinician for his stupidity. Moments later, perhaps when the abused child self has emerged and is curled up weeping on the couch, the therapist becomes a rescuer, fantasizing about tucking the patient under a warm quilt. In the end, it is the clinician's ability to assume, enact, observe, and, ultimately, to help to make explicit all of the relational stances taken on by each member of the therapeutic dyad without becoming locked into any particular role or relational paradigm, that moves the treatment along, facilitating the patient's identification, working-through, and integration of long-fragmented self and object representations.

CHAPTER 10

Transference and Countertransference: A Case Example

TO CLARIFY FURTHER the way in which transference and countertransference develop and are analyzed within the treatment of a sexual abuse survivor, this chapter is devoted to an extended case vignette.

Belinda is a strikingly attractive, 36-year-old woman who has long, wavy black hair and big green eyes. She has been in twice weekly psychoanalytic psychotherapy for 6 years.

This patient was the only child in an upper middle-class family in which both parents were successful professionals. After graduating summa cum laude from a small, regional college, Belinda's mother attended on scholarship an Ivy League professional graduate school where she met Belinda's father, Timothy. Angela and Timothy married the week after they graduated, and Belinda was born 3 years later. The pregnancy was unplanned and resented by Angela who felt that it had cost her an important promotion. Timothy, on the other hand, welcomed the birth of his daughter.

Belinda's perspective on her parents' marriage was that Angela belittled her husband for failing to live up to his potential and to promises he had made to her before they were married. Although successful, he was not as career-driven as his wife, and Angela apparently resented this. By the time Belinda was 7, her mother's verbal denigration of Timothy was consistent and vicious. Angela worked later and later more and more often; Timothy frequently slept in the guest room, and he began to drink heavily at night. Belinda now surmises that her mother engaged in one or more extramarital affairs during Belinda's childhood.

Belinda's childhood relationship with her mother seemed focused around a morning ritual during which the child watched in fascination as her mother carefully attended to dressing and arranging her hair and makeup. Except for this daily interaction, Belinda saw little of her mother and was left primarily in the care of her father and a series of nannies. Belinda's sense was that, as a child, she yearned to be as important to her mother as Angela's career seemed to be. Belinda felt inadequate and somehow "wrong" for her inability to win her mother's interest or affection.

On the other hand, Belinda adored her father and also felt sorry for him. They often dined alone together in the evening. Sometimes, Belinda sat in her mother's chair and "toasted" her father as she had seen the grown-ups do at parties. After dinner, father and daughter frequently watched TV together; eventually, Belinda learned to mix her father's scotch and sodas. Occasionally, when Angela returned home and found Timothy and Belinda together, she made sarcastic remarks that positioned her husband and daughter as a couple. Belinda recalled one such remark, delivered scathingly by her mother, "Well, isn't this a lovely little domestic scene. I must admit, Tim, she's about your speed. But, Belinda, darling, you could do so much better." Belinda was 6 years old at the time.

When Belinda was 7 years old, her father began to sexually abuse her. As they watched TV together, with Belinda on Timothy's lap, he kissed her inappropriately, licked her ears and neck, and fondled her thighs, telling her how soft and sweet she was and calling her "Daddy's special little lovey." One night, shortly after these activities had begun, Belinda awoke to the smell of scotch and found her father lying next to her, pressing against her with his erect penis. Terrified, confused, but also wanting to care for her father, Belinda lay still while Timothy placed his penis between her legs and moved both of them back and forth until he had orgasm and ejaculated. As time went on, the molestations began to occur almost nightly and escalated to include fondling of Belinda's breasts, digital penetration of her vagina, fellatio, and cunnilingus. The abuse ended abruptly when Belinda was 13 after her father had intercourse with her for the first time. After that incident, which may have frightened Timothy, Belinda perceives that her father withdrew from her completely; he was seldom at home, spending most of his evenings at a downtown bar.

Once, when she was 9 years old, Belinda tried to tell her mother about the abuse. She said to her mother, "Mommy, Daddy sometimes comes into my room at night and his thingy gets big, and he rubs it on me." To this, Angela sarcastically responded, "Belinda, please, don't be ridiculous. Your father is totally incapable of getting it up, even with a 9-year-old. You just wish he was that much of a man. But he never was, and he's not now. So we're both out of luck."

At some point, Belinda began to dissociate her father's abuse and also split off her mother's hostilely neglectful response to her disclosure. By the time she arrived at boarding school, a year after the sexual abuse ended, Belinda had few memories of the sexual traumas and, in fact, recalled few specific details about her childhood at all. Her parents seemed like dreamlike figures to her with whom she would feel vaguely uncomfortable during visits home. Belinda began to arrange to spend holidays at the homes of friends, stayed at school for two summers, ostensibly to take extra courses, and convinced her parents to send her away as a camp counselor for another two summers.

At boarding school, Belinda performed well academically and made two close friendships that have lasted into adulthood. Other than these two girls, Belinda remained removed from most of her classmates; she remembers being on the periphery of a number of groups but never entered the center of any of these. During her high school years, she dated a number of boys from a brother boarding school; she did not engage in sex with any of these young men, and, in fact, several relationships ended because the boys found her sexually unresponsive. At the same time and unknown to any of her school friends, Belinda was sexually promiscuous with "townies," older, working-class boys and young men she met in a bar in the city in which her school was located. During her boarding school years, Belinda also began to drink; by her senior year, she was consuming more than a pint of scotch every night. Although she tried marijuana once or twice, she never became involved in any drug except alcohol. Also during her high school experience, Belinda began to cut herself occasionally with a razor, carefully making non-lethal slits in her upper thighs, between her legs where her father had once placed his penis. In addition, she developed a bulimic pattern of bingeing on sweets several times a week, after which she vomited. After vomiting or cutting, Belinda would "feel better," although she was never sure in what way she felt "bad"; she simply remembered a release of tension after the self-destructive activities.

After graduating from boarding school, Belinda attended a Seven Sisters college where she majored in literature and history. Repeating her boarding school experience, she did well academically, made two close friends while remaining only peripherally connected to other women, and split her relationships with men between primarily nonsexual dating relationships with college men and promiscuous sexual adventures with working-class, usually older men. By the end of college, her drinking had escalated to a fifth of scotch a day, and she continued to cut and binge and purge.

After commencement, Belinda spent several months in Europe at her parents' expense. These 6 months are still a blur of drunken partying, hang-overs, and sexual promiscuity to Belinda. Often, she awoke with a man and had no memory of who he was or how they had ended up together for the night. Frequently, these were older men, sometimes married, whom she had met at parties or in a bar.

Returning to the United States, Belinda obtained a job as an assistant to an account executive for a major advertising agency. Professionally, Belinda did very well, quickly being promoted until she reached a position of account executive for one of the agency's most important clients. She was respected by agency and account people alike for her ability to understand and address both the business and creative needs of the client. A persistent criticism during performance reviews, however, was that Belinda drank too much during the entertaining that was a part of her job. Unfortunately, her alcoholism worsened during the 6 years she was with the agency; when she was 29, she was fired. At that point, she was drinking more than a quart of scotch a night. The following year, she began therapy.

During the 6 years she worked in advertising, Belinda lived alone. She maintained relationships with her four friends from boarding school and college, seeing one or more of them weekly, but, beyond that, had no friendships with women. Belinda also continued her pattern of nonsexually dating "nice" men while promiscuously sleeping with older men, many of whom were married, heavy drinkers whom she met in bars. Occasionally, she never learned the name of a man with whom she had spent the night. She had little contact with her parents through these years, and she periodically continued to cut herself and to binge and purge.

Shortly after she was fired from the advertising agency, one of her boarding school friends had a serious talk with her. This woman confronted her about her drinking, about the episodic bulimia, and about her sexual acting out, which Belinda's friend suspected despite Belinda's attempts to keep it a secret, even from herself. Something about this woman's concern moved Belinda; the next morning, she attended her first AA meeting. Over the next year, Belinda became well connected in AA, selecting and working with a caring sponsor. As she sobered up, she began to examine the chaos and contradictions in her life; she also started to experience disturbing physical sensations—her vagina contracted whenever she saw a bottle of scotch, she sometimes felt her thighs get big and swollen, and she became intensely nauseated at the smell of Old Spice men's cologne. Finally, she dissociated; she often felt numb and "spacy," with time taking on a dreamlike quality. An AA associate, who was an incest survivor, recommended that Belinda go into therapy. She decided to do so and obtained a therapist's name from another therapist who conducted an intake and suspected a sexually traumatic background.

Belinda was almost 30 when she presented for treatment. Despite the years of drinking and self-abusive behaviors, she was strikingly attractive. For a long time, she arrived for sessions dressed alternately in very tight jeans, high-heeled boots, and provocatively low-cut, usually red or black tops; in loose-fitting, pastel sweat suits that evoked in the therapist an association to children's playclothes; or in expensive, sharply tailored, "preppy" clothing. The therapist would later learn that these outfits reflected different parts of Belinda's ego organization and, in turn, bespoke shifting levels of functioning.

For the first 6 months of therapy, Belinda was in crisis. She was besieged by unsymbolized traumatic memories, body memories, and dissociative episodes that terrified and disorganized her. She wondered if she were going crazy. Often, the only way she could end a disturbing experience was to cut herself; this would temporarily return her to "normal" functioning. Transferentially, she sought in the therapist an omnipotent rescuer onto whom she could collapse and on whom she could depend to relieve her suffering. More subtly, she looked to the therapist to take control of her mind, body, and functioning so that she would not have to experience the pain and chaos with which she was trying to cope. The clinician responded to Belinda by assuring her that the disorganizing experiences she was having contained meaning, meaning that therapist and patient together could discover. Increasingly, these reassurances soothed her, reducing the panic she felt about the experiences.

It was primarily outside of the sessions that Belinda experienced dissociations, unsymbolized body memories, and intense affects. In the consultation room, the patient usually sat rigidly still, reporting these events with absolutely no affect. Split off from her feelings, Belinda conveyed the emotional wallop of her experiences through projective identification; it was the therapist who felt nauseous, terrified, spacy, and who had seemingly inexplicable physical sensations such as vaginal pain and contractions and perceived shifts in body size.

As Belinda became convinced that the therapist believed her experiences held meaning and indicated an ability to tolerate the power of that meaning, the patient began to associate to rather than simply report what was happening to her. When she did this, she started to recover the memories of her father's sexual abuse and her mother's hostile neglect. This occurred primarily through the emergence of a dissociated abused child imago.

It was during this period of treatment that the therapist realized that there were, in fact, three aspects to Belinda's organization of self. The adult patient, embodied in Belinda's preppy look, had only hazy, impressionistic memories of her traumatic past. Interpersonally isolated, highly intellectualized, affectless, it was this part of Belinda who had worked successfully, organized the financial side of her life, and dated "nice" men. A dissociated traumatized child ego state, concretely represented by Belinda's playclothes, was much more primitively organized than the adult patient; it was this part of Belinda that remembered the childhood traumas. Finally, an adolescent part of Belinda, bespoken by tight jeans and sexy tops, acted out the rage and hatred associated with the traumas. It was this aspect of Belinda that drank, cut, vomited, and engaged in dangerously promiscuous sex.

A typical session during this phase of treatment often included the sequential emergence of all three aspects of Belinda. The adult part of her usually arrived for session. Her primary transference to the therapist encapsulated a yearning for the clinician to make sense of her experiences, to think when she could not and to integrate for her that which was fragmented. At the same time, Belinda feared the therapist's very ability to penetrate the chaos and confusion that, after all, protected her from knowledge of her traumatic past. Both these transferences of the adult patient had a distant, intellectualized quality to which the therapist internally responded with distance and some indifference. Here, transference to the clinician as a hoped-for rescuer and an abuser was conveyed by the patient through an identification with and enactment of her internalized mother's unavailability. In turn, the therapist also felt mildly indifferent toward Belinda, repeating, albeit to a much lesser extreme, Belinda's mother's neglect.

When the dissociated abused child aspect of the patient emerged to verbalize and enact the trauma, more intense transference-countertransference constellations were set into play. There were two primary transferences of the abused child imago to the therapist. One was to the clinician as an idealized, omnipotent rescuer who would finally listen and alleviate the pain and terror inside which this child had long been trapped and isolated. To this transference, the clinician responded with intense feelings of wanting to save and nurture. Deeply moved by this abused child self's pain, neediness, and resiliency, the therapist often fantasized about mothering this aspect of Belinda.

Another transference of the dissociated traumatized child was to the therapist as victimizer, one more adult who would ultimately betray or abuse her. Most specifically, the child part of Belinda feared that the clinician would "make" her get closer to the patient's adult part. Acknowledging that as the ultimate therapeutic goal, the therapist felt like an abuser and betrayer of childlike trust. Sometimes, the therapist was tempted to abandon the analytic work by promising to care forever for the dissociated abused child. This, of course, also would repeat Belinda's father's insistence that his daughter remain tied to him in a way that precluded growth and autonomy.

Yet other transference-countertransference configurations coincided with the emergence and work with adolescent aspects of Belinda. Identified with the omnipotence, rage, and underlying terror enacted by both her parents, the adolescent part of the patient consciously and defensively viewed the therapist with contempt, as a bumbling, ineffectual intruder who only could "screw up the works" for her. Less consciously, the adolescent part of Belinda yearned for and simultaneously feared an adult figure who would set appropriate limits on her compulsive wrecking by helping her to contain and express her rage in more hopeful ways. In other words, the adolescent self longed to hope but, trusting no one other than herself, smashed hope in order to maintain control and to stave off a bitter, inevitable disappointment. This adolescent part of the patient also railed at the clinician who was experienced as trying to seduce Belinda into believing empty promises that healing could occur through the therapeutic work. In turn, the therapist frequently felt intimidated by the power of the adolescent self's rage and by the impressive array of acting-out behaviors this part of the patient displayed. When Belinda "proudly" displayed a fresh gouge she had inflicted on herself hours after the last session or "bragged" about sleeping with a newcomer to AA, thus enacting her father's abusiveness, the therapist experienced herself as viciously attacked, abused, helpless, and impotently enraged. On the other hand, when the clinician attempted to elicit cooperation and trust from Belinda, she often felt shamelessly seductive and wondered if, in fact, she was beguiling the patient with a promise of hope and healing on which she could never deliver.

As the adult Belinda became aware more fully of the heretofore dissociated child and adolescent aspects of her and became more conscious of their memories, motives, and defenses, she felt betrayed by the therapist who she experienced as forcing her to look at and work with memories and self and object representations of which she wanted no part. Why could not the clinician and the other parts of her just go away and leave her in peace? Frequently, the clinician identified with the hope the patient was afraid to feel and incongruently responded with optimism to the patient's pessimism and anger. Sometimes, this replicated Belinda's neglectful mother, narcissistically preoccupied with professional success, and thus out of touch with Belinda's internal states and affects.

In addition to the transferences and countertransferences between the therapist and each aspect of Belinda, there were transferences and countertransferences bespeaking each part's reactions to the others. For example, Belinda the adult utterly hated the little girl part of her, blaming her for the current pain and disorganization, as well as for the original abuse. Belinda wanted to "kill that kid right out of me." The child self, on the other hand, felt that Belinda the adult had betrayed her by growing up and, thus, could not be trusted. In session the child self would petulantly refuse to share her memories with her adult counterpart, feeling that the adult Belinda would only hold them in contempt as once her mother did. Belinda's adolescent self, on the other hand reacted to the child with a superior protectiveness. She agreed that the adult should stay out of the kid's life, asserting that she, the adolescent, would take care of both the child and herself. The child, on the other hand, feared the adolescent's rage and potential for acting out encapsulated within the adolescent aspects of the patient while respecting the feistiness of this part of Belinda. The adolescent self held the adult patient in complete contempt, berating her for her "wimpiness" and refusal to acknowledge the sexual abuse. The adult patient, at the same time, feared the intense rage and hatred embedded within more adolescent parts of her; Belinda the adult wanted to just let the adolescent self "be." It was the therapist's task and challenge to introduce each part of Belinda to the others in a new way, interpreting the motives, fears, pain, and defenses of each to the others.

At the end of about 4 years, the therapy entered a new phase. By now, the adult, child, and adolescent parts of the patient were acquainted and shared mental contents (e.g., traumatic memories, knowledge of each other's activities and moods). Although the patient was far from whole, disparate elements of her had achieved a modicum of acknowledgment and accommodation. The crisis period of extreme extratherapeutic dissociation and the recall of trauma through unsymbolized and body memories had passed. It seemed as if Belinda, now conscious of many aspects of her childhood abuse and neglect, once again put the sexual trauma to the side in order to more fully explore and work through her pre- and posttrauma relationship with her mother.

For a protracted period of time, Belinda's therapy centered on her relationship with her narcissistically involved, hostilely neglectful mother. During this phase of treatment, Belinda often identified with her internalized mother, withholding from and depriving the therapist. There were long silences on the part of the patient during which she deflected any attempt by the clinician to make contact. Frequently, the therapist felt ravenously hungry after a session and, in general, experienced herself as rejected, frustrated, and in despair at not being able to connect with Belinda. The therapist found herself working harder and harder to engage with her patient, countertransferentially enacting Belinda's attempts to elicit her mother's attention and involvement.

During this period of treatment, there was also a transference to the therapist as victim and as victimizer. Certain that she was incredibly toxic, Belinda recurrently fantasized that she was filled with small, filthy, black bugs that might crawl out onto her body, shocking and disgusting the therapist. The bugs represented remnants of the poisonous psychological feedings Belinda had received from both parents; she felt possessed by them and feared that they would frighten and disorganize the clinician as Belinda was once terrorized and rendered internally chaotic. When Belinda talked about her bugs, the therapist experienced a wish to rescue; she fantasized about cradling Belinda in her arms, gently picking off the bugs, or about allowing Belinda to vomit the bugs into the waste basket while she held her hair back out of her way.

Beneath the transference to the therapist as victim of Belinda's toxicity was, of course, a paranoid fear that the clinician, reacting to Belinda with disgust, would victimize the patient by abandoning her. In fact, Belinda sometimes verbalized her fear that the therapist would "throw (her) out of therapy." This transference included elements of the therapist as seductress, offering an availability and constancy that was tenuous and could be shattered, and of the clinician as hostile mother who would abusively abandon the patient to her bugs as her mother once abandoned her to her father. Sometimes, the therapist responded to these transferences as an omnipotent rescuer and felt guilty about such necessary "abandonments" as vacations or sick days. At other times, the clinician experienced herself as victimized by Belinda's implicit demand that she continously prove and reprove her willingness to stay in relationship with the patient for the duration of the treatment.

Toward the end of this phase of treatment, Belinda risked becoming more vulnerable with the therapist, explicitly expressing both loving and hateful feelings. Now, the clinician became in the transference a long yearned-for good-enough mother, neither ideal nor narcissistically neglectful. Belinda, at this point, seemed to move out of a paranoid/schizoid relationship with the therapist into a depressive position in which gratitude and disappointment could coexist, inform each other, and be openly expressed. The establishment of the therapist as a good-enough mother ushered in a phase of therapeutic work in which the sexual abuse was once again of paramount importance.

Signaling entry into this period of treatment was Belinda's repeated discussion of extratherapeutic interactions that were portrayed as abusive or, conversely, spoken of with a contempt that betrayed underlying fear of both their power and their attractiveness. At the same time, Belinda wondered why the therapist would want to work with incest survivors, suggesting that perhaps the clinician "got off on" stories of abuse. Sometimes, the therapist felt abusive and unnecessarily voyeuristic, and questioned her own motives for involving herself in this work. Belinda frequently expressed fury at and contempt for interventions she experienced as intrusive or as ridiculously impotent. Here, Belinda unconsciously bespoke an identification with her internalized mother, belittling the clinician as inadequate as Angela had once devalued Timothy. At another level, however, Belinda adaptively was giving voice to the fury at having been abused that she had never been able to convey openly during the childhood victimizations. Now, the adolescent aspect of her grew closer to the adult patient, as Belinda transferentially hurled hate and rage at the therapist rather than self-destructively acting it out. Although the power of Belinda's anger was impressive, the therapist was excited and enlivened by the patient's free verbalization of these feelings. It should be noted that, during this phase of treatment, Belinda would at times defensively retreat to enactment of transference reactions more reflective of her relationship with her mother.

As Belinda's working through of her fury waned, she entered a phase of intense mourning for her lost childhood, and new transference-countertransference paradigms were set into play.

During this period of treatment, Belinda acutely experienced the pain of her lost childhood, as well as the loss of her compensatory fantasied good parents. Now, the dissociated little girl became closer to the adult patient who keenly felt childlike neediness and bereavement. Belinda, at this point, reacted to the clinician as an evil seductress, who, promising healing and health, had stripped Belinda of her defenses, leaving her aware and alone. Also experiencing the therapist as a vicious abuser, Belinda accused her of taking control of an innocent patient and forcing her to face things that might have been better left untouched. The therapist, railed Belinda, knew what would happen if treatment went on, and now look at what had happened. Belinda's world was shattered. She knew too much. She knew more than she had ever wanted to know. And what, Belinda wanted to know, was the therapist going to do about all this. Now that she had robbed Belinda of her childhood and her defenses, how was the clinician going to make up for all this loss? Frequently, the therapist experienced the full measure of guilt that Belinda's parents should have felt for betraying, abusing, and negelcting her. She found herself fantasizing about all kinds of ways to make reparation, from bringing Belinda home with her to bake chocolate chip cookies, to planning trips to Disneyland that she and Belinda would share. It was difficult but, as the therapist knew, imperative to avoid truncating the patient's mourning process. At the same time, however, she encouraged Belinda to fantasize about and express ways in which she wanted the analyst to come through with reparation. Belinda and the therapist then played with these fantasies in session, with the clinician tacitly acknowledging the legitimacy of her patient's needs and relational strivings. Eventually, as Belinda's grief was worked through, the patient transferred her longings to appropriate extratherapeutic objects; she got a roommate, made new friends, and began dating an emotionally available and playful man, for the first time combining sexual and emotional intimacy in one relationship.

Now, another phase of treatment began during which Belinda experienced and reworked an oedipal conflict. During this period, Belinda's transference to the therapist was as a fantasied romantic partner, a possible abuser who would inappropriately put into action romantic fantasies, and as a potentially dangerous sexual competitor. Romantic feelings about the clinician were primarily communicated nonverbally, through looks, tone of voice, and small gifts of flowers and food. Derivatives bespoke Belinda's attraction to the therapist as pretty and full of life. The patient also more overtly expressed jealousy about other patients with whom she had to share the therapist and about the clinician's husband, who had not been mentioned by the patient until this time. Countertransferentially, the therapist delighted in Belinda's shyly expressed romance and felt protective toward the patient, wanting nothing to disrupt the natural unfolding of this work.

Derivatives, including references to a friend who had been sexually abused by a psychiatrist with whom she was in treatment, allowed the therapist to know that Belinda was unconsciously attuned to the clinician's reactions to her, alert to any signs that the therapist might sexually abuse her. This increased her sense of protectiveness toward Belinda.

At the same time that Belinda was engaging the therapist in an oedipal romance, derivatives suggested that she also was reacting to her as a potentially envious and dangerous competitor who would narcissistically crush her childlike sexuality. The clinician had a recurrent fantasy of herself as Snow White's wicked stepmother, so threatened by a child's loveliness that she was driven to have her killed.

Finally, at least in terms of the transference and countertransference issues discussed in these chapters, Belinda moved into a period of startlingly powerful adolescentlike sexuality, during which she seemed totally immersed in identifying and experimenting with herself as a sexual being. She arrived for sessions appropriately yet seductively dressed, sporting new perfumes, colors, hairstyles, and makeup. Her transference to the therapist vacillated between come-hither seductiveness, competition, and terror that the clinician would either cling to her possessively or reject her entirely.

Within the seductive transference to the therapist, Belinda's flirtations were more clearly sexually tinged than ever before, and she sometimes seductively draped herself on the couch, exposing more of her legs than usual. To this, the therapist responded with frank sexual arousal and wry amusement at the sexy teenager her once-terrified patient had become. At the same time, Belinda also competed with the clinician. She sometimes compared their outfits or hairstyles, subtly (or not so subtly!) devaluing the therapist as just not quite fashionably "with it." The therapist, in turn, found herself wondering if, in fact, it was not time for a new wardrobe and a makeover. In addition, the clinician experienced envy, but also appreciation, of Belinda's newfound sexual freedom and vitality; it was clear that, for the first time in her life, Belinda was finding comfort in her sexuality. Finally, Belinda openly expressed concern that the therapist disapproved of her deepening relationship with her boyfriend, indicating a fear of the clinician's potential possessiveness. Belinda also worried that the therapist might feel that she no longer needed therapy, thus abandoning her as her father once did. In fact, the clinician experienced deep satisfaction, albeit combined with a sense of loss and some envy, that Belinda was involved in a wonderful extratherapeutic romance. The therapist also recognized, however, that continued therapy would be needed for some time.

This clinical vignette presents examples of the emergence of various transference and countertransference configurations in the psychoanalytically oriented treatment of one adult survivor of childhood sexual abuse. It is necessarily somewhat schematic and does not reflect all the shifts, dramatic and subtle, that occurred over the course of an extensive treatment. We think, however, that the work with Belinda outlined here does provide the flavor of the myriad of relational paradigms with which the analyst is confronted in psychoanalytic treatment with this population.

CHAPTER 11

Technical Considerations in Treatment

IN EACH OF THE CHAPTERS presented thus far we have looked at the psychoanalytically oriented treatment of adult survivors of childhood sexual abuse from one of a series of different, often overlapping perspectives. At the risk of being occasionally redundant, such a format best communicates our belief that, although every treatment is a unique experience between patient and therapist, work with adult survivors involves the recapitulation of certain characteristic issues that the working clinician can come to anticipate with some degree of confidence. The manifestations of these issues as they emerge in the transference-countertransference unfolding serve the therapist as points of reference, beacons of light through the enshrouding fog of passionate, shifting, and endlessly mind-boggling reenactments as they occur in therapy. Ultimately, we hope to familiarize clinicians with the implications of certain therapeutic choice points, at a time when the capacity for quiet reflection and introspection are undisrupted by the heat of the transference-countertransference moment.

In this chapter and the next, we wish to move toward the evolution of a treatment model for psychoanalytically oriented work with adult survivors of childhood sexual abuse. In so doing we wish to shape a model that has the fluidity to move with the contours of each particular therapeutic interaction yet serve as an effective map for traversing what we have come to know as a particularly hazardous course. Although the map allows room for many routes via which different patient-therapist dyads can reach a common point, critical choices along the way must be made with an eye toward the strengths and weaknesses of the particular travelers, as well as the respectful recognition that each route involves the necessary negotiation of certain critical, equally precarious and potentially explosive obstacles.

We will begin with a review of the assumptions made throughout this book about the particular psychic organization of our patients, the nature of the therapeutic experience, and our beliefs about the mutative factors implicit in our notion of treatment. Where such a review becomes redundant to the reader, we apologize; we viewed such an attempt to synthesize and integrate the treatment recommendations scattered throughout this work as a pressing clinical need, worthy of some repetition.

Assumptions about the Patient

The adult survivor of childhood sexual abuse is a victim of chronic trauma that varies only by degree and is subject to all the long-term sequelae we have come to associate with PTSD and delayed PTSD, such as dissociation, sudden regression, disorganization of thought processes, visual and somatic representations of as-yet unformulated memory. We maintain that a psychoanalytically oriented treatment is the best way to resolve the now-internalized system of pathological identifications and counteridentifications that volley in dissociated form between therapist and patient with truly dizzying rapidity and to work through the reality/distorting/preserving system of defenses established to maintain a sense of integrity against overwhelming ego assault. However, such treatment needs to incorporate without exception a familiarity with clinical research on traumatic responses and to reach an accommodation between such contemporary research and the conduct of the psychoanalytic encounter.

Any such treatment must, above and beyond all else, take into account the primacy of dissociative mechanisms around which the adult survivor has organized her internal world. The separate and mutually exclusive organizations of particular aspects of self in relationship to often disparate representations of significant others emerges from the literature as the single most common way in which adult survivors attempt to recapture the perplexity born of the fact that their abusers and those who ignored or permitted their abuse were often, at other times and places, loving and beloved objects. Only through dissociation can the adult survivor find the capacity to maintain such irreconcilable and disparate experiences of significant others and to accommodate the representations of self that grow out of such polar experiences with others. The earlier the abuse, the more chronic the abuse, and the closer the relationship between abuser and victim, the more pervasive the dissociative structure of the personality will be.

Where such dissociation becomes the hallmark of personality organization, some, most, or all of the patient's memories of childhood sexual abuse come to be cordoned off into a separate internalized system of self and object representations that can then either be maintained unformulated and out of awareness or coexist in alternative, yet mutually exclusive, patterns of accessability to consciousness. These dissociated states also involve different affects, different levels of ego organization, and different physiological states incorporating the unsymbolized somatic representations of intense danger and the bodily memories of specific abuse. Such separately structured and dissociated states, organized around inescapable threats to the patient's ego integrity, prove to be particularly sensitive to external environmental triggers reminiscent of the original trauma. Certainly, the reenactment of early relational paradigms in the transference-countertransference experiences that unfold within psychoanalytic treatment can serve as powerful examples of such triggers, signaling the return of state-dependent memories unique to the traumatogenic experiences. The return of such experiences may occur as the accessibility of memories previously forgotten, but is equally as likely to involve a reenactment whose meaning will be formulated for the first time as the situation is interpreted by patient and therapist together.

The clinician unfamiliar with the return of such previously dissociated material may initially become alarmed by its particular qualities. Dissociated material intrudes disruptively and without apparent meaning. It has never been symbolized, and its appearance is unexpected, triggered by arbitrary and, at first, unidentified events. Such events may be external or part of the transference-countertransference enactment between patient and therapist. Either way, the manifestations are often intense, disruptive, only vaguely embedded in any kind of identifiably meaningful context, and are all too often confused with the early symptoms of a burgeoning psychotic process. The difficulty with such a formulation is that, in equating it with serious mental disturbance, therapist and family are often moved toward heroic efforts to recontain and silence the emergence of these alarming states, thus foreclosing for a second time on the all-important opportunity to establish meaningful connections between these experiences and past events. Hospitalization, excessive or inappropriate medication, even shock treatments have been used in well-meaning, though misguided, attempts to avoid what initially looked like a severe decompensation. Although we believe that medication and occasionally hospitalization may be necessary in helping the patient to effectively contain the reemergence of traumatic events, it is imperative for the success of the treatment that such efforts be made with a knowledge and understanding of dissociative processes, and in the spirit of containment—not foreclosure. In this chapter, as we focus on specific treatment strategies, we will consider ways in which the therapist can help the patient to contain such unbearable anxieties and, in so doing, facilitate the patient's availability for treatment. Such containment is a necessary precondition for further work but it is not in itself a goal of therapy.

Assumptions about the Therapist's Role

Our assumptions about the nature of the therapist's role in the treatment of adult survivors begin with the fundamental belief that such traumatic disruption in early object bonds as that which we have come to associate with childhood sexual abuse can only be ameliorated within the confines of an intense therapeutic relationship—specifically, the kind we know to occur in psychoanalysis and psychoanalytically oriented psychotherapy. Although the full, emotionally charged abreaction of traumatic memory is essential to successful treatment, we also know it to be insufficient in accomplishing the kind of long-term changes we seek in the patient's current interpersonal world. Such changes require not only a thorough recovery of otherwise dissociated traumatic object relationships and related fantasy—via the triggers embedded in transference-countertransference reenactments—but also a systematic working-through of the particular constellation of pathological defenses used by the patient to preserve some semblance of adequate external functioning despite the most intense forms of external and internal pressures.

The art of such a treatment rests with the therapist's capacity to strike an optimal balance between reworking the old and cocreating the new. Although we do not aim at reparenting the patient—in fact, regard such attempts as seriously inhibiting the mourning process intrinsic to our treatment model—we do consider the establishment of a safe holding environment against which passionate, often violent, enactments can safely occur to be imperative to therapeutic success. As Winnicott (1954–1955) believed that each baby required two mothers, "an environment mother" and "an object mother," we hold that each adult survivor of traumatic abuse requires two therapists: one who will, like the environment mother, hold, integrate, regulate, and modulate, and another who, like the "object mother," will survive the onslaught of intensely passionate and violent reenactments ultimately drawn upon herself.

By allowing for, even encouraging, such a dissociative split in the patient's experience of the transference, within transference-countertransference reenactments, therapists are capable of reproducing the same coexistent levels of meaning that define the adult trauma survivor's experience of both the internal object world and the external world of interpersonal relationships. Within such a construction of the analytic frame, analysts can evoke multiple, yet simultaneous, experiences of self and other that make possible the maintenance of an erratic and unpredictable but set course through the powerfully turbulent storm. As the "environment therapist" functions adequately in such a role, new structure-building experiences of other and self in relation to other are forged and internalized. This process occurs in synchrony with the most violently disruptive reenactments between patient and "object therapist" imaginable. It is, paradoxically, the moments of most savage and frenzied reenactment that speak to and strengthen the extraordinary holding powers of the adequately functioning "environment therapist." As the vehemence of each untamed crisis gives way to understanding born of active interpretive work, the patient is strengthened by the growing capacity to withstand and, ultimately, transcend. In seemingly endless progression, the self and object world are torn apart by traumatic reenactments, working toward the illusive reconfiguration of the old internal matrices, but always with the only vaguely perceptible presence of a secondary transference-countertransference constellation that holds, soothes, heals, and ultimately potentiates new, integrative organizations of such traumatically sundered internal representations. We believe that in such a way the age-old controversy between the therapist as creator of new and healthier experience and the therapist as interpreter of old and pathological experience can finally come together and coexist with fluid grace.

The Treatment Model

In chapter 1, we outlined five components we believe to be endemic to the treatment of adult survivors of childhood sexual abuse. Although we do not believe that such components involve specific and orderly stages of the work, we do believe that they comingle, moving in and out of positions of primacy as different issues take shape within the therapeutic interaction. These constituent elements are: (1) containment; (2) recovery and disclosure of traumatic memories and fantasied elaborations; (3) symbolization and encoding of memory and experience; (4) integration of disparate self and object systems and of other reality-distorting defenses; and (5) internalization of a new object relationship.

Containment

One defining feature of work with patients who suffer from previously dissociated aspects of traumatic states is the psychologically and physiologically mediated states of terror and hyperarousal that repeatedly flood attempts at therapeutic clarification. The activation of such regressive states of disorganization and confusion by unidentified conditioned stimuli in the environment and within therapy renders the patient unavailable for the kinds of ego-mediated, cognitive interventions relied on in traditional psychoanalytic work. The resurgence of such uncontained states of hyperarousal during the course of treatment are concretely experienced by the patient as retraumatizations by the therapist who stands by, apparently ineffectually, while the patient is overwhelmed by the same states of meaningless terror that once accompanied experiences of abuse. Such perceived helplessness on the part of the therapist reinvokes the image of the ineffectual parent who could do nothing to protect her child from extreme forms of abuse. Interpretations, at such times, are at best ineffective and at worst are experienced as foreign and hostilely motivated penetrations of the patient by the therapist/abuser in the transference-countertransference enactment. In either case, such regressive states of confusion, disorientation, terror, and hyperarousal render the patient unavailable for analytically oriented interventions.

Clearly, the therapist must be active in helping the patient to contain such disorganizing and repetitive experiences of terrifying regression. Such activity, we believe, involves the action of both the "environment" therapist and the "object" therapist. Ultimately, it becomes the task of the "environment" therapist, facilitating emotional and cognitive availability on the part of the patient, that will allow the treatment to progress from interventions aimed at symptom abatement to those focusing on insightful reconstruction and interpretation of the abusive and counterabusive reenactments in the transference and countertransference. As the "environment therapist" helps to contain and achieve cognitive availability on the part of the patient, the "object therapist" draws to herself the recapitulation of toxic introjects, working from the inside to diffuse via reenactment and active interpretation their reality-distorting potential. Therapists are always shifting between "holding" from the outside and reworking from the inside; between the background of containment and integration and the foreground of active interpretation of transference-countertransference paradigms, ever conscious of the patient's struggle to contain traumatic levels of highly sexualized overstimulation. This is by no one's standards an easy task, especially as one of the defining features of "trauma" rests in its pernicious and tenacious assault on the experienced integrity and survival of self. However, the struggle to maintain a sense of control during the recapitulation of abusive childhood traumas does persist as a thematic subtext throughout the course of such turbulent treatments. It falls to the therapist undertaking this work to play both melody and harmony in concert with the patient's as yet unstudied attempts at a counterpoint duet.

In the end, the new, intense, and trusting bond between patient and therapist—that which survives and emerges out of the maelstrom of relentlessly hazardous exposure to transference-countertransference challenges and threats—will, it is hoped, come to serve as the most reliable and intransigent buffer between the patient and her world of traumatic objectlessness. Internalization of the therapeutic relationship will forever change the patient's internal system of self and object representation organized around traumatic memories. For, as these memories are reenacted and worked through with the therapist, they no longer exist in the world of isolation and despair that was for so long the home of the abused child. However, such steadfastness of object constancy in the face of the kinds of therapeutic interactions we have described is a goal of the treatment, not a bedrock of the therapeutic process either at its initial stages or as it traverses some of the dangerous terrains to be anticipated.

Certain specific interventions can be helpful when the holding functions of treatment and of the therapist are strained to the limits. (Any therapeutic attempts to enhance the patient's experience of control, mastery, and competence in the face of terrifying disorganization can only facilitate the therapy.)

Certainly, the analyst must learn extreme patience, allowing the patient to control the timing and progression of reconstructive work, as she struggles to keep anxiety and panic within tolerable limits. Seen as the concrete symbolic embodiment of the abusing other, the analytic process must not be allowed to overtake the patient's ego-coping mechanisms. At first, the responsibility for timing and pacing lies with the therapist, but one of the therapeutic tasks is the slow and steady relinquishment of this ego function. By assisting the patient to time and control the emergence of traumatic memory, the treatment process symbolically speaks to the patient's growing capacity to control and set limits for her abuser. Such control is often further enhanced by helping the patient to anticipate when the return of certain memories or the reenactment and interpretation of certain events in the treatment situation may trigger a period of particularly regressive experiences. For example, memories themselves can become equated in the patient's mind with the powers of the abusive other; certain therapeutic strategies can help to contain the disorganization that often accompanies memory.

Amelia was a 29-year-old law student whose treatment had focused on a prolonged period of rather sadistic sexual abuse at the hands of her maternal grandfather. Between the ages of 5 and 7, when her family had been forced to move in with her maternal grandparents, Amelia's grandfather had terrified and overwhelmed the child by insisting on various forms of painful sexual contact. The patient never told her parents or her grandmother, as she was unwilling to destroy what she described as an otherwise close-knit family; and although she remembered the fact of the abuse, she had been unable thus far to recall specific incidents with full emotional accessability during therapy. Her experience, however, was that her grandfather's presence had dominated her life, that "even the happiest times were infused with his dangerous and powerful presence."

Amelia's upcoming wedding to a fellow classmate was scheduled one month prior to the time in treatment to be described. Approximately a year earlier, her fiancé had been diagnosed with a life-threatening illness that required extensive surgery and a long recuperative process. As the surgery had been judged a complete success and the doctors had just announced Amelia's fiancé to be entirely "disease free," the upcoming wedding was likely to be a singularly joyous occasion in the patient's life, a dual celebration for the couple and for the families involved.

As the day of her wedding approached, Amelia became plagued by a series of nightmares that began to portend the reemergence of many of the specific memories that she had sought in her treatment. As one would expect, her moods became erratic, her nights sleepless, her anxiety was reaching unmanageable limits, and she was plagued by vague yet painful and inexplicable somatic symptoms. The therapist was in a quandary. Clearly, the analytic work was moving toward the recovery of some critical material, and yet the timing of this "breakthrough" could not have been worse. The patient herself felt what she described as an "urgent, driven pressure to continue remembering, whatever the cost!" It was the therapist who ultimately had to call a moratorium of sorts on the work of recovering traumatic memories, reminding the patient that somehow her grandfather's presence had ruined so many significant and potentially happy moments for her. "It's as if the grandfather within you has planned the return of these memories; he cannot allow you this uniquely joyous time without somehow exerting his presence on the proceedings." The therapist went on to add, "We have so much time after the wedding, after your honeymoon; why not wait. Why not tell your grandfather that we are not going to let him spoil this occasion like he's spoiled so many others?" The patient began to cry quietly. She clenched her fists as if ready for a fight, saying only, "That's right, this is mine . . . this is mine."

While the patient was away, she sent the therapist a brief note: "There was a lurking presence; the hint of a shadow. He was there, but only in the background. It was clear that for the first time I had the upper hand; I had to be aware, stay in control . . . but in the end the day belonged to me." When the patient returned, she had no difficulty resuming the work that had been interrupted in this way. Indeed, the work seemed easier; the patient was in more control of dosing and containing traumatic memories; and there were fewer times when she became overwhelmed and disorganized by them.

In most situations, such a complementary and shifting focus on containment and interpretation will be sufficient in dealing with the emerging clinical material. However, where the abuse was particularly overwhelming to the child, either because of a particularly sadistic process, a particularly early onset, or because of the nature of the relationship between victim and abuser, the patient and therapist may be unable to fend off the disorganization and regression that accompany any attempt to deal with this material. Here the therapist must resort to other techniques that will enhance the patient's sense of control and prevent the experience of retraumatization.

We have found that many patients do well with a combination of behavioral and psychoanalytic techniques. Although we do not recommend the use of hypnosis by the therapist in facilitating disclosure, as this is often viewed by the patient as a form of therapeutic domination and invasive contol and has proven to be unnecessary in facilitating the disclosure of traumatic memories, it has been our experience that such techniques can be used *by the patient* to enhance her experience of control and containment (Spiegel, 1986). The patient is taught any of a number of deep-relaxation exercises, processes akin to self-hypnotic techniques, that promote a form of physical and mental self-control and sense of well-being and can be used before, during, and after the disclosure of traumatic memories. In a typical case, the therapist chooses a relaxation technique and teaches it to the patient in session until it can be used effectively to help the patient to modulate gradually escalating degrees of anxiety, working up, eventually, to experiences of sexualized traumatic overstimulation. This technique can also be used by the patient outside of therapy in dealing with uncontrollable flashbacks and experiences of panic secondary to such flashbacks. It is important that the therapist explain the relaxation technique as a process designed to enhance the patient's self-control. It empowers the patient to do clinical work without an experience of disorganization and retraumatization that otherwise could not be done. If the process is used only to help the patient to control this anxiety and later on to more effectively shut down the repetitive flashbacks that plague her extratherapy hours, it is not likely to arouse a paranoid suspicion of violation and attempted control. If it is attempted too early, or if the therapist is less than scrupulous in the ways such techniques are used, it may have the effect of fortifying the patient's paranoid defenses, and prevent further clinical work. If used effectively, self-hypnosis can serve a crucial role in preventing unnecessary regression, avoiding the need for excessive medication or even hospitalization during the working-through process.

Although the specifics of such techniques are well beyond the scope of this book, many excellent texts describe the use of behavioral techniques in the treatment of PTSD (see, for example, Spiegel & Spiegel, 1978). We recommend that analytically trained clinicians working with adult survivors of any childhood trauma familiarize themselves with these methods and think through before the need arises any resistances they may have to using them in the context of an analytically oriented treatment. In working with adult survivors, crises emerge erratically and unpredictably; and there are many occasions in which some nontraditional parameter must be used to fend off a complete decompensation. Schooling the patient in noninvasive, deep-relaxation techniques prior to the crisis often gives the clinician a relatively benign way of helping the patient to cope with the panic without foreclosing on the emergence of the problematic clinical material.

Within the context of a psychoanalytically oriented treatment, such exercises can be used to serve another, primarily symbolic function. If patient and therapist have worked together in achieving the kind of deep relaxation that can facilitate the emergence and containment of traumatic memory, the exercise itself will come to symbolically evoke the therapist's presence at critical times when she is not available to the patient. The ability to symbolically evoke the therapist's presence, particularly at times of crisis but also between sessions, in the middle of the night, during vacations, and so on, fortifies a growing capacity for object constancy that renders the traumatic isolation of the abused child less toxic. As the patient becomes increasingly able to evoke the therapist's symbolic presence at times of intense hyper-arousal, she is assuming responsibility for her own psychic survival and is, by so doing, also addressing the often desperate dependency she feels on the therapist—in and of itself a source of dangerous overstimulation.

Adequate containment also involves dealing in a protective way with the patient's violent, self-abusive, and suicidal threats. Failure to do so involves a reenactment of the role of the denying and unseeing parent, but attempts at too strident an intervention suggest experiences of domination and inva-sive control. Either contribute to a decreased experience of safety and con-tainment for both patient and therapist and threaten to abruptly terminate the therapeutic endeavor through transference or countertransference acting out. In addition to the active transference-countertransference interpretation required to identify the place of such violence in the psychic equilibrium of abused patients, the relaxation techniques offer the patient a concrete substi-tute for the sedating, self-regulatory aspects of self-abusive behaviors de-scribed in chapter 7.

When all else fails, the therapist must be ready to use medication and, ul-timately, hospitalization to contain the patient's unbearably painful or vio-lent and self-abusive behaviors. Many medications can be effective in help-ing to contain experiences of panic, dissociation, and depression (Courtois, 1988, van der Kolk, 1988;), and active research continues with new drugs and new applications of already available substances. A psychiatric consul-tation may be necessary when states of traumatic hyperarousal become un-manageable; however, the referring clinician should make sure that the psy-chiatrist chosen is familiar with the treatment of traumatic stress disorders and capable of adequately differentiating them from other psychotic processes.

Where hospitalization becomes unavoidable, the therapist should make sure that this occurs at a facility where she will be able to continue treating the patient in concert with the hospital's treatment team. It is almost un-avoidable that the patient will view such a hospitalization as a therapeutic abandonment in which the therapist was either unwilling or unable to tri-umph over the patient's internalized abuser; and in which, simultaneously, via dissociative processes, the patient was cast out by an angry therapist, dis-appointed with the patient's therapeutic efforts. Only a continuing therapeu-tic accessability will maximize the potential value of a brief hospitalization and allow for the interpretation of these transference-countertransference patterns. Where the inpatient team views the patient's hospitalization as a therapeutic failure, so informing the patient and preventing continued con-tact between patient and therapist, such transference-countertransference distortions are reinforced and dissociative processes strengthened. Though therapeutic failures will undoubtedly be seen by inpatient teams, a working familiarity with the kinds of transference-countertransference paradigms enacted by adult survivors must be used to evaluate the patient's and the therapist's representation of the events leading up to hospitalization and to prevent a possible premature, abortive, and ultimately destructive cessation of the ongoing treatment. Whenever possible, the inpatient treatment team can serve as consultant to the therapist-patient dyad, attempting to clarify the problematic aspects of their interaction and, in so doing, "unsticking" the embeddedness of the transference-countertransference enmeshment that may have precipitated the hospitalization. Such cooperation, consultation, and, when necessary, training and supervision are almost always preferable to a new referral for the patient. Although necessary on occasion, the traumatic potential of such a move should always be a factor in the deliberation of the hospital team. Asking a patient to choose between an old and a new therapist, or forcing a patient to turn against an ambivalently loved former therapist are situations replete with the potential for unnecessary retraumatization.

Recovery and Disclosure of Memories and Fantasied Elaborations

Recovery and disclosure of memories are obviously among the most significant aspects of work with adult survivors of childhood sexual abuse. Although it is not in itself sufficient in accomplishing the kinds of necessary long-term characterological changes in the internal organization of the patient's self and object world, it is nonetheless the bedrock of therapeutic action. There is some controversy in the field about how to best promote the return of pathogenic memory. It is our contention that the elusively shifting interplay in the transference-countertransference configurations played out between patient and therapist remain the most powerful way to potentiate the reemergence of traumatically dissociated experience. If allowed to wend their way unrestricted through the internal map of the patient's and therapist's memory, experience, and fantasy pool, all forms of long-forgotten or unformulated history will be recreated within the analysis. In such a transitional arena, the potential is unlimited, shaped only by the unconscious, dissociated, and unformulated aspects of experience contained within the bounds of the particular patient-therapist dyad.

Cognitive psychologists posit that memories are often state-dependent; that is, they can only be retrieved under conditions reminiscent of those in which the experience was first embedded. How then to recreate an experience of traumatic child abuse without retraumatizing the patient? Is this possible? An infinite number of memories are systematically encoded and organized around separate categories of self- and object-related experiences and will emerge into consciousness if such a self and object constellation is triggered by some internal or external event. Such triggers, frequently intense and passionate, often outwardly meaningless and arbitrary, are best unearthed in the free, open, and mutual play between patient and therapist. It is inherent in the process that trauma, when trauma there is, will impress the particularities of its template on the malleable surface of the analytic experience; that it will be embossed there, in stark relief for those familiar with its interpersonal imprint, as its manifestations emerge in specific, trauma-related transference-countertransference paradigms.

In assessing the role of the therapist in psychoanalytically oriented treatment of adult survivors, it is impossible not to respond to current controversies regarding the reliability of early memories and the subtle ways in which therapists can suggest certain formulations that, via the power of the transference, become unconsciously incorporated into the patient's personal narrative (Loftus, 1992). Reconstruction of any kind in analytic work must take into account the therapist's transferentially derived power to dangerously distort and misshape the patient's evolving understanding of personal history. Likewise, one should not underestimate the primary importance of fantasied elaborations of the traumas suffered by victims of childhood sexual abuse. Nor is it an easy matter to untangle memories from their fantasy-imbued versions. However, fantasied elaborations of traumatic memories most often evolve from the real event, rather than from the transformation of instinctual drives, and they are designed to protect in some way the patient's internalized self and object relations. Our position on the issue may be one of emphasis; when listening to what our patients say, we attune ourselves to the traumatic experiences endured, rather than turning our ears primarily toward the fantasies elaborating the facts. In so doing, we remember that we are working with people who as children often disclosed their abuse to an adult who ignored, vilified, or disbelieved them. Although in the end both fantasy and reality must be analyzed, we feel that these patients need therapists who are prepared to hear and bear witness with them to the reality of their horrific childhood experiences.

It is nevertheless important to make perfectly clear our position that it is *never the therapist's task to tell the patient that she was sexually abused.* Analysts cannot tell their patients what did or did not happen to them. We have no special capacity to see into the past. The most elegant reconstructions can be wrong. Analysts are often made anxious by stories of abuse, because they presume that it is their task to distinguish what actually happened from fantasied elaborations. In truth, this is impossible.

Any reconstruction that includes childhood sexual abuse can arise only out of the therapeutic reenactment within the transference-countertransference paradigms, observed jointly by therapist and patient in their shared roles as actors in and observers of their own unfolding drama. It is the patient's task to discover and define personal meaning. As we attend to the pathological defenses and disruptions in reality-testing functions secondary to early trauma, the patient becomes a more acute observer of this process and stands ready to believe in her own explanatory constructions. Such a construction, which includes the possibility or even the likelihood of traumatic sexual abuse, will emerge out of the unfolding treatment. It must not be the therapist's veiled agenda to lead the patient to such a determination.

As analysts, we are open to what we hear; we reflect without prejudice the possibility of certain explanatory reconstructions; we presume an intermingling of reality and fantasy in all of our patients' communications. We also, however, bring to our work a knowledge of developmental processes and of the long-term consequences of childhood abuse, and a familiarity with the appearance of dissociation in clinical work and the inextricable link between dissociation and child abuse. We learn to identify certain symptoms as we listen to our patients' narratives, and, finally, we watch with great care the emergence of the transference-countertransference reenactments that we have come to associate with histories of traumatic childhood abuse. In short, we become increasingly informed and thoughtful about those phenomena and processes that should alert us to the possibility of traumatic abuse. In the end, we listen with a different ear to our patients' associations and stand ready, when necessary, to validate the experiences that emerge honestly from the analytic work.

The Symbolization and Encoding of Experience

Throughout the complex task of helping the patient to piece together the dissociated fragments of her personal history, the clinician must remember that truly traumatic memories are rarely, if ever, semantically encoded in memory. As described so many times, most memories of childhood sexual abuse recur as intrusive eidetic imagery, strange and inexplicable mood shifts, undiagnosable somatic complaints, dissociative episodes, ideational and or emotional flooding with only vague and seemingly arbitrary precipitants. The more terrifying and sadistic the abuse, the more confidently one can make this statement, because fear itself comes to mediate the forms of regressive disorganization that render verbal capabilities inoperative. This phenomenon can be accounted for along a multidimensional axis.

It is as if the memories of abuse and the entire system of self and object representations organized around those memories come to be trapped, encased within a wordless world. In the first place, the actuality of the sexual abuse is rarely, if ever, spoken of between victim and abuser—and certainly not in the wider family, where it threatens to destroy the entire familial system. The patient is warned repeatedly that only continued silence will guarantee the continuity of the family as she knows it and her continued existence within its protective embrace. With the victim's survival at stake the victim's continued secrecy is all but assured. In addition, sexual abuse usu-

ally occurs at night, when the patient is already in a somnolent, dreamlike state; and it is, therefore, never clearly differentiated from dream states, hypnogogic states, and fantasy states. Darkness, wordlessness, and the extreme discontinuity of the patient's object world as it appears in this form compared to its more protoypical daytime personification also contribute to the profound sense of unreality, an unreality that defies verbal representation.

It is, therefore, unusual for adult survivors of childhood sexual abuse to be able to recall their experiences in a clearly articulated form. The psychologically and physiologically mediated forms of terrifying hyperarousal, often perversely sexualized, give rise to an ego regression and subsequent disorganization that make linguistic symbolization of experience virtually impossible. The images are, therefore, hidden, like embedded pictures, in the intricately woven pattern of clinical material, more easily articulated as foreground against background when the observer is relatively familiar with the patterns that may emerge. In the absence of words, such patterns leave their mark on the analytic relationship, creating a steady flow of traumatic reenactment in this arena. Via projective-introjective mechanisms, actively potentiated by the inaccessability of language, patient and therapist alternate in their roles as subject and object, as victim abuser, savior, and neglectful other.

It is only as traumatic scenarios replay themselves within the analyic relationship that meaning can emerge out of the chaos and panic of continuously frenzied reenactments. Between patient and therapist, words can finally be used to represent the activity that replays itself between them with such consistency; words can likewise be used to provide meaningful links between these reenactments and the events, as well as the possible events, of the patient's past. As past and present are brought together, each elucidating the other, the intrusive imagery, extreme mood shifts, somatic symptoms, and so on that have plagued the patient's life with meaningless suffering can at last be placed within a contextual frame bearing on internalized relations and their contemporary external manifestations. The first therapeutic task is, thus, not simply the analysis of fantasied elaborations of actual instances of sexual abuse but also, insofar as that abuse is traumatic, the forging of historical and interpersonal intelligibility out of overwhelming chaos and disorder. The construction of meaning must here precede its analysis. Therapist and patient together must learn to listen to an unfamiliar language of images, moods, and somatic experiences—a language, in large part, strange and unfamiliar to practicing psychoanalysts. Patient and therapist together must also come to believe in the notion that such phenomena are as much a part of the memories that must be woven together as are those the patient can verbalize. Memories that recur in the form of recurring intrusive images, mood shifts, night terrors, bodily sensations, and so on are simply manifestations of experience that have been mentally preserved in a different way and at a point in time when appropriate words failed.

The importance of verbally encoding and symbolizing the kinds of experiences that overwhelm many survivors of childhood abuse cannot be overemphasized. Ultimately words must be found to describe and make sense of these moments. Such semantic symbolization must facilitate the patient's capacity for self-reflective awareness, ultimately serving to reinforce her profoundly incapacitated sense of reality. For how can we expect the patient to believe in something about which she has never been able to speak? Such a process also facilitates communication between the dissociated aspects of the patient's world. That system of internalized representations of self and other, existing within the context of ongoing abuse and dissociatively split off from the rest of consciousness, can at long last speak of the terror, the betrayal, the loss of control, and even at times the loss of consciousness. Such experiences can be shared with another internalized system dissociatively shut off from this knowledge and with a therapist, who, by her very presence and empathic resonance, stands ready to relive the devastating and unfathomable experience of horrifying aloneness endemic to the traumatogenic ordeal. It is only via the use of language that such debilitating breaches of consciousness and of experiencing self and other can be mended.

Another issue is the omnipotent destructiveness with which many incest survivors imbue their words. Because the patient has maintained such a painful silence about her abuse, over so many years under the threat of exposure, retaliation, or expulsion from the family unit, her words themselves become symbolically infused with fantastically intensified potential for destructiveness and devastation. The patient believes that speaking of the abusive events carries in the present the same power to destroy her world that it did when she was a completely dependent child. As patient and therapist name together the traumatic events and those who perpetrated them, as they express the rage, helplessness, and terror, at the same time working through associated experiences of guilt and fantasied participation, words become divested of their power to destroy. Again, there is a shoring up of the critical distinction between the symbolic and the actual. As the therapeutic pair survive the use of such angry words directed at the abuser, they can begin to direct angry words at each other, as well, without the previously ubiquitous dread of abandonment or annihilation.

Running parallel to our emphasis on symbolization is the equally compelling proviso that the words chosen must be the patient's own—carefully selected, always subject to change and reformulation. The therapeutic process, like a piece of sculpture, brings the patient ever closer to a final construction with which she can feel satisfied; but the work remains "in progress" for some time. We remain cognizant here that each word spoken between patient and therapist captures a piece of the patient's nightmarish world; yet, in so defining experience, it also limits that which can be understood through the analytically experienced and understood illusion.

Integration of Dissociated Self and Object Systems

One of the primary goals of working with adult survivors of childhood sexual abuse from a psychoanalytic position is the opportunity of working through via transference-countertransference reenactment and interpretation the split-off systems of self and object representation secondary to traumatic childhood abuse. Although the literature on traumatic responses makes clear the undeniable association between trauma and dissociation, most of the treatment literature focuses on the need to help the patient to recover memories of the abusive situations. However, although such recovery of traumatic memory is necessary, it is barely sufficient to accomplish the necessary character changes in interpersonal functioning and inner harmony which we seek. Our position remains that traumatic abuse results in the dissociation not only of memories but of the entire system of complicated self and object representations associatively linked to those chronic abusive circumstances. It is the enactment, semantic encoding, and ultimate working-through of these internal matrices of self and object that account for true and long-lasting structural change for adult survivors. The patient must ultimately come to understand not only what happened but also how those events became a template for the internal organization of all subsequent experience.

We are often asked about the place of hypnosis in the recovery of traumatic memories. We have several concerns and believe that our treatment strategy of evoking traumatic memories through the triggers embedded in the transference-countertransference enactments offers a preferable alternative. It is our experience that trancelike states emerge naturally and regularly in working with adult survivors of childhood abuse. After all, dissociation is a state of trance, and it has become a very natural and central aspect of the adult survivor's defensive armamentarium. As specific transference-countertransference paradigms related to the abusive circumstances are reenacted during therapy, the patient will gently fall into such states without the introduction of any artificial induction. After all, the transference itself is an alteration of consciousness that permits illusion to temporarily preempt an interpersonal reality.

On the other hand, the dangers of using a formal hypnotic induction procedure are complex. Surely, the patient would feel invaded by a powerful and disarming force. The relinquishment of control could be reexperienced as a traumatic submission to the all-powerful therapist/abuser, and the recovery of memory as yet another violation of mind and body. Memory must emerge only as the patient sees fit and feels ready. She must feel herself to be in control of the process of recovering memories. Indeed, one of the most problematic aspects of flashbacks to abusive situations is that they tend to flood the patient's experience and leave her feeling invaded by intruding and uncontrollable thoughts. It is the therapeutic task to help the patient to feel more in control, so that memories can reemerge slowly and be reintegrated into the patient's experience. Techniques that try and overcome such defenses can only fail, even if they offer an initial appeal to patient and therapist alike. Our use of hypnosis is thus restricted to deep-relaxation techniques described above, techniques designed to enhance rather than overwhelm the patient's capacity to contain the reemergence of traumatic memory.

Internalization of a New Object Relationship to the Therapist

Underlying our philosophy of treating adult survivors of childhood abuse is a more broad-based therapeutic belief that memories of all kinds are ultimately organized around the significant object-related experiences of an individual's life. It is, therefore, a natural extension of this perspective to believe that the soothing, undoing, and redoing that must be accomplished with adult survivors can only proceed and be internalized in the context of a significant object relationship between patient and therapist. Traumatic memories can be "abreacted," but abusive relationships cannot be so easily excised.

It is extremely important that the therapist working with an adult survivor understand that, by dint of his very presence, the original traumatogenic situation is altered. As the therapist bears witness to the reemergence of traumatic memory, as he validates the patient's memories as they resonate with his own countertransference experiences, as he helps to demystify the sense of unreality that pervades the patient's waking experiences, he permanently alters the survivor's experience that pain, fear, and rage can only be safely experienced in isolation. In an abusive home, the child's helplessness is ensured by the flooding of internal resources and the unavailability of auxiliary ego support within the family. Where there is someone to listen, to share, to confirm, and ultimately to assist with containment, the pathognomic effects of such helpless solitary confinement become reconfigured.

Within this therapeutic relationship between patient and therapist, it is not only the past that is reworked but a future prematurely foreclosed that is once again reopened. We witness a growing capacity to resonate with the emotional timbre of significant other; to trust in their essential goodness, at the same time that anger, envy, greed, and other negative feelings can be experienced and known as essential aspects of interpersonal contact without the fear of destroying or being destroyed. We also see the willingness to know and be known by the other without the disorganizing anxiety secondary to an experience of hostile penetration. To touch and be touched by, to move and be moved by, to influence and be influenced by, can all, once again, or perhaps for the first time, emerge as significant aspects of the interpersonal negotiations by dint of which we all strive to carve out a safe sanctuary in our otherwise anonymous worlds.

The reemergence and containment of traumatic memories; the symbolic formulation and verbal encoding of these memories; the integration of previously irreconcilable self and object representations organized around these traumatic experiences; and the participation and ultimate internalization of the all-important self and object representations organized around the analyst all are essential aspects of the therapeutic work to be done. We are reminded of a particularly lucid effusion of primary process, uttered by a highly intelligent, schizophrenic woman with whom one of the authors had been working. Following a particularly moving session in which both patient and therapist had felt riveted to the material emerging, the patient got up to leave with the following words: "Well, thank you, doctor. . . . You certainly have given me food for thought . . . or maybe it would be more accurate to say thought for food. . . . Oh, I don't know which it is . . . probably both. . . . What I'm trying to say is that, today, we certainly did some good work together, you and I."

CHAPTER 12

Concluding Thoughts: Theoretical Implications and Reconsiderations

A YOUNG WOMAN sits in her therapist's office. She is in her late twenties, depressed, slumped over, relatively expressionless, and, as usual, rather noncommunicative. She is overweight, sloppily groomed, and untidily dressed. Her speech is garbled and her words almost inaudible. The therapist struggles with her own sense of hopelessness and frustration. The patient is enormously successful at a job that requires her to be both articulate and intellectually disciplined; yet, in the therapy hours, she is almost intolerably slow and obtuse. The patient has been coming twice a week for over 6 months, and, yet, the therapist believes that she knows little about this woman's life. She has tried any number of ways to engage with her patient, but all efforts have failed. There seems to be little she can do but wait.

Suddenly, the patient leans forward; her eyes begin to fill with tears; she emits a plaintive sigh and opens her mouth as if to speak. The therapist is aware that her heart has begun to beat a little faster, that she leans slightly forward in her own chair, striving to meet her patient's unconscious expression of diminishing distance with excited anticipation. Perhaps, this will be the moment. A second, fleeting though it may be, of some authentic emotional engagement. A revelation, perhaps that will reward her for the long months of oppressive and deadening isolation. The therapist feels alive for the first time in this session, as she strains to catch those first precious words.

For a moment, there is eye contact between patient and therapist. An ephemeral fusion of genuine need and therapeutic receptivity. An experience that will clearly not go unmarked by the two participants in this endeavor. But just at this moment of precise emotional complementarity, the tide begins to recede. The therapist watches in horrifying disbelief as the patient's eyes reabsorb her tears, just at the instant they promise to spill over and resuscitate the parched analytic interior. The patient sighs again, vehemently shaking her head, "No," and slumps back in her chair. She turns to her therapist, again establishing a fleeting eye contact, and in that second communicates the pain of a lifetime filled with endless numbers of such failed attempts. The therapist herself feels close to tears.

During the next year of treatment, such exchanges repeat themselves in monotonous, wavelike, almost hypnotizing repetitions of this unverbalized pattern; long, unbroken periods of dejection and withdrawal, made tolerable only by such fleeting yet tantalizing windows of access to the patient's palpable pain and longing. Experiences of hopelessness, despair, engagement, and arousal, fatigue, boredom, guilt, and reengagement localize themselves alternately in the inner experience of patient and therapist, switching perspectives with a dizzying rapidity. Because they exist to a large degree outside the dialog of this treatment, which remains focused on gaining access to the patient's past life and on understanding how these past experiences inform the present transference manifestations, such parallel experiences of transference and countertransference, embedded as they are in the present, remain virtually unformulated. This, despite the fact that the intense emotional valence carried by such experiences contains the only shared reality that exists between patient and therapist.

In an effort to remain therapeutically alive and engaged, the therapist initiates a series of three consultations, which parenthetically and retrospectively seem to mirror the unfolding trends in psychoanalytic theory. The first supervisor listens with growing concern that the therapist's active attempts to engage the patient in a dialog have unwittingly provided the patient, in identification with her aggressor, with an ever-ready venue for manipulative control and sadistic frustration of the therapist, essentially, a negative therapeutic reaction in the form of a sadomasochistic deadlock. This consultant recommends increasing the patient's sessions to three times a week, insisting that she use the couch, and limiting the therapist's participation significantly, thus reestablishing what he terms, "the temporarily lost atmosphere of therapeutic neutrality and abstinence." From the vantage point of the present, we might partially agree with the supervisor's assessment of the clinical situation, but understand his prescription to represent a countertransferentially induced counterattack on the patient, given credibility by its embeddedness in conventional classical technique.

The second consultant is empathically tuned in to this patient's endless search for and destruction of hope in the therapeutic relationship. She is impressed with what she sees as the gross deficiencies in this patient's early life (though relatively little is recalled) and speaks to the need for a therapeutic holding environment that will facilitate the emergence of developmentally delayed ego capacities and of experiences of self in gratifying relation to another. She emphasizes the importance of remaining empathically involved with the patient's struggle and being particularly alert to the kinds of countertransferentially spurred retaliatory responses she believes to be indicated by the first supervisor's recommendations.

The therapist is now completely bewildered. Both consultants have many years of teaching experience and are well respected in the analytic community; yet, it appears that they have recommended diametrically opposite courses of treatment. The therapist herself feels uncomfortable with the first suggestion because of the retaliatory overtones already mentioned, and the second appears to her not terribly different from the approach she has been following, that is, maintaining some empathic resonance with her distant and uncommunicative patient. She struggles for some time more and in desperation tries one more consultation.

There is an immediate rapport between the therapist and the third consultant. Together, they are able to establish an atmosphere of unusual openness and mutuality; one that feels itself to be a safe place for fertile self-disclosure. This supervisor listens to the clinical material and remarks, "I am struck with how much you do know about your patient. I think the problem is that you are spending too much time waiting for her words. She is not telling you about herself, she is showing you. She herself has no words. Perhaps she is waiting for yours. Go back and speak to her about herself. I think that she is waiting for you to do that." The therapist presses for clarification, What should she say? "I don't know what she has told you. And you won't either unless you listen in a different way; not to the words or absence of words but to the entire situation; the moods, the body, the gestures, the silences. . . . Come back in a few weeks, and we will speak again."

It is difficult to concretize the effects of this input on the therapeutic work. The therapist began to speak of her own experiences in the sessions with her patient, of her own moments of hope and despair, her experiences of being helpful to the patient and her sense of frustration and ineptitude. She shared her belief that the patient wanted desperately to reach out but somehow couldn't find the words with which to accomplish this. Of course, this was slowly dosed out over time. As it was new to the therapist, who was here reaching beyond her own accustomed way of working, we can assume a certain degree of awkwardness and error in the approach. Nonetheless, changes in the therapeutic work were palpable. Essentially both the patient and the therapist woke up. The therapist reported feeling alive, involved, alert to the nuances of the therapeutic exchange that had gone unnoticed previously. Years later, the patient described her experience:

> It was as if I had always seen the world and related to it through a haze . . . a film or gauze that was translucent. It allowed me to see light, but there were no shapes or forms. Everything was fluid . . . I would identify it, and it would change. I could not speak or find words for such a thing. When you began to speak with me about these things, I began to feel that I could somehow hold on to them too . . . at least long enough to feel them . . . to understand what they might be.

Three months after this shift in the therapy, what then seemed like a remarkable thing occurred. The patient came into the session noticeably anxious. She reported that, although it had honestly not struck her as important before, there was something that the therapist might find it important to know. She went on to describe that the only problem was that she could not tell the therapist what she needed to in spoken words. At that point, she took a piece of paper out of her briefcase, wrote something on it, and handed it to the therapist. Given the context of this book, it will not surprise the reader, as it did the therapist, that written on the paper was the single word *Incest*.

The patient continued, "Now I will take the paper back, and we will not speak of this again, for I cannot know about it. I thought you might need to know, but I cannot. Please don't say a word." The therapist, respectful of the patient's wishes, handed the paper back to her, and before the therapist's unbelieving and dumbstruck eyes, the patient tore the paper into tiny pieces and proceeded to eat it.

After months of struggling to really understand and apprehend this new way of working, the therapist felt the sudden emergence of some clarity. "I think you just helped me to understand from inside myself, what it feels like to witness and participate in something that desperately presses to be spoken about, yet where solemn promises and commitments make that an act of betrayal." The patient smiled and again looked tearful. It occurred to the therapist after the session had ended that this was the first time she had ever seen this particular patient smile.

We present this lengthy and dramatic clinical summary as an allegory of sorts: one therapist's search to find a method with which to approach and give voice to that which remains unspeakable or even unsymbolizable by the patient. It is a true story, shared with the authors, and coming from a time in the recent history of psychoanalysis when active use of the countertransference was rarely if ever mentioned—certainly not as active a part of the psychoanalytic dialog as it is today. We include it here, because we believe that it highlights some of the most active controversies in the field today. Although these controversies are not unique to work with adult survivors of childhood sexual abuse, this particular area of work with its emphasis on the rapidly shifting and always intense and regressive transference-countertransference enactments makes the clinical and theoretical resolution of such controversey an ongoing imperative for the working clinician.

We thus conclude our work by setting forth our own theoretical resolution of some of these issues and by anticipating some of the reader's questions, concerns, and criticisms about (1) the therapeutic interplay of illusion and reality, with particular regard to what we have termed "the child persona"; (2) a reappraisal of the traditional concepts of abstinence and neutrality in working with a population of abuse victims; (3) some thoughts on the pathogeneity of projective identification in abused children, and the posture of psychoanalytic inquiry; and finally (4) a reconsideration of the place of oedipal dynamics in psychological development and the therapeutic stance that evolves from such a reconsideration.

The Interplay of Illusion and Reality

It is our hope that the very poignant vignette presented in the preceding section makes explicit our overriding belief that psychoanalytic work and change involve the successful creation of a potential space (Khan, 1971; Winnicott, 1957), within which analyst and patient together cocreate an illusory world, where past, present, and future, the real, the fantastically elaborated, and the otherwise irreducible, can come alive, occupying for a time center stage, in this mutually accessible reality. In a world where experience has defied words, where it has never been adequately encoded, experienced, and repressed, emergence must come via reenactment. In myriad ways, transference-countertransference reenactment—intrusive ideation and flashbacks, somatic symptoms, dreams, fantasies, and so on—the pressures of the past will make their presence wordlessly felt in this transitional arena. Not every patient will be as behaviorally articulate as our patient, who literally ate her own words, but all will find a way of impressing what they simultaneously know and don't know on the actively receptive medium of psychoanalytic discourse.

In the case described, progress was ultimately made by engaging the "child persona," by commiserating with the burden of her terrible silence and consequent solitude, and gently and empathically drawing out her experiences of the rather brutal incest she had suffered. Initially, the therapist had to speak for the child, kept carefully closeted by the "adult"; but, ultimately she was able to speak with the child of all that had happened to her, to process with her all the ways in which the two of them reenacted the various sides of self and object representations specific to the previously dissociated abusive experiences, the fantasies of victim, abuser, savior, and neglecting other.

When this child self appeared, the analyst spoke as one would to a traumatized child, gently, slowly, and reassuringly. She did what was necessary to protect the child, symbolically and actually, from any dangers that threatened her. These included her own self-destructive and self-neglectful behaviors; unnecessarily dangerous counterphobic behaviors, attitudes, and postures that threatened the continuity of the treatment; assaults on the effectiveness of the therapist; and so on. They played first on safe territory, with ideas about the past and present, with ideas about what they might be thinking, feeling, imagining. As the relationship felt safer, they began to play with angrier thoughts and feelings, eventually giving way to the kinds of passionate reenactments of abusive and counterabusive scenarios described earlier in the book. Such reenactments eventually shed their patina of "play" and became very real and deadly battles for the survival of the treatment-child. Therapist and patient faced repeated exposure to psychic death within that analytic interior.

We hold that with such reenactments, past and present are fused, as together the patient and therapist explore the terror and incomprehensability of the love, dependence, hatred, and betrayal that mark the organizing experiences of the patient's internal world and, therefore, the boundaries of the reality within their shared illusory space. In essence, the treatment itself becomes an illusory home for the abused child who has never and will never know any other such safe sanctuary. Such a home allows for a background of safety and containment, while simultaneously permitting, even encouraging, the emergence of the bitterest moments of betrayal; the most unspeakable terrors of childhood abuse; the most profound experiences of abject hate, in the context of otherwise dependent, sometimes loving attatchments to another.

Some object to our depiction of the child persona as anything more than a metaphor (Shengold, 1992); however, for us, the child who emerges time and time again when we undertake the treatment of an adult survivor is a palpably real and essential figure in the clinical work. Surely, we do not believe that there truly is a little person inside of the big person who comes for treatment any more than we believe we can isolate the physiological locus of the ego. However, for the working analyst, the child persona is a *clinical reality*, albeit a reality born of illusion. She does not usually live in the world of others but makes her home in the transitional space created between patient and therapist. In this space, she remembers, relives, and at least partially redoes, those traumatic relationships which were precipitously foreclosed as abusive events became dissociated. In an eloquent paper on the virtue of sustaining paradox in psychoanalytic work, Emmanuel Ghent (1992) writes:

> However true it is that there is no baby living in the adult patient . . . so often it happens that the route to truth is through the intensity of illusion. Is not analysis a veritable playpen for transference and countertransference, and what are these if not vehicles for finding truth by knocking on the walls of illusion? Are not dreams the quintessential illusions, fictions? Are not most art forms—lines on a flat plane or ambiguous words in blank verse or people playing roles on stage—are not these all built on illusion? And do not all these lead us, through illusion, to encounter a level of truth and reality that is otherwise inaccessible? (p. 139).

Ghent states with poetic cadence the need to suspend our reliance on rationality, in order to reach more powerful truths in our clinical work. We believe the presence of the child persona represents just such a form of irrational truth. It is only within the confines of this carefully constructed irrationality that the emergence of traumatic childhood memories and their dissociated self and object representations will make their fullest appearance. We believe, then, that it is only when the analyst can create a home for and then wholeheartedly enter into the illusory world of the dissociated child that analytic progress will ensue.

Returning to the patient we are presenting, the reader will be interested in how and under what circumstances the powerful vow of silence was first breached between patient and therapist. Almost 3 months after the above events, during which time neither patient nor therapist spoke of what had transpired between them, the following events occurred. The patient entered the session one day in what appeared to be an uncharacteristically "chatty" and "upbeat" mood. She was quite amused with herself for having confused two important pieces of correspondence at work and completely forgetting the deadline on another project. She seemed unusually "dizzy" and appeared to be enjoying this state, not at all like the meticulously careful and sober-minded perfectionist she usually presented. The therapist became aware that she "seemed like a different person." (Such an experience should always alert the therapist to the possible presence of dissociated material.) As the therapist mused, she heard the patient say with some excitement and laughter:

PATIENT: It's amazing to me that sometimes I can just block important things out of my head like this. They're gone entirely!

THERAPIST: It would seem to have been a carefully developed survival technique for you. There were some things you just had to keep out of your head.

PATIENT: Oh now, you be careful . . . you're speaking of something else entirely . . . we made a deal, and a promise is a promise, you know.

THERAPIST: I'm to be a good girl and never speak of the things I know about. This is very hard you know, and it feels more than a little bit crazy.

PATIENT: I don't know what you mean.

THERAPIST: Oh, but I believe that some part of you does. I'd venture to say that some part of you knows just what I'm saying . . . just what I'm feeling. I think that that particular part of you is very little . . . and she's watching to see if I'll be bad . . . because if I am, then maybe it would be safe for her to speak and to be bad with me.

PATIENT: [Here the patient lifts her legs up and literally curls herself into a ball on her chair. She covers her face with her long hair and for a moment almost appears to be sucking on her thumb. Her voice quality is strikingly different from any the therapist has heard before.] Are you bad? Do you ever do bad things?

THERAPIST: Lots of times. When I was little, sometimes I did bad things that I didn't even know were bad. Now, I guess I still do bad things sometimes.

PATIENT: When I was little, I did big girl bad things.

THERAPIST: Can you tell me about them? It might feel better if you could.

PATIENT: Do you have a bathroom here [the patient, of course, had used the bathroom on many occasions]. I feel like I'm going to be sick. [The patient is silent and sits with her hand covering her mouth.] What did you ask me, again?

THERAPIST: [Noting the dissociative switch] I asked if you wanted to tell me about the bad things . . . if you thought that might help.

PATIENT: I really feel nauseous . . . like I'm going to throw up.

THERAPIST: Like something inside wants to come out?

PATIENT: It was my father . . . [the patient is crying now, and her whole body begins to shake uncontrollably] I can't stop this. I think that's all I can say now. . . .

THERAPIST: You can say one word a day if that's how you need to do this.

PATIENT: [Silent for a few minutes, still crying.] It hurted me. [She is unaware of her use of language.]

THERAPIST: I'm sure it did, it must have hurt you a lot.

PATIENT: [Making eye contact now, and nodding a very childlike yes, still crying.]

THERAPIST: You know it hurts to hear about it too . . . to see you in so much pain . . . but, even then, it doesn't feel as crazy as both of us knowing this thing that we can't speak about. . . .

And so it went.

This paradox of the interplay between fantasy and illusion leads us to yet another dilemma. If patients suffer from serious deficits in reality testing, how can so much of the therapeutic work needed to repair such deficits occur in a world of illusion? Will this not compound the problem? The answer can only be an unequivocal no. We are asked often about those patients who show all the symptoms of having been sexually abused, whose dreams and fantasies seem reflective of experiences of actual abuse, and where all of the powerful transference-countertransference reenactments we have described play themselves out in the analytic work; but, unlike the patients being described she is never able to recover actual memories of such abuse. Certainly, such cases exist, and we can never be completely sure of what happened in the childhoods of such patients, of why they remain unable to recover their memories.

The luckiest of our patients have their memories verified by family members or by the abuser himself (Herman & Shatzow, 1987). Next, come patients who are capable of recovering, in full or in part, specific pictorial memories of their abuse. But one should not assume that such recovery in itself resurrects the battered sense of reality that has permeated the patient's growing-up years. Even here, it is almost universal in work with survivors of childhood abuse that at many points along the way, patients will question the veracity of their statements, the reality of their memories. "I must be making this all up," is commonly heard. Or "How do we know that I'm telling the truth, this could all be a fantasy." Certainly, these doubts are the worst for patients who never get to their specific memories, but they exist and continue to exist for all those who suffer from dissociative disorders.

Here it is essential to remember that childhood sexual abuse is not only an intrusion into the body but also a transgression of the mind, in which the intruding other shapes and defines the child's experience. Via projective identifications from a parent whose own boundary functions are severely impaired, the child comes to precociously know all forms of experience over which she or he feels no ownership. It is not the recovery of abusive memories per se that is essential for the reparation of such ego functioning, although such memory recovery is helpful, but the moment-to-moment interpretation and negotiation of an illusory reality shared between patient and therapist that ultimately provides the second chance for such developmental achievements.

Here one can turn to a model of psychoanalysis that appreciates the developmental importance of reaching a stage of intersubjectivity (Benjamin, 1988, 1990) and of incorporating the need for such an achievement at the heart of the therapeutic frame. The patient will have a point of view; will come to "know" her experience of the analytic encounter and of the analyst's participation in this encounter. She will have her perspective on the state of the analyst's subjective experience within their interaction. The analyst on her part will have to greater or lesser degrees a different perspective on the interaction itself, as well as on the patient as object and subject. Given the nature of the patient's experiences, she will either have little confidence in her own perceptions, or she will cling to them with a ferocity that speaks to her repetitive experiences of mental invasion. The analyst may err in the direction of too much confidence in her particular point of view.

Within a relational model, this will be the jumping off point for the kind of negotiation that lies at the heart of the therapeutic action of psychoanalysis (Mitchell, 1991). At times, analyst and patient will concur on their perception of an event. This, of course, will nurture the patient's conviction in her own perceptions. At other times, the patient's perceptions will hold sway against those of the analyst, perhaps even bringing about a change in his particular point of view. At yet other times, the patient will come to change her perspective, and in so doing learn that she can surrender a point without mentally losing herself in the experience of another. As patient and analyst work together to interpret the illusory world they have cocreated, a kind of sorting out process ensues, whereby the experiences of each mind come together, comingle, and ultimately assume a clearly differentiated integrity. From out of this process, one can hope to see the partial restoration of boundaries that were so weakened by the early traumatic abuse and by the constant barrage of projective identifications that flood the experience of mental and physical integrity within these patients.

The Concepts of Abstinence and Neutrality

We find it significant to remember that Freud's earliest formulations about psychoanalytic process and technique were based in large measure on his work with a group of patients he believed to have been victims of prepubertal sexual abuse. Although we no longer hold such abuse to be at the heart of all psychoneurosis, we have in large numbers been returning to the view that Freud's early, hysterical patients were sexual abuse victims. In fact, Freud tells us (1896) that in many of these cases, he and the patient were able to obtain external confirmation of these assumptions.

In working with adult survivors of childhood sexual abuse today, the reader should bear in mind that many of the basic assumptions at the foundation of psychoanalytic theory and technique were specifically derived against this very unique backdrop. For example, the absolute importance of neutrality and steadfast abstinence on the part of the analyst were articulated against the background of intense transference and countertransference enactments, such as extraordinary proclamations of love in the transference. Freud was not about to forget that Breuer's countertransferential response to Anna O's declaration of transference love (including what appeared to be a hysterical pregnancy) was to send his colleague fleeing the country on a second honeymoon with his wife. Breuer was not to return to his pioneering interest in psychoanalysis on his return. If we assume Freud and Breuer to have been confronted with the kinds of intense and relentless enactments and reenactments in the transference and countertransference that we have articulated in chapter 9, Breuer's flight and Freud's compelling response appear in a somewhat new perspective. It was, after all, in his paper "Observations on Transference-Love," that Freud (1915) first articulated the "rule of abstinence." From the same paper also comes contextual support for the notion that Freud was not writing about simple experiences of tenderness, romantic fantasy, and yearning we now recognize as common to so many analyses. We propose that he was, indeed, describing the kinds of erotized reactions that reenact in the transference and countertransference the sorts of violent boundary transgressions common to adult survivors of sexual abuse (Blum, 1973; Davies & Frawley, 1992; Levine, 1990). Freud (1915) states:

There can be no doubt that the outbreak of a passionate demand for love is largely the work of resistance. One will have long since noticed in the patient the signs of an affectionate transference, and one will have been able to feel certain that her docility, her acceptance of the analytic explanations, her remarkable comprehension and the high degree of intelligence she showed were to be attributed to this attitude towards her doctor. Now all this is swept away. She has become quite without insight and seems to be swallowed up in her love (p. 162).

It is in relation to this description that Freud first spells out his famous injunction. He says:

I have already let it be understood that analytic technique requires of the physician that he should deny to the patient who is craving for love the satisfaction she demands. The treatment must be carried out in abstinence. By this, I do not mean physical abstinence alone, nor yet the deprivation of everything that the patient desires, for perhaps no sick person could tolerate this. Instead, I shall state it as a fundamental principle that the patient's need and longing should be allowed to persist in her, in order that they may serve as forces impelling her to do work and to make changes, and that we must beware of appeasing those forces by means of surrogates. (p. 165)

Though Freud later (1919) broadened his view of abstinence as a necessary background against which all analyses should be conducted, many contemporary psychoanalysts maintain a definition of the analytic privation that would appear broader and more all-inclusive than even Freud intended. Greenson (1967), for example, cautions that overgratification of the patient by the analyst can cause the transference and countertransference to become stalemated with the patient in a passive, submissive role and the analyst in the role of an all-giving savior. Levine (1990), writing specifically of the treatment of adult survivors, warns the reader that the dangers of overstimulating the patient by gratifying certain aspects of the transference far outweigh the dangers of narcissistically injuring the patient by interpreting her wishes vis à vis the therapist. Levine states that, although a departure from what he terms "the requisite stance of abstinence, neutrality, and analytic inquiry" may stimulate feelings of intense narcissistic injury in the patient, a failure to maintain such a position "may stimulate the analysand's fears of the analyst's corruption or seducibility" (p. 200).

As we move from a classical position to a more relational one, we deemphasize the implicit necessity for frustration and abstinence (as originally defined) as we broaden our singular reliance on the primacy of interpretation of instinctual wishes as the modus operandi of all therapeutic change. We draw into our understanding of the therapeutic action of psychoanalysis or psychoanalytically informed psychotherapy an emphasis on the centrality of the very "dangers" we are cautioned to avoid. We assume that reenactments will occur in the transference-countertransference unfolding, and rather than attempting to purify the analytic space to sidestep such experiences, we in

fact wait patiently for their emergence. We accept that at some point patient and therapist will become locked into a stalemate with the patient in a passive submissive role and the analyst in the role of an all-giving parent/savior, as articulated by Greenson. Contrary to the position assumed by Levine, we actually hope that in our treatment of adult survivors, certain patient-therapist interactions will stimulate fears about the analyst's corruptability and seducibility. For what could be more important to analyze in the therapeutic work with an adult survivor of sexual abuse?

It is of paramount importance that the emergence of such necessary transference-countertransference paradigms not be viewed as due to "analyst error" but as watershed markings that the therapeutic process is unfolding in a way that will allow for the understanding and reintegration of such significant object-relational matrices. For us the notion of therapeutic neutrality lies in countertransferentially maintaining the capacity to extricate the patient-therapist dyad through interpretation and negotiation from the stalemated and entrenched position and, in so doing, make possible a completely different yet equally problematic interaction. The notion of abstinence rests, we believe, on the therapist's ability to protect the illusory quality of the transitional space in which transference and countertransference play themselves out, to guard against becoming entrenched in actual, behavioral confirmations of the patient's transference experience, unconsciously reenacted outside the province of therapeutic interpretation and negotiation. Such actualization of what should remain symbolic in therapy could bring about a dangerous collapse of the transitional arena and seriously impede further therapeutic progress.

Knocking on the door of illusion, calling forth the participation of the child persona within the adult, we run head on into these contemporary psychoanalytic conundrums. Most practicing clinicians today would agree that the idea of conducting an analysis without gratifying many of the patient's spoken and unspoken needs is impossible, if not absurd. The very nature of treatment, the fact that the patient is in possession of the analyst's undivided, empathic attention, renders such a conceptualization inconceivable. As we literally slog our way through the kaleidoscopic shifting of rageful, bitter, entitled, empty, and deadening transference and countertransference reenactments—reenactments that shift rapidly and unexpectedly through the volleying of projective-introjective mechanisms—we find that it behooves us as clinicians to have carefully thought through our position on some of these issues ahead of time. These include whether or not to gratify what we perceive to be early developmentally frustrated needs and the place and extent of the analyst's participation in the course of treatment—impositions of the analyst's perception where it differs from that of the patient, explicit countertransference disclosures, and so on. We find that "the heat of the moment" is not conducive to quiet and introspective reflection.

Having found certain forms of gratification acceptable, therapists find themselves groping for some guidelines, some reestablishment of appropriate boundaries within which to conduct the treatment. In an attempt to answer such a need, much has been written about where the analyst responds and where he refrains from doing so. Much of the debate has centered around the attempt to distinguish between what have been termed "libidinal wishes" and "developmental needs." In the first case, common wisdom would have us believe we frustrate, in the second, gratify. We will, for the sake of parsimony and because the question has been so well articulated elsewhere (Ghent, 1992; Mitchell, 1991; Shabad, 1993), sidestep the distinctions between needs, wishes, and drives, stating simply our belief that no patient will ever call forth the therapist's desire to nurture and restore as will the adult who has suffered serious childhood abuse. Given such an endemic countertransferential pressure and such confusion in the psychoanalytic literature, what are we to do?

Gratification and Mourning

How do we steer a course between rigid adherence to an antiquated caricature of treatment and the kind of countertransferential acting out that can lead to intense overstimulation in the transference, including all forms of actual rather than symbolic reenactments (including the sexual revictimization of the patient by the therapist more common among adult survivors of sexual abuse than among any other single group [Kluft, 1990b]. We can attempt an answer by looking at both sides of the problem, or why we must avoid both undergratification and overgratification.

Certainly, work with adult survivors requires certain gratifications within the transference. Experiences of nurturing, holding, containing, protecting are intrinsic to work with both the child and the adult persona. The analysis will simply not proceed without emotional availability on the part of the analyst. Such experiences not only create the potential for the emergence of traumatic material into the analysis but also carry another essential function. Such experiences of gratification in the transference essentially awaken long-denied desires within the patient. All those who work with adults who were traumatically abused as children know that the combination of wild overstimulation in the context of otherwise neglectful parenting has rendered them as adults virtually. dead to experiences of hunger and desire of any kind. Their salvation was bought at the expense of the most stringent counterdependent defenses, and, like anorexic patients, they no longer experience feelings of hunger. Any approach that clings to notions of abstinence and total nongratification serve merely to intensify such defenses, as well as the shame and humiliation that accompany any experience of need in the therapeutic relationship.

On the other end of this dialectical tension is the analyst who believes that he or she can make up for all the patient has suffered, that, with the emergence of the child persona, he or she can redo, reparent, in essence salvage, a childhood that has been permanently lost. We believe this to be impossible. In chapter 9 we articulated in great detail how such an attempt—an identification with the patient's internalized savior—calls forth the sadistic introject in his most treatment-destroying incarnations. Ultimately, the persistence of such an attempt at salvation interferes with the mourning process and with the patient's relinquishing of childhood fantasies revolving around a perfect compensatory childhood of complete and total parental indulgence. When such a fantasy is allowed to remain unanalyzed in dissociated form, it imposes itself on all other gratifying relationships in the patient's life and ultimately renders them disappointing and empty. For a moment, the analyst remains all important, but eventually he too will be brought down and rendered helpless and inept by the abuser within the patient.

Last, although we all strive to consider the developmental deficits of our patients in the difficult process of negotiating such therapeutic decisions, we believe that it is all too common to ignore the fact that the therapist's own states of need have had a profound impact on the decision to gratify or not gratify the patient's needs. All too often, we couch our decisions not to gratify a particular request in terms of how we understand the patient's needs and wishes, not in terms of how such enactments would impinge on our own needs and desires. Such formulations are terribly confusing to patients whose internal experience of self and of reality has been so buffeted by repetitive projective-introjective cycles. They have been told what they want, what they don't want, what they feel, and what they don't feel. They have been told that the sexual abuse they hate is what they really want, and ultimately they end up hating whatever they come to truly want. Often, there has been only minimal correspondence between the labels given to the patient's internal experience and the patient's own definition of internal realities. The therapist who maintains an approach that focuses exclusively on interpretation of the patient's needs and desires without including his own desires as part of the final decision-making process merely repeats the trauma of presuming he knows what it is that the patient needs and wants.

In the case being discussed in this chapter, the patient, at a point much further along in her treatment, decided that she must have at least a month of her therapy free of charge. She argued persuasively and passionately that she could never feel secure that the therapist really cared about her unless she was willing to engage in such an arrangement. The therapist attempted to interpret the request from every possible perspective; the patient's wish to be special above all other patients; the patient's identification with her abuser; the wish to engage the analyst in some form of illicit activity; greed, envy, and so on all found their way into the therapeutic discourse on this matter. The patient's demand continued, however, unabated, in a way that was experienced as relentless and belligerent by the analyst. In desperation and anger, she yelled back one day, "Look, I just don't want to, okay; I can't afford it, I won't do it, and I won't discuss it any further!" The therapist felt that she had completely lost control. However, the patient was quiet for the first time with regard to this issue. Her only response was, "Oh, I guess that makes sense. . . . Why didn't you say so originally. . . . If you can't, you can't." She never discussed the issue again, unless it was raised by the therapist, and then she always responded matter-of-factly, "It's a closed issue, you said so."

Some years later, the patient was able to discuss the event with some equanimity and great insight:

> PATIENT: You kept telling me what I needed . . . what I wanted. You'd never done that before. I felt like you were making me crazy. I think you felt guilty about saying no, and I was very demanding . . . so I think you put it all on me. I can't tell you how that felt . . . it was like you were trying to be inside of me . . . like my father. . . . I felt paralyzed and betrayed. When you finally got angry and just said you plain didn't want to, I was incredibly pissed off. But that was okay . . . we were just like any two people having a fight. I knew what you wanted, so then I could be clear about what I wanted. . . . Angry at you, not at myself. [With a laugh] I had to push you a long way . . . but you came through for me in the end.

Oedipal Dynamics and Sexual Abuse

One final issue that warrants reconsideration in work with individuals who have been sexually abused as children is the finer distinction between more normative and more pathological resolutions of traditional oedipal dynamics. Such distinctions become essential in successfully working through these developmental issues with adult survivors. In its simplest and most paradigmatic form, the theory informs us that the positive Oedipus complex involves the child's erotic and sexual longings for the opposite-sex parent and the inhibitory terror of competition with and retaliation by the parent of the same sex. It is the fear of such competition and retaliation that ultimately leads to resolution of these erotic longings and pushes the child along into latency, where such erotic stirrings are quelled and, at least temporarily, held in check by the stern injunctions of the superego.

Let us pause here, and reflect for a moment on the child's and parents' oedipal experience in a more or less typical family. There is little as safely as-

sured in life as the relatively nonneurotic pleasure parents experience in response to the first tender unfoldings of their child's sexual journey. When such romantic ideation is directed at the parent of the opposite sex, success is all but assured. The child experiences herself to be the most delightful of seductresses; her parent, it would appear, is utterly besotted by her most naive and guileless attempts to seduce and cajole. In this best of all possible worlds, each has found in the other the perfect lover, passionate, tender, bemused, and without rival. Such love affairs exist only in fantasy, and it is only within this fantasy that they are permitted to flourish unspoiled.

Danger to such illusory perfection in the positive oedipal situation can come from two directions: the jealous impingement of the same-sex parent, whose sexual insecurity encourages an experience of her child as a powerful competitor for her spouse's attentions, or the same-sex parent's inability or feared inability to keep this affair within the safe confines of psychic fantasy. Both of these dangers are realized in the case of actual sexual abuse. In a situation where the child unconsciously experiences or perceives the same-sex parent's jealousy or the opposite parent's discomfort over her sexual strivings, such experiences of her sexual self will become frought with anxiety and ambivalence and come to be associated with object-related experiences of anger or disapproval. Any such future experience of sexual stirring will revivify these relational paradigms around which her early sexual experiences were organized. In cases where there is an actualization of oedipal dynamics in the real sexual contact or overwhelming overstimulation of the child, there is likely to be a complete foreclosure of such loving and romantic potentialities. The more tender erotic oedipal experiences come to be replaced by an identification with the transgressing parent and it is ensured that the patient's sexual longings will be similarly expressed (when they are allowed to be expressed at all) in violent and intrusively demanding ways.

It is at this juncture that we call into question Freud's (1924) belief in the "dissolution" of the Oedipus complex and take some objection to the idea that it is primarily superego injunction and fear of castration or loss of love that brings about the destruction of the complex. Although this may certainly explain the fate of events in families where jealous impingements and boundary transgressions have been the hallmark of the Oedipus situation, it is unlikely to represent the normal course of events in families where the young child's emergent sexuality has been graciously welcomed and enjoyed. One may prefer Loewald's (1980) concept of the "waning" of the complex, namely, that it moves in and out of a position of primacy at different points in the individual's lifetime. However, the possibility exists that the fundamental oedipal experiences are not subject to "resolution" at all. When drive theory takes a back seat—and the need for renunciation of infantile libidinal attachments is called into question—we are freed to believe that Oedipus is not destroyed that the residues of the richly erotic oedipal years are merely transcendent, that they form the rich and fertile soil in which mature love can flourish. Although the superego may become heir to an Oedipus complex marked by jealousy, guilt, impulsivity, and boundary transgression, a more positive experience and result lead from early oedipal romance to the evolution of an ego capacity for passionate and erotically charged mature love based on healthy identifications with two parents comfortably at peace with their own sexualities (see Searles [1959b] for a related point of view). Might Freud's theories be subject here too to the particular coloration given them by his early work with adult survivors? Clinical experience demonstrates the tenaciously stubborn recurrence of oedipally colored crushes, idealizations, and love affairs. Indeed, the early intensely erotic and passionate beginnings of most love relationships bear many of the hallmarks of the individual's unique oedipal situations. Such experiences are not ruled out by successful analyses; on the contrary, such analytic work often potentiates the possibilities for such love.

How one understands the optimal fate of the oedipal dynamic powerfully influences the content and timing of certain interpretations, as these dynamics play themselves out in the patient-therapist relationship. In an earlier paper (Davies & Frawley, 1992a) we stated that work with adult survivors of childhood sexual abuse would force patient and therapist alike to "think long and hard, during the course of their work together, about the nature of abuse and the differences between benign and malignant seduction" (p. 30). We suggest here that "malignant seduction" is in essence an identification with the transgressing abusive or overstimulating parent or with the jealous, retaliatory parent, reenacted in the transference-countertransference dyad. Its hallmarks are vengeful, retaliatory eroticized assaults, relentless demands for actual gratification, and a countertransference response of needing to be ever vigilant to attempts at invasive transgression of the therapeutic boundaries.

The therapist must interpret actively the appearance of such a sadistic introject—the abusive parent reincarnated in the persona of the beseeching, seductive, highly eroticized patient, pleading relentlessly for any and all forms of inappropriate gratification on the part of the therapist. Here, the countertransference response most naturally and powerfully evoked informs and directs a therapeutic stance protective of the therapeutic boundaries and vigilantly attuned to not gratifying the patient's experiences of sadistic omnipotence vis à vis the therapist. For the patient, there is little as empathically powerful as identifying and helping to contain through interpretation the omnipotent infantile ragings of the internalized aggressor with whom the patient has identified. This is especially true as via dissociation such a persona can turn its assaultive stance against the patient herself as well as against the therapist. Such a paradigm should be suspected whether the manifestation of such a position in the transference is openly attacking or, as is equally likely with adult survivors, is unrelenting in its attempts at eroti-

cized boundary impingements and transgressions. Caught within such a transference-countertransference enactment, an informed and thoughtful adherence to the rules of abstinence and a focus on interpretively unlocking the therapeutic stalemate follow naturally.

Of concern here is the way in which such a paradigm can become entrenched, so that the therapist identifies the whole patient with the demands of the sadistic introject, thus assuming a sadistically withholding retaliatory and overly interpretive stance vis à vis any of the patient's expressed wishes. This can be disastrous in such treatments; although given the frequency with which this particular transference-countertransference paradigm emerges, it is, unfortunately, all too common.

One of the simplest yet most tragic effects of early childhood sexual abuse is that the child learns to equate her sensual and sexual desires with the actualities of the abuse. She believes that had she not permitted herself such thoughts, the incest would not have occurred. Such a child learns not to play with her own thoughts (Bollas, 1989), that fantasy and reality come too dangerously close to permit such free reign. In such a context, there is no oedipal romance; the child is not free to luxuriate in the exquisite sweetness of childhood infatuation. The mutuality of benign seduction endemic to oedipal love finds no voice, and such interactions are forever associated with malignant penetration and overstimulation, rather than playfulness, sensuality, and sexual pleasure.

When such oedipal experiences begin to emerge in the treatment setting, such benign flirtation must be receptively met with a mood of innocence and playfulness. The analyst in such a scenario must resonate with the harmless pleasure of the interaction and move from the foreground of active transference interpretation to the background of protecting and containing a transitional space, wherein such a prematurely foreclosed developmental necessity can emerge and flourish. Such a shift is enormously difficult, particularly for the therapist who has been contending with overly eroticized demands in the transference. He or she will hold fast to an interpretive mode aimed at supplanting insight for the ungratifiable, ultimately self-destructive demands of the patient and may well miss the important shift from intrusive demands to playful ones, that is, from real to illusory modes of interaction. The therapist working with an adult survivor of childhood sexual abuse must, therefore, be vigilant in his or her attention to the emergence of such changes in the transference. When intrusive seduction is met with active and accurate interpretation of the patient's identification with her own aggressor, the result will be an enhanced experience of safety and containment within the therapeutic relationship. On the other hand, the active interpretation of a benign and flirtatious overture toward the therapist will surely humiliate the patient and set back, if not again foreclose, the development of a healthy and heartfelt oedipal love.

Although we are surely aware that even a benignly flirtatious interplay between patient and therapist is likely to increase the patient's anxiety, as well as her experience of the therapist as dangerous and seductive, we believe, as stated earlier, that such a distortion is inevitable. In the absence of any inappropriate gratifications that would actualize such a perception, this transference distortion can be clarified via accurate interpretation of the patient's fears. However, narcissistic injury secondary to an overactive interpretation of the patient's fledgling oedipal attempts will viscerally resurrect experiences of humiliation and shame over which words appear to have no assuaging powers. The capacity to distinguish between experiences of playful flirtatiousness and dangerously intrusive seduction represents an important piece of the analytic work, and nowhere can it be done more effectively than within the transference-countertransference experience.

Having stressed the importance of developing the capacity to distinguish and negotiate between the benign and malignant manifestations of seductive behavior, therapists should recognize the difficulty in shifting from a countertransference position cautiously guarded against assault and penetration to one that is receptive to the tentative, fledgling flirtations of an emerging oedipal romance. It is frequently in the countertransference that we are best able to identify these often subtle shifts. We notice a shift from the demand for concrete gratifications that allows the therapist more playful latitude in the realm of symbolic exchanges. In this symbolic and highly illusory place, the true oedipal unfolding can finally be expressed.

In the case explored in this chapter, it was only after patient and therapist had fully explored the meaning of their battles over the analytic fee and the patient's demands for a month of free therapy that a different kind of wish for gratification could emerge in the treatment setting. As already discussed, this working-through process involved not only the meaning of the demands as experienced by the patient but also the therapist's experience of such demands in the countertransference. As the patient became reassured by the therapist's ability to own and monitor her own experiences without resorting to an unconscious use of projective defenses and a retaliatory reliance on an overly interpretive stance, she became more able to search for the more profound and hard-to-verbalize wishes beyond her aggressive demands. A highly romanticized fascination with the nuances of the therapist's life and the wishes to be special, to be loved, to be valued above all others began to emerge as never before in this treatment. The patient was able to sustain increasingly intense experiences of vulnerability in this interpersonal arena, because she became less and less wary of what she feared as aggressive penetration via interpretation. Such interpretations for this patient were experienced as reenactments of her mother's aggressive assaults; in actuality they were projections of her own unacceptable identifications.

As such experiences of real intimacy grow in the therapeutic relationship, moments of true mutuality and shared pleasure can be expressed despite the accompanying vulnerability of both patient and therapist. The patient is once again—or perhaps for the first time—safely able to yearn, fantasize, and dream; and she ultimately becomes able to bring such aspects of her self experience into an interpersonal arena where they are most risky. In the end, we hope that the patient will ask for things that the therapist can give, as an indication that the patient is once again approaching her own desires with some belief that gratification is possible. Again, we have no illusions of compensating the patient for early parental betrayal or of recreating a childhood that was filled with nightmarish terror and betrayal. This would be an act of the most profound therapeutic grandiosity. Rather, we view the simultaneous unfolding of mutually pleasurable and loving feelings in the patient and therapist as indicative of the successful reconfiguration of the relational matrices that are the pathological defensive consequences of traumatic abuse in early childhood. Here in stark contrast to the hideous reenactments that have recurred as a leitmotif throughout the transference-countertransference struggles is an intensely charged object relationship in which romance, desire, fantasy, and benign seduction can be safely enjoyed.

In closing, let us return to where we began, to the woman who had to swallow her own words, to the patient who could not cry. Perhaps our point is best made in what we believe was a pivotal therapeutic exchange. At a point in treatment, during which the patient became particularly aware of the therapist's availability and concern, the following interchange took place:

> PATIENT: I feel like you've managed to touch me. I don't know how. Touch always hurt so much . . . I wouldn't let myself feel it. I was dead to touch. [Again with tears almost, but not quite spilling over] But you've touched me, and it doesn't hurt, and I don't feel wildly overstimulated and crazy. Just touched . . . just touched. [The patient begins to cry for the first time.]
>
> THERAPIST: You know, don't you, that you've touched me, too.
>
> PATIENT: No! [Looking frightened] How? How have I touched you?
>
> THERAPIST: We've worked together for a long time, and we both know that there are some things that words can't encompass. You'll just have to believe me that you have. I think it still frightens you a bit. You look a little frightened . . . but touching doesn't have to be bad. Being touched by you doesn't hurt either.

Here the patient began to sob for the first time in her long years of therapy. Throughout her reliving of years of chronic and sadistic abuse, she had maintained an intense and ultimately exhausting self-control. As the patient sobbed, the therapist realized that she too was breathing more deeply and more freely than she had ever done before in the course of this treatment. In her own body, there was a resonant release of tension and control that only became palpable in its absence. The therapist was aware that in the patient's tears, freely flowing, and in the resonance she felt with such an experience of release, she felt life and hope. She could, for the first time with this patient, see past the years of deadening brutality and the finalities of parental betrayal to a future filled with living possibilities.

References

Abend, S. M. (1986). Sibling loss. In A. Rothstein (Ed.), *The reconstruction of trauma* (pp. 95–104.) Madison, CT: International Universities Press.

Adams, P. R., & Adams, G. R. (1984). Mt. Saint Helens ashfall: Evidence for a disaster stress reaction. *American Psychologist, 39,* 252–260.

American Psychiatric Association (1987). *Diagnostic and statistical manual of mental disorders.* Washington, DC: author.

Amir, S., Brown, Z. W., & Amit, Z. (1980). The role of endorphins in stress: Evidence and speculations. *Neurosciences and Biobehavioral Review, 4,* 77–86.

Armstrong, L. (1978). *Kiss daddy goodnight.* New York: Pocket Books.

Aron, L. (1991). The patient's experience of the analyst's subjectivity. *Psychoanalytic Dialogues, 1,* 29–51.

Bagley, C., & Ramsay, R. (1986). Sexual abuse in childhood: Psychosocial outcomes and implications for social work practice. In *Social work practice in sexual problems.* Binghamton, NY: Haworth Press, 33–47.

Balint, M. (1979). *The basic fault.* New York: Brunner/Mazel.

Barocas, H. A. (1975). Children of purgatory: reflection on the concentration camp survival syndrome. *International Journal of Social Psychiatry, 21,* 87–92.

Baum, A., Gatchel, R. J., & Schaeffer, N. A. (1983). Emotional, behavioral, and physiological effects of chronic stress at Three Mile Island. *Journal of Consulting and Clinical Psychology, 51,* 565–572.

Benjamin, J. (1988). *The bonds of love: Psychoanalysis, feminism, and the problem of domination.* New York: Pantheon.

Benjamin, J. (1990). An outline of intersubjectivity: The development of recognition. *Psychoanalytic Psychology, 7* (Suppl.), 33–46.

Bergman, M. S., & Jucovy, M. C. (Eds.). (1982). *Generation of the holocaust.* New York: Basic Books.

Bernstein, A. E. (1990). The impact of incest trauma on ego development. In H. B. Levine (Ed.), *Adult analysis and childhood sexual abuse* (pp. 65–92). Hillsdale, NJ: The Analytic Press.

Bion, W. (1962). Learning from experience. In *Seven servants* (pp. 1–111). New York: Aronson.

Blum, H. (1973). Erotized transference. *Journal of the American psychoanalytic Association, 21* 61–76.

Bollas, C. (1987). *The Shadow of the object.* London: Free Association Press.

Bollas, C. (1989). *Forces of destiny: Psychoanalysis and human idiom.* London: Free Association Press.

Bowlby, J. (1969). *Attachment and loss. Vol. 1: Attachment.* New York: Basic Books.

Bowlby, J. (1973). *Attachment and loss. Vol. 2: Separation.* New York: Basic Books.

Braun, B. G. (Ed.). (1986). *Treatment of multiple personality disorder.* Washington, DC: American Psychiatric Press.

Braun, B. G., & Sachs, R. G. (1985). The development of multiple personality disorder. In R. P. Kluft (Ed.), *Childhood antecedents of multiple personality disorder.* Washington, DC: American Psychiatric Press.

Brenner, C. (1986). Discussion of the various contributions. In A. Rothstein (Ed.), *The reconstruction of trauma.* Madison, CT: International Universities Press.

Briere, J. (1988). The long-term clinical correlates of childhood sexual victimization. *Annals of the New York Academy of Sciences, 528,* 327–334.

Briere, J. (1989). *Therapy for adults molested as children.* New York: Springer-Verlag.

Briere, J., & Runtz, M. (1986). Suicidal thoughts and behaviors in former sexual abuse victims. *Canadian Journal of Behavioral Science, 18,* 413–423.

Briere, J., & Runtz, M. (1988). Symptomatology associated with childhood sexual victimization in a non-clinical adult sample. *Child Abuse and Neglect, 12,* 51–59.

Briere, J., & Zaidi, L. Y. (1988, August). *Sexual abuse histories and sequelae in psychiatric emergency room patients.* Paper presented at the Annual Meeting of the American Psychological Association, Atlanta, GA.

Bromberg, P. (1991). On knowing one's patient inside out: The aesthetics of unconscious communication. *Psychoanalytic Dialogues.* 1(4): 399–422.

Brunngraber, L. S. (1986). Father-daughter incest: Immediate and long-term effects of sexual abuse. *Advances in Nursing Science, 8,* 15–35.

Burgess, A. W., & Holmstrom, L. L. (1974a). Rape trauma syndrome. *American Journal of Psychiatry, 131,* 981–985.

Burgess, A. W., & Holmstrom, L. L. (1974b). *Rape: Victims of crisis.* Bowie, MD: Robert J. Bradly.

Burgess, A. W., & Holmstrom, L. L. (1978). Recovery from rape and prior life stress. *Research in Nursing and Health, 1,* 165–174.

Burland, J. A., & Raskin, R. (1990). The psychoanalysis of adults who were sexually abused in childhood: A preliminary report from the discussion group of the American Psychoanalytic Association. In H. B. Levine (Ed.), *Adult analysis and childhood sexual abuse* (pp. 35–44). Hillsdale, NJ: The Analytic Press.

Card, J. J. (1983). *Lives after Vietnam: The personal impact of military service.* Lexington, MA: Lexington Books.

Cole, C. (1988). Routine comprehensive inquiry for abuse: A justifiable clinical assessment procedure. *Clinical Social Work Journal, 16,* 33–42.

Cooper, A. M. (1986). Toward a limited definition of psychic trauma. In A. Rothstein (Ed.), *The reconstruction of trauma* (pp. 41–58). Madison, CT: International Universities Press.

Courtois, C. A. (1980). Studying and counseling women with past incest experiences. *Victimology, 5,* 322–334.

Courtois, C. (1988). *Healing the incest wound.* New York: Norton.

Davies, J. M., & Frawley, M. G. (1992a). Dissociative processes and transference-countertransference paradigms in the psychoanalytically oriented treatment of adult survivors of childhood sexual abuse. *Psychoanalytic Dialogues.* 2(1): 5–36.

Davies, J. M., & Frawley, M. G. (1992b). Reply to Gabbard, Shengold, & Grotstein. *Psychoanalytic Dialogues,* 2(1): 77–96.

Dickes, R. (1965). The defensive functions of an altered state of consciousness. *Journal of the American Psychoanalytic Association, 13,* 356–403.

Dowling, S. (1986). Discussion of the various contributions. In A. Rothstein (Ed.), *The reconstruction of trauma* (pp. 205–218). Madison, CT: International Universities Press.

Dupont, J. (1988). *The clinical diary of Sandor Ferenczi* (M. H. Balint & N. Z. Jackson, Trans.). Cambridge, MA: Harvard University Press.

Ehrenberg, D. B. *The intimate edge.* New York: Norton.

Eitinger, L. (1980). The concentration camp syndrome and its late sequelae. In J. E. Dimsdale (Ed.), *Survivors, victims, and perpetrators: Essays on the Nazi Holocaust.* New York: Hemisphere.

Erikson, E. H. (1963). *Childhood and society.* New York: Norton.

Fairbairn, W. R. D. (1943). The repression and return of bad objects. In *Psychoanalytic studies of the personality* (pp. 59–81). London: Tavistock/Routledge, 1990.

Fairbairn, W. R. D. (1954). Observations on the nature of hysterical states. *British Journal of Medical Psychology, 27,* 105–125.

Fast, I. (1985). *Event theory: A Piaget Freud integration.* Hillsdale, NJ: Lawrence Erlbaum.

Fenichel, O. (1945). *The psychoanalytic theory of neurosis.* New York: Norton.

Ferenczi, S. (1932). Confusion of tongues between adults and the child. *International Journal of Psychoanalysis, 30,* 225.

Ferenczi, S. (1932). *The passions of adults and their influence on the character development and sexual development of children.* Paper presented at the International Psycho-Analytic Congress, Wiesbaden.

Figley, C. R. (Ed.). (1978). *Stress disorder among Vietnam veterans.* New York: Brunner/Mazel.

Figley, C. R. (Ed.). (1986). *Trauma and its wake (Vols. 1 and 2).* New York: Brunner/Mazel.

Fine, C. G. (1990). The cognitive sequelae of incest. In R. Kluft (Ed.), *Incest related syndromes of adult psychopathology* (pp. 161–182). Washington, DC: American Psychiatric Press.

Finkelhor, D. (1984). *Childhood sexual abuse.* New York: The Free Press.

Finkelhor, D., & Brown, A. (1985). The traumatic impact of childhood sexual abuse. *American Journal of Orthopsychiatry, 55,* 530–541.

Fish-Murray, C. C., Koby, E. V., & van der Kolk, B. A. (1987). Evolving ideas: The effect of abuse on children's thought. In B. A. van der Kolk (Ed.), *Psychological trauma* (pp. 89–110). Washington, DC: American Psychiatric Press.

Fliess, R. (1953). The hypnotic evasion. *Psychoanalytic Quarterly, 22,* 497–511.

Frank, E., Turner, S. M., and Duffy, B. (1979). Depressive symptoms in rape victims. *Journal of Affective Disorders, 1,* 269–297.

Frawley, M. G. (1988). The sexual lives of adult survivors of father-daughter incest. *Dissertation Abstracts International, 49.* (University Microfilms No. 88–06,
   457)

Freud, A. (1967). Comments on psychic trauma. In *The Writings of Anna Freud*
   (Vol. V, pp. 221–241). Madison, CT: International Universities Press.

Freud, S. (1896). The aetiology of hysteria. In J. Strachey (Ed. and Trans.), *The
   standard edition of the complete psychological works of Sigmund Freud* (Vol. 3, pp.
   189–221). London: Hogarth Press, 1961.

Freud, S. (1915). Observations on transference love. In J. Strachey (Ed. and
   Trans.), *The standard edition of the complete psychological works of Sigmund Freud*
   (Vol. 12, p. 159). London: Hogarth Press, 1961.

Freud, S. (1919). Lines of advance in psycho-analytic therapy. In J. Strachey (Ed.
   and Trans.), *The standard edition of the complete psychological works of Sigmund
   Freud* (Vol. 17). London: Hogarth Press, 1961.

Freud, S. (1924). The dissolution of the Oedipus complex. In J. Strachey (Ed. and
   Trans.), *The standard edition of the complete psychological works of Sigmund Freud*
   (Vol. 19, p. 173). London: Hogarth Press, 1961.

Fromuth, M. E. (1986). The relationship of childhood sexual abuse with later psychological and sexual adjustment in a sample of college women. *Child Abuse
   and Neglect, 10,* 5–15.

Furst, S. S. (Ed.). (1967). *Psychic trauma.* New York: Basic Books.

Furst, S. S. (1986). Psychic trauma and its reconstruction with particular reference
   to postchildhood trauma. In A. Rothstein (Ed.), *The reconstruction of trauma*
   (pp. 29–40). Madison, CT: International Universities Press.

Gabbard, G. O. (1992). Commentary on "dissociative processes and transference-
   countertransference paradigms" by Jody Messler Davies and Mary Gail
   Frawley. *Psychoanalytic Dialogues, 2,* 37–47.

Gartner, R. (1993, April). *Considerations in the psychoanalytic treatment of men who
   were sexually abused as children.* Paper delivered at the Thirteenth Annual
   Meeting of the Division of Psychoanalysis (39) of the American Psychological
   Association, New York City.

Gay, P. (1988). *Freud.* New York: Doubleday.

Gediman, H. (1991). Seduction trauma: Complemental intrapsychic and interpersonal perspectives on fantasy and reality. *Psychoanalytic Psychology, 8,*
   381–402.

Gelinas, D. (1983). The persisting negative effects of incest. *Psychiatry, 46,*
   312–332.

Ghent, E. (1992). Paradox and process. *Psychoanalytic Dialogues, 2,* 135–160.

Gill, M. M. (1982). *Analysis of Transference, Vol. 1.* Madison, CT: International
   Universities Press.

Gill, M. M., & Hoffman, I. Z. (1982). *Analysis of Transference. Vol. 2:* Madison, CT:
   International Universities Press.

Gold, E. (1986). Long-term effects of sexual victimization in childhood: An attri-
   butional approach. *Journal of Consulting and Clinical Psychology, 54,* 471–475.

Graff, H., & Mallin, R. (1967). The syndrome of the wrist cutter. *American Journal
   of Psychiatry, 124,* 74–80.

Grand, S. (1992). On doubting and knowing in the psychoanalytic treatment of incest survivors. Unpublished manuscript.

Green, B. L. (1982). Assessing levels of psychological impairment following disaster. *Journal of Nervous and Mental Diseases, 170,* 544–552.

Green, B. L., Grace, N. C., Titchener J. L., & Lindy, J. G. (1983). Levels of functional impairment following a civilian disaster: The Beverly Hills Supper Club fire. *Journal of Consulting and Clinical Psychology, 51,* 573–580.

Green, B. L., Wilson, J. P., & Lindy, J. G. (1985). Conceptualizing post-traumatic stress disorder: A psychosocial framework. In C. R. Figley (Ed.), *Trauma and its wake,* Vol. 1 (pp. 53–72). New York: Brunner/Mazel.

Greenacre, P. (1949). A contribution to the study of screen memories. In *Trauma, growth and personality* (pp. 188–203). Madison, CT: International Universities Press.

Greenacre, P. (1950). The prepuberty trauma in girls. In *Trauma growth, and personality.* (pp. 204–223.) Madison, CT: International Universities Press.

Greenacre, P. (1967). The influence of infantile trauma in genetic patterns. In S. S. Furst, (Ed.), *Psychic trauma* (pp. 108–153). Madison, CT: International Universities Press.

Greenberg, J. (1991). Countertransference and reality. *Psychoanalytic Dialogues, 1,* 52–73.

Greenberg, J., & Mitchell, S. (1983). *Object relations in psychoanalytic theory.* Cambridge, MA: Harvard University Press.

Greenson, R. (1967). *The technique and practice of psychoanalysis.* Madison, CT: International Universities Press.

Grotstein, J. S. (1985). *Splitting and projective identification.* Northvale, NJ: Jason Aronson.

Gunderson, J. G. (1984). *Borderline personality disorganization.* Washington, DC: American Psychiatric Press.

Herman, J. L. (1981). *Father-daughter incest.* Cambridge, MA: Harvard University Press.

Herman, J. L. (1992). *Trauma and recovery.* New York: Basic Books.

Herman, J. L., & Shatzow, E. (1987). Recovery and verification of memories of childhood sexual trauma. *Psychoanalytic Psychology 4,* 1–14.

Herman, J. L., Perry, C. C., & van der Kolk, B. A. (1989). Childhood trauma in borderline personality disorder. *American Journal of Psychiatry, 146,* 490–495.

Hilgard, E. R. (1977). *Divided Consciousness.* New York: Wiley.

Hoffman, I. Z. (1983), The patient as interpreter of the analyst's experience. *Contemporary Psychoanalysis, 19,* 389–422.

Hoffman, I. Z. (1991), Discussion: Toward a social-constructivist view of the psychoanalytic situation. *Psychoanalytic Dialogues, 1,* 74–105.

Janet, P. (1889). *L'Automatisme psychologique.* Paris: Balliere.

Janet, P. (1894). Histoire d'une idée fixe. *Revue de Philosophie, 37,* 121–168.

Janet, P. (1898). *Névroses et idées fixes* (2 vols.). Paris: Alcan.

Janet, P. (1907). *The major symptoms of hysteria.* New York: Macmillan.

Janet, P. (1909). Problèmes psychologiques de l'émotion. *Revue de Neurologie, 17,* 1551–1687.

Janet, P. (1911). *L'état mental des hystériques,* (3rd ed.) Paris. Alcan: [Reprint: Marseille: Lafitte Reprints, 1983].

Janoff-Bulman, R. (1985). The aftermath of victimization: Rebuilding shattered assumptions. In C. R. Figley (Ed.), *Trauma and its wake* (Vol. 1, pp. 15–35). New York: Brunner/Mazel.

Jehu, D. (1988). *Beyond sexual abuse.* Chichester, U.K.: Wiley.

Jones, E. (1961). *The life and work of Sigmund Freud.* New York: Basic Books.

Joseph, B. (1989). *Psychic equilibrium and psychic change.* New York: Routledge.

Kardiner, A. (1941). *The traumatic neuroses of war.* New York: P. Hoeber.

Kernberg, O. (1976). *Object relations therapy and clinical psychoanalysis.* Northvale, NJ: Jason Aronson.

Kernberg, O. (1984). *Severe Personality Disorders.* New Haven, CT: Yale University Press.

Kestenberg, J. (1985). Child survivors of the Holocaust—40 years later. *Journal of the American Academy of Child Psychiatry, 24,* 408–412.

Khan, M. M. (1960). Regression and integration in the analytic setting. In *The Privacy of the Self.* Madison, CT: International Universities Press, pp. 13–26, 1974.

Khan. M. M. (1969). Vicissitudes of being, knowing, and experiencing in the therapeutic situation. In *The Privacy of Self.* Madison CT: International Universities Press, pp. 203–218, 1974.

Khan. M. M. (1971a). To Hear with Eyes. In *The Privacy of Self.* Madison, CT: International Universities Press, pp. 234–250, 1974.

Khan. M. M. (1971b). The role of illusion in the analytic space and process. In *The Privacy of Self.* Madison, CT: International Universities Press, pp. 251–269, 1974.

Kilpatrick, D. G., Veronen, L. G., & Resick, P. (1979). The aftermath of rape: Recent empirical findings. *American Journal of Orthopsychiatry, 49,* 658–669.

Klein, M. (1952). Some theoretical conclusions regarding the emotional life of the infant. In *Envy and Gratitude.* New York: Delacorte Press, 1975.

Kluft, R. (1984). Multiple Personality in Childhood. *Psychiatric Clinics of North America, 7,* 121–134.

Kluft, R. P. (Ed.). (1990a). *Incest related syndromes of adult psychopathology.* Washington, DC: American Psychiatric Press.

Kluft, R. (1990b). Dissociation and subsequent vulnerability. *Dissociation, 3,* 167–173.

Kluft, R. (1990c). *Incest related syndromes of adult psychopathology.* Washington, DC: American Psychiatric Press.

Kluft, R. (1990d). Incest and subsequent revictimization: The case of therapist-patient sexual exploitation, with a description of the sitting duck syndrome. In R. Kluft (Ed.), *Incest related syndromes of adult psychopathology.* Washington DC: American Psychiatric Press.

Kohut, H. (1971). *The analysis of the self.* Madison, CT: International Universities Press.

Kolb, L. (1987). Neuropsychological hypothesis explaining post-traumatic stress disorder. *American Journal of Psychiatry, 144,* 989–995.

Kramer, S. (1983). Object-coercive doubting: A pathological defense response to maternal incest. In H. Blum (Ed.), *Defense and resistance* (pp. 325–362). Madison, CT: International Universities Press.

Kramer, S. (1990). Residues of incest. In H. B. Levine (Ed.), *Adult analysis and childhood sexual abuse* (pp. 149–170). Hillsdale, NJ: The Analytic Press.

Kramer, S. (1991). Psychopathological effects of incest. In S. Kramer and S. Akhtar, (Ed.), *The trauma of transgression*. Northvale, NJ: Jason Aronson, 1991.

Kramer, S., & Akhtar, S. (Eds.). (1991). *The trauma of transgression*. Northvale, NJ: Jason Aronson.

Krull, M. (1986). *Freud and his father*. New York: Norton.

Krystal, H. (1978). Trauma and affects. *Psychoanalytic Study of the Child, 33,* 81–116.

Krystal, H. (1988). *Integration and self healing*. Hillsdale, NJ: The Analytic Press.

Laufer, R. S., Frey-Wouters, E., & Gallops, M. S. (1985). Traumatic stressors in the Vietnam War and Post-traumatic Stress Disorder. In C. Figley (Ed.), *Trauma and its wake* Vol. 1, (pp. 73–89). New York: Brunner/Mazel.

Levine, H. B. (Ed.). (1990). *Adult analysis and childhood sexual abuse*. Hillsdale, NJ: The Analytic Press.

Lifton, R. J. (1967). *Death in life: Survivors of Hiroshima*. New York: Simon & Schuster.

Loewald, H. (1980). The waning of the Oedipus complex. In *Papers on psychoanalysis*. New Haven: Yale University Press.

Loftus, E. (1992). Address to the American Psychological Association, 100th Annual Meeting, Washington, DC.

Masson, J. M. (1984). *The assault on truth*. New York: Farrar, Straus, & Giroux.

Masson, J. M. (Ed.). (1985). *The complete letters of Sigmund Freud to Wilhelm Fliess, 1887–1894*. Cambridge, MA: The Belknap Press of Harvard University Press.

Masterson, J. F. (1976). *Psychotherapy of the borderline adult*. New York: Brunner/Mazel.

McDougall, J. (1989). *Theaters of the body*. New York: Norton.

McGrath, W. G. (1986). *Freud's discovery of psychoanalysis*. Ithaca, NY: Cornell University Press.

Meissner, W. W. (1988). *Treatment of patients in the borderline spectrum*. Northvale, NJ: Jason Aronson.

Miczek, K. A., Thompson, M. L., & Shuster, L. (1982). Opioid-like analgesia in defeated mice. *Science, 215,* 1520–1522.

Miller, A. (1981). *Prisoners of childhood*. New York: Basic Books.

Miller, A. (1983). *For your own good*. New York: Farrar, Straus, & Giroux.

Miller, M. (1984). *Thou shalt not be aware*. New York: Farrar, Straus, & Giroux.

Mitchell, S. A. (1988). *Relational concepts in psychoanalysis: An integration*. Cambridge, MA: Harvard University Press.

Mitchell, S. A. (1991). Wishes, needs and interpersonal negotiations. *Psychoanalytic Inquiry 11,* 147–170.

Newirth, J. (1992, August). *Psychotherapy with the sexually abused patient: The use of countertransference*. Paper presented at the 100th Annual Meeting of the American Psychological Association, Washington, DC.

Ogden, T. H. (1979). On projective identification. *International Journal of Psycho-Analysis, 60,* 357–373.

Ogden, T. H. (1986). *The matrix of the mind.* Northvale, NJ: Jason Aronson.

Ogden, T. H. (1991). *Projective identification and psychotherapeutic technique.* Northvale, NJ: Jason Aronson.

Pattison, E. M., & Kahan, J. (1983). The deliberate self-harm syndrome. *American Journal of Psychiatry, 140,* 867–872.

Perry, R., & Lindell, M. (1978). The psychological consequences of natural disaster: A review of research on American communities. *Mass Emergencies, 3,* 105–115.

Perry, J. C., Herman, J. L., van der Kolk, B. A., & Hoke, L. A. (1990). Psychotherapy and psychological trauma in borderline personality disorder. *Psychiatric Annals, 20,* 33–43.

Piaget, J. (1968). *Six psychological studies.* New York: Vintage.

Pine, F. (1981). In the beginning: Contributions to a psychoanalytic developmental psychology. *International Review of Psychoanalysis, 8,* 15–33.

Pitman, R., Orr, S., Laforgue, D., and De Jong, J. (1987). Psychophysiology of PTSD imagery in Vietnam combat veterans. *Archives of General Psychiatry, 44,* 940–976.

Porder, M. (1987). Projective identification: An alternative hypothesis. *Psycho - analytic Quarterly, 56,* 431–451.

Putnam, F. (1989), *The diagnosis and treatment of multiple personality disorders.* New York: Guilford Press.

Pynoos, R. S., & Eth, S. (1985). Developmental perspective on psychic trauma in childhood. In R. C. Figley (Ed.), *Trauma and its wake.* New York: Brunner/Mazel.

Racker, H. (1968). *Transference and countertransference.* Madison, CT: International Universities Press.

Rakoff, V. A. (1966). A long-term effect of the concentration camp experience. *Viewpoints, 1,* 17–22.

Rosenthal, R. J., Rinzler, C. & Wallsh, R. (1972). Wrist-cutting syndrome: The meaning of a gesture. *American Journal of Psychiatry,* 128; 47–52.

Ross, C. A. (1989). *Multiple personality disorder.* New York: Wiley.

Ross, D. R., & Lowenstein, R. J. (Eds.) (1992). Perspectives on multiple personality disorder. *Psychoanalytic Inquiry,* 12(1).

Russell, D. E. H. (1986). *The secret trauma.* New York: Basic Books.

Sandler, J. (1987), *Projection, identification, projective identification.* Madison, CT: International Universities Press.

Saunders, E. A. (1991). Rorschach indicators of chronic childhood sexual abuse in female borderline in-patients. *Bulletin of the Menninger Clinic, 55,* 48–71.

Scharff, D. E. (1982). *The sexual relationship.* Boston: Routledge & Kegan Paul.

Searles, H. F. (1959). Oedipal love in the countertransference. In *Collected Papers on Schizophrenia and Related Subjects.* Madison, CT: International Universities Press.

Searles, H. F. (1975). The patient as therapist to the analyst. In P. Giovancchini (Ed.), *Tactics and techniques in psychoanalytic psychotherapy. Vol. II: Countertransference* (pp. 95–151). Northvale, NJ: Jason Aronson.

Searles, H. F. (1986). *My work with borderline patients.* Northvale, NJ: Jason Aronson.

Shabad, P. (1993). Resentment, indignation, and entitlement: The transformation of unconscious wish into need. *Psychoanalytic Dialogues, 3*(4).

Shearer, S. L., Peters, C. P., Quaytman, M. S., & Ogden, R. L. (1990). Frequency and correlates of childhood sexual and physical abuse in adult female borderline in-patients. *American Journal of Psychiatry, 147,* 214–216.

Shengold, L. (1963). The parent as sphinx. *Journal of the American Psychoanalytic Association, 11,* 725–751.

Shengold, L. (1967). The effects of overstimulation: Rat people. *International Journal of Psychoanalysis, 48,* 403–415.

Shengold, L. (1971). More about rats and rat people. *International Journal of Psychoanalysis, 52,* 277–288.

Shengold, L. (1979). Child abuse and deprivation: Soul murder. *Journal of the American Psychoanalytic Association, 27,* 533–559.

Shengold, L. (1989). *Soul murder.* New Haven: Yale University Press.

Shengold, L. (1992). Commentary on "Dissociative processes and transference-countertransference paradigms ... " by Jody Messler Davies and Mary Gail Frawley. *Psychoanalytic Dialogues, 2,* 49–59.

Silver, J. M., Sandberg, D. P., and Hales, R. E. (1990). New approaches in the pharmacotherapy of Posttraumatic Stress Disorder. *Journal of Clinical Psychiatry, 51,* 33–38.

Simpson, C. A., & Porter, G. L. (1981). Self-mutilation in children and adolescents. *Bulletin of the Menninger Clinic, 45,* 428–438.

Slavin, J. H. (1992, April). *The rediscovery of trauma.* Paper presented at the Twelfth Annual Meeting of the Division of Psychoanalysis (39) of the American Psychological Association, Philadelphia, PA.

Spiegel, D. (1990). Trauma, dissociation, and hypnosis. In R. Kluft (Ed.), *Incest related syndromes of adult psychopathology.* Washington, DC: American Psychiatric Press.

Spiegel, D. & Spiegel, H. (1978). *Trance and treatment: Clinical uses of hypnosis.* Washington, DC: American Psychiatric Press.

Spiegel, D. (1986). Dissociation, double binds, and posttraumatic stress in multiple personality disorder. In B. G. Braun (Ed.), *Treatment of multiple personality disorder* (pp. 61–78). Washington, DC: American Psychiatric Press.

Steele, B. (1986). Child abuse. In A. Rothstein (Ed.), *The reconstruction of trauma.* Madison, CT: International Universities Press.

Stern, D. N. (1985). *The interpersonal world of the infant.* New York: Basic Books.

Stolorow, R. D., & Atwood, G. E. (1992). *Contexts of being.* Hillsdale, NJ: The Analytic Press.

Stone, M. H. (1990). Incest in the borderline patient. In R. P. Kluft (Ed.), *Incest related syndromes of adult psychopathology* (pp. 183–204). Washington, DC: American Psychiatric Press.

Stone, M. H., Unwin, A., Beacham, B., & Swenson, C. (1989). Incest in female borderlines: Its frequency and impact. *International Journal of Family Psychiatry, 9,* 277–293.

Sullivan, H. S. (1956). *Clinical studies in psychiatry.* New York: Norton.

Surrey, J., Swett, C., Michaels, A., & Levin, S. (1990). Reported history of physical and sexual abuse and severity of symptoms in women psychiatric outpatients. *American Journal of Orthopsychiatry, 60,* 412–417.

Sutherland, S., & Scherl, D. J. (1970). Patterns of response among rape victims. *American Journal of Orthopsychiatry, 40,* 503–511.

Tansey, M. J., & Burke, W. F. (1989). *Understanding countertransference: From projective identification to empathy.* Hillsdale, NJ: The Analytic Press.

Terr, L. C. (1979). Children of Chowchilla. *Psychoanalytic Study of the Child, 34,* 547–623.

Terr, L. C. (1983). Chowchilla revisited: The effects of psychic trauma four years after a school bus kidnapping. *American Journal of Psychiatry, 140,* 1543–1550.

Terr, L. C. (1990). *Too scared to cry.* New York: Harper & Row.

Terr, L. C. (1991). Childhood traumas: An outline and overview. *American Journal of Psychiatry, 148,* 10–20.

Ulman, R. B. & Brothers, D. (1988). *The shattered self.* Hillsdale, NJ: The Analytic Press.

Van der Hart, O., & Horst, R. (1988). The dissociation theory of Pierre Janet. *Journal of traumatic stress, 2,* 397–412.

Van der Hart, O., & Horst, R. (1989). The dissociation theory of Pierre Janet. *Journal of traumatic stress, 2,* 397–412.

van der Kolk, B. A. (1988). The trauma spectrum: The interaction of biological and social events in the genesis of the trauma response. *Journal of Traumatic Stress, 1*(3), 273–290.

van der Kolk, B. A. (1989). The compulsion to repeat the trauma. *Psychiatric Clinics of North America, 12,* 389–411.

van der Kolk, B. A., Herman, J., & Perry, C. (1984). Traumatic antecedents of borderline personality disorder. Paper presented at the Fourth Annual Meeting of the Society for Traumatic Stress Studies, Baltimore.

van der Kolk, B. A., & Ducey, C. P. (1989). The psychological processing of traumatic experience: Rorschach patterns in PTSD. *Journal of Traumatic Stress, 2,* 259–274.

van der Kolk, B. A., & Greenberg, M. S. (1987). Psychobiology of the trauma response: Hyperarousal, constriction, and addiction to trauma reexposure. In B. A. Van der Kolk (Ed.), *Psychological trauma* (pp. 63–88). Washington, DC: American Psychiatric Press.

van der Kolk, B. A., & Kadish, W. (1987). Amnesia, dissociation, and the return of the repressed. In B. A. Van der Kolk (Ed.), *Psychological trauma* (pp. 173–190). Washington, DC: American Psychiatric Press.

van der Kolk, B. A., Brown, P., & Van der Hart, O. (1989). Pierre Janet on post traumatic stress. *Journal of traumatic stress, 2,* 365–378.

Volkan, V. D. (1976), *Primitive internalized object relations.* Madison, CT: International Universities Press.

Volkan, V. D. (1987). *Six steps in the treatment of borderline personality organization.* Northvale, NJ: Jason Aronson.

Weiss, J. M., Glazer, H. I., Pohorecky, L. A., et al. (1975). Effects of chronic exposure to stressors on subsequent avoidance/escape behavior and on brain norepinephrine. *Psychosomatic Medicine, 37*, 522–524.

Wilson, J. P., Smith, W. K., & Johnson, S. K. (1985). A comparative analysis of PTSD among various survivor groups. In C. R. Figley (Ed.), *Trauma and its wake* (Vol. 1). New York: Brunner/Mazel.

Winnicott, D. W. (1960a). Ego distortion in terms of the true and false self. In *The maturational processes and the facilitating environment* (pp. 140–152). Madison, CT: International Universities Press, 1965.

Winnicott, D. W. (1960b). Counter-transference. In *The maturational processes and the facilitating environment* (pp. 158–165). Madison, CT: International Universities Press, 1965.

Winnicott, D. W. (1947). Hate in the countertransference. In *Through Paediatrics to psychoanalysis*. New York: Basic Books.

Winnicott, D. W. (1951). Transitional objects and transitional phenomena. In *Through Paediatrics to psychoanalysis*. New York: Basic Books.

Winnicott, D. W. (1954–1955) The depressive position in normal emotional development. *Through Paediatrics to psychoanalysis*. New York: Basic Books.

Winnicott, D. W. (1955). Clinical varieties of transference. In *Through Paediatrics to psychoanalysis*. New York: Basic Books.

Winnicott, D. W. (1960). Ego distortion in terms of true and false self. In *The maturational processes and the facilitating environment*. Madison, CT: International Universities Press, 1965.

Winnicott, D. W. (1962). Ego integration in child development. In *The maturational processes and the facilitating environment*. Madison, CT: International Universities Press, 1965.

Winnicott, D. W. (1971). *Playing and reality*. New York: Tavistock.

Wolf, E. K., & Alpert, J. (1991). Psychoanalysis and child sexual abuse: A review of the post Freudian literature. *Psychoanalytic Psychology, 8*, 305–329.

Wyatt, G. (1985). The sexual abuse of Afro-American and white women in childhood. *Child Abuse and Neglect, 9*, 507–519.

Yager, T., Laufer, R. S., & Gallops, M. S. (1984). Some problems associated with war experience in men of the Vietnam generation. *Archives of General Psychiatry, 41*, 327–333.

Young, M. B. (1988). Understanding identity disruption and intimacy: One aspect of posttraumatic stress. *Contemporary Family Therapy, 10*, 30–43.

Index